NUCLEAR EXPORTS AND WORLD POLITICS

The proliferation of nuclear weapons is a question closely tied to the international trade in nuclear goods. The issues have been vividly underscored by such events as India's atomic test of 1974 and Israel's attack on the Iraqi reactor in 1981.

As countries in the Third World see nuclear energy as vital to their future economic development, so western supplying states face increasing dilemmas about the desirability of exporting nuclear reactors, materials, fuel and technology to potentially unstable regimes and to areas of sharp regional tension. And western nations are themselves by no means agreed on the best path to a more viable international nuclear regime. The 1970s were marked by a number of tensions and crises in the relations between the United States and Europe on this question.

In this book an international group of specialists in nuclear politics examines recent trends in the nuclear supply policies of six western nations: the United States, France, West Germany, Canada, the United Kingdom, and Australia. Each focuses on the policy process in a particular country, exploring such issues as the balancing of export earnings and security risks, the impact of shrinking domestic markets, and roles of various nuclear actors in the making of export policy. Approaches to the international nuclear regime are discussed in the light of the International Nuclear Fuel Cycle Evaluation (INFCE) completed in 1980. Two chapters assess challenges and problems facing this regime in the 1980s and the issues posed by the spread of nuclear energy capabilities in the south.

The book will be of value to students of international politics, strategic studies, energy politics, and north–south relations.

NUCLEAR EXPORTS AND WORLD POLITICS
Policy and Regime

Edited by

Robert Boardman
Centre for Foreign Policy Studies
Dalhousie University

and

James F. Keeley
Department of Political Science
University of Calgary

in association with the
Centre for Foreign Policy Studies,
Dalhousie University

St. Martin's Press   New York

St. Martin's Press, Inc., 175 Fifth Avenue, New York, NY 10010
Printed in Hong Kong
First published in the United States of America in 1983

ISBN 0–312–57976–4

Library of Congress in Publication Data

Main entry under title:

Nuclear exports and world politics.

    Includes index.
    Contents: Nuclear export policies and the non-proliferation regime/
Robert Boardman and James F. Keeley — Four decades of living with
the genie/Arnold Kramish — Giscard's legacy/Pierre Lellouche —
[etc.]
    1. Nuclear nonproliferation — Addresses, essays, lectures. I.
Boardman, Robert. II. Keeley, James F.
JX1974.73.N75 1983   327.1'74   82-10779
ISBN 0–312–57976–4

Contents

v

Part IV   Conclusions

Preface

Canada and the United States were among the countries which attempted to take initiatives to check nuclear weapons proliferation during the 1970s. While the immediate context of such moves was debate within and between the nuclear exporting nations on the most appropriate response to the continuing demands of less developed countries for nuclear power following the Indian test of 1974, the issues came to encompass the full range of questions involved in nuclear policy. This kind of broader reassessment was already beginning to get under way in several advanced industrial states in the mid-1970s, though non-proliferation concerns were central to shifts in public attitudes towards nuclear power generally in only a few. By the end of the decade, however, no clear way forward seemed to have emerged, even though some of the tensions much in evidence only a few years earlier seemed to have been eased. Disaffection on the part of many developing nations towards existing non-proliferation regimes appeared widespread and irremovable; and dissension among the western group of nuclear exporting and consuming countries, while cooled somewhat by the International Nuclear Fuel Cycle Evaluation (INFCE) inspired by the Carter Administration's anxiety-laden view of world nuclear developments in 1977, remained beneath the surface of inter-allied relations.

The focus in the main body of this book is on policies and policy-making processes in a selected number of western nuclear exporting countries. It formed no part of our aims in planning the volume to add to the stock of policy and international regime recommendations and proposals that now forms a quite substantial part of the literature on non-proliferation. An assumption underlying the study was that the orientations of the leading nuclear supplying states merit a more central position in the analysis of international nuclear politics and non-proliferation, and that a broader comparative approach was a useful and relatively under-exploited tool for this task. Two succeeding chapters then deal respectively with the perspectives of less developed countries on nuclear energy and non-proliferation regimes,

vii

and with some of the major issues and problems involved in the development and viability of such regimes.

The contributions of the two editors owe much to a programme of research originally carried out in the Centre for Foreign Policy Studies, Dalhousie University, on the problems facing Canada in the post-1974 period. We should like to thank in this connection the Donner Foundation of Canada, and to acknowledge support given through the Military and Strategic Studies Programmes of the Department of National Defence at the Universities of British Columbia and Calgary. Mrs Doris Boyle was an invaluable source of assistance throughout the project. Since events in this field can move rapidly, we should add that final versions of most chapters were completed in the late summer of 1981. The views expressed in the chapters by Dr Ashok Kapur and by Dr P. R. Johannson are those of the respective authors, and do not reflect those of institutions with which either is associated.

"Billion" has been used throughout to indicate one thousand million.

The editors and publishers wish to thank the following who have kindly given permission for the use of copyright materials: the Royal Institute of International Affairs, for the figure and table from T. J. Connolly *et al.*, *World Nuclear Energy Paths*, ICGNE, 1979; the Stockholm International Peace Research Institute, for the table from *SIPRI Yearbook*, 1980; Handelsblatt GmbH, for the table from *Atomwirtschaft-Atomtechnik*, 26, 1981; the International Atomic Energy Agency, for the table from *Power Reactors in Member States*, 1979, 1980, 1981; and Europa Union Verlag GmbH, for the material from *Arbeitspapiere zur Internationalen Politik*, 12, 1980.

December 1981   R. B.
                                                                     J. F. K.

The Contributors

Robert Boardman is Professor of Political Science and Director of the Centre for Foreign Policy Studies at Dalhousie University, Nova Scotia. He completed his doctorate at the University of London. He has taught at the Universities of Leicester and Surrey and from 1977 to 1978 was a Research Associate of the Centre de Recherches sur les Institutions Internationales, Geneva. His books include *Britain and the People's Republic of China, 1949–74* and *Foreign Policy Making in Communist Countries: A Comparative Approach* (edited with Hannes Adomeit).

Malcolm Grieve is Lecturer in Political Science at the University of British Columbia. He graduated from the University of Bristol, and then took a Master's degree at Dalhousie University where he is also currently a doctoral candidate. He has published several articles dealing with African and international political economy, and is at present conducting research into problems of public policy making in developing countries.

Erwin Häckel was born in Bayreuth, and is currently Heisenberg Fellow at the Deutsche Gesellschaft für Auswärtige Politik, Bonn, and Senior Lecturer in Political Science at the University of Konstanz. He has also been a Research Fellow of the Center for Science and International Affairs at Harvard University (1980 to 1981), and a Research Associate at the International Institute for Strategic Studies in London (1969 to 1970). His writings have dealt with energy policy, nuclear weapons proliferation, international organisations and German foreign policy.

P. R. Johannson was born and educated in Vancouver, British Columbia. Following a career in broadcast journalism he completed undergraduate work at the University of British Columbia and then Master's and Ph.D. degrees at the School of Advanced International Studies, Johns Hopkins University. He is the author of *Nuclear Exports and Canadian Foreign Policy* (forthcoming), and has published many articles in Canada. He was until recently a Post-Doctoral Fellow at the Institute of International Relations, University of British Columbia, and has since joined the staff of the Bank of Montreal.

Ashok Kapur is Associate Professor of Political Science at the University of Waterloo, Ontario. He is the author of *India's Nuclear Option* (1976) and *International Nuclear Proliferation* (1979), as well as numerous articles and papers on related subjects. From 1980 to 1981 he was a member of the United Nations Group of Experts tasked to study Israeli nuclear armament.

James F. Keeley is Assistant Professor of Political Science at the University of Calgary, Alberta. He was born in Winnipeg, and following undergraduate work at the University of Manitoba received Master's and Ph.D. degrees from Stanford University. He has also been a Post-Doctoral Fellow at the Institute of International Relations, University of British Columbia, and at the Centre for Foreign Policy Studies, Dalhousie University. His research interests have centred on Canadian nuclear export policy, nuclear proliferation and Canadian–American relations.

Arnold Kramish has been engaged in nuclear research and policy since the Manhattan Project in 1944. He has held a Guggenheim Fellowship and has been a Research Fellow at both the International Institute for Strategic Studies and the Council on Foreign Relations. As Science Counselor of the Department of State he was attached to the United States Missions to UNESCO and OECD. He holds technical patents and has authored many articles and books, including *The Peaceful Atom in Foreign Policy* and *Atomic Energy in the Soviet Union*.

Pierre Lellouche is Head of Strategic Studies at the Institut Français des Relations Internationales, and a columnist for the French weekly *Le Point*. He is a graduate of both the law school and the Institut d'Etudes Politiques in Paris, and obtained his doctorate in law from Harvard University. From 1974 to 1978 he was a Research Fellow in Harvard's programme for science and international affairs and at GERPI, Maison des Sciences de l'Homme, Paris. His main areas of work are European security issues, arms control and strategic problems, and he is the author of several books and articles dealing with defence matters and various aspects of non-proliferation.

Russell B. Trood received his LL.B. from the University of Sydney, in which city he later practised as a solicitor. He holds a Master's degree in strategic studies from the University of Wales, Aberystwyth, and is presently carrying out research on Australian–United States relations during the Vietnam war as a doctoral candidate at Dalhousie University.

List of Abbreviations

AAEC	Australian Atomic Energy Commission
AEA	Atomic Energy Authority
AECL	Atomic Energy of Canada Ltd.
AGR	Advanced gas-cooled reactor
ALP	Australian Labor Party
BNEE	British Nuclear Export Executive
BNFL	British Nuclear Fuels Ltd.
BWR	Boiling water reactor
CANDU	Canadian deuterium uranium reactor
CAS	Committee on Assurances of Supply (IAEA)
CDFR	Commercial demonstration fast reactor
CEA	Commissariat à l'Energie Atomique
CEGB	Central Electricity Generating Board
CFDT	Confédération Française Démocratique du Travail
CNPE	Council on Foreign Nuclear Policy
DFR	Dounreay fast reactor
EDF	Electricité de France
EEC	European Economic Community
ENDC	Eighteen-Nation Disarmament Committee (UN)
EURATOM	European Atomic Energy Community
FBR	Fast breeder reactor
FOE	Friends of the Earth
GEC	General Electric Co.
HTR	High temperature reactor
IAEA	International Atomic Energy Agency
INFCE	International Nuclear Fuel Cycle Evaluation
IPS	International plutonium storage
KWU	Kraftwerk Union
L–NCP	Liberal and National Country Parties
LWR	Light water reactor
MLF	Multilateral nuclear force
MUF	Material unaccounted for
MW	Megawatt
NEA	Nuclear Energy Agency

NNC	National Nuclear Corporation
NNPA	Nuclear Non-proliferation Act
NPT	Treaty on the Non-proliferation of Nuclear Weapons
NSG	Nuclear Suppliers Group
NNWS	Non-nuclear weapon state
NWS	Nuclear weapon state
OECD	Organisation for Economic Cooperation and Development
PFR	Prototype fast reactor
PWR	Pressurised water reactor
SGHWR	Steam-generating heavy water reactor
SGN	Société Générale pour les Techniques Nouvelles
SIPRI	Stockholm International Peace Research Institute

Part I Introduction

1 Nuclear Export Policies and the Non-proliferation Regime

Robert Boardman and James F. Keeley

Few technologies have promised the extremes of danger and benefit, or generated the fear and the enthusiasm, presented by and associated with nuclear power. Domestically, the hope for cheap, abundant energy has been set against environmental and safety concerns. Internationally, nuclear power as an instrument of economic growth and of energy independence has been set against the memory of Hiroshima and Nagasaki, and the fear of nuclear weapons proliferation. In the last decade, the unfavourable aspects of this duality have been strengthened. Domestic opposition to nuclear power development, reinforced by the potent symbol of Three Mile Island, has had devastating results in some countries, while the economic virtues of nuclear power have been rendered ambiguous at best by inflation and stricter regulation. And India's test of a nuclear explosive device in May 1974 signalled – though it did not of itself cause entirely – the start of a period of increasing doubt about the effectiveness of the non-proliferation regime. Nuclear exporters, individually and collectively, began to reconsider their policies – a process which created tension not only among suppliers but also between nuclear haves and have-nots. The prospects of increasing use of nuclear power, of growing stockpiles of plutonium, and of the development of national enrichment capabilities raised fears that weapons-usable material would be more readily available and less easily controlled than formerly.

The Israeli attack on and destruction of Iraq's French-supplied Osirak reactor in June 1981 merely put a final touch to a period of uncertainty. The raid was prompted not only by Israeli distrust of Iraqi intentions, but also by a lack of confidence in the international non-proliferation regime. Both domestic nuclear programmes and this

3

regime have thus come under increasing pressure in the last several years. These pressures are related. Historically, the non-proliferation regime has been founded upon and profoundly dependent upon nuclear exports as both a main channel for the diffusion of nuclear technology and as a chief mechanism for the international control of that technology. The nuclear exporters have played a central role in the creation and the evolution of the regime. However, the development of nuclear capabilities, through both indigenous efforts and international transfers, has come to threaten that regime and to undermine the position of the nuclear suppliers. For the latter, moreover, a weakening domestic market can mean increased reliance on exports: if the international market is itself weak, suppliers can thus be led to soften their terms of export in order to secure sales and, by so doing, to assist – and perhaps save – their own nuclear power programmes and national nuclear industries.

NON-PROLIFERATION AND THE DIFFUSION OF NUCLEAR CAPABILITIES

The major focus of the non-proliferation regime has been on preventing the use of civilian capabilities for proscribed military purposes. The early safeguards systems tried to do this for nuclear exports and IAEA-assisted projects: if states wished to develop nuclear weapons, it would be through their own, unassisted efforts. The Non-proliferation Treaty extended the principle to include even purely domestic capabilities of non-nuclear weapons states. These, if party to the treaty, bound themselves neither to acquire nor to develop nuclear explosives, and accepted a safeguards system as a means of verifying that pledge.

A diversion of a purely civilian programme to weapons production is not the only route to nuclear weapons, nor is it necessarily the best. The five nuclear powers (India is a sixth by courtesy, to some degree) all used explicitly military programmes as a means of developing weapons capability. Indeed these programmes helped shape later civilian developments. The American light water reactor had its origins in submarine propulsion systems, and the early British nuclear programme rested on a need to produce plutonium for military use. As commercial nuclear power has developed, moreover, the degree of separation between military and civilian programmes has widened. Civilian technology is more expensive and more demanding than military for the production of fissionable materials. The materials requirements of civilian programmes and their operating practices differ from those of military programmes. Civilian power reactors generally use either low-enriched or natural uranium, neither immediately usable for weapons purposes. While plutonium from civilian reactors may be weapons-usable, the short burn-up time and the frequent refuelling need to produce high-quality weapons-grade plutonium interfere with economic power production. As Arnold Kramish aptly observed in 1964, "One cannot have efficient bombs and low-cost power at the same time."[1]

None the less, civilian programmes do present a number of weapons-relevant options. A state may violate safeguards, through clandestine diversion or the use of clandestine facilities. As the volume of material handled increases, the effectiveness of safeguard systems may be eroded. The materials accounting system at the heart of current safeguards leaves some percentage of material unaccounted for; but the critical mass needed for an explosive device is an absolute quantity, so that at high volumes it may be possible to divert without being detected. Efforts are, of course, being made to meet this problem, through, for example, improved containment and surveillance measures. At the extreme, there is the threat of "smash and grab" seizures of materials. More generally, the development of an open, legitimate nuclear industrial capability can also be seen as a potential threat, for it may provide a state with the basic technical capability to back up the selection of a weapons option at some future time. John Maddox has argued that Canada's contribution to the Indian test was less the poorly safeguarded reactor in which the plutonium was produced than the general assistance which Canada gave to the Indian nuclear industry.[2] Another writer concluded in 1979 that:

> In effect, any state which has a small nuclear power industry, the sophisticated industrial infrastructure and skilled manpower which are the preconditions of a nuclear power industry, or the political will to divert the resources necessary to create such an industry, regardless of high opportunity costs, has the potential to become a nuclear weapon state by the year 2000.[3]

Lists of the two or three dozen states technically capable of becoming nuclear weapon states during the 1980s and 1990s[4] are useful, but may also be misleading. The increase in nuclear weapon states has lagged behind the spread of capabilities and the growth of stockpiles of fissile materials.[5] The acquisition of nuclear weapons, it cannot be emphasised too often, is more than a matter of capabilities. Some states – the Canadas, Finlands, Austrias or Hungaries – are most unlikely to develop nuclear weapons under any remotely probable circumstances. Others might develop them only under such circumstances – such as the erosion or the withdrawal of the American nuclear umbrella – as would themselves be extremely unsettling. Even popular favourites in the nuclear-weapons-race listings – Iran before the fall of the Shah, perhaps, or Iraq before the Israeli raid – are subject to nobbling by fate or rivals. Consideration of technical, economic, scientific and industrial capabilities, then, should not obscure the political factors behind a decision to go nuclear. On the other hand, control through the non-proliferation regime of potential proliferators could become increasingly difficult as the number of "self-suppliers" or even exporters grows. We shall return to this point shortly.

Whether the focus is on the simple increase in the number of technically capable states, the regime-eroding effects of diffusion or (an additional worry) the increased availability of fissionable materials for nuclear terrorism, the spread of nuclear capabilities and the growth in the volume of nuclear materials handled have been major concerns in recent attempts to reform the non-proliferation regime. Aside from the tightening of safeguards requirements (among other things to include transfers of technology) efforts have gone into controlling the transfer and the indigenous development of "sensitive" technologies at key points in the nuclear fuel cycle – above all for reprocessing and enrichment – and the development of fast breeder reactors. One of the issues in INFCE was whether certain reactor types and their associated specific fuel cycles were particularly resistant, or particularly vulnerable, to proliferation risks by diversion, terrorism or other means. It was their differing views on these problems that led to the conflicting approaches of the United States and of Europe in the second half of the 1970s to the future of nuclear power. But at all points in such debates political and technical arguments have been inextricably mixed. At what point, for example, does one set limitations or controls on the concentration of U–235? Twenty per cent has gradually become the magic figure here, but debate on the figure has not been entirely divorced from wider political considerations. Similarly, the weapons-usability of reactor-grade plutonium has blurred the distinction between civilian and military nuclear programmes, and lay at the heart of US concern during the Carter Administration about the plutonium economy; but designating certain reactor systems as "diversion-resistant", and thus as preferable to others, inevitably has commercial implications (as well as giving would-be proliferators useful clues on how best to do it). Before and during INFCE, attempts to slow or halt the development of fast breeders, or of local enrichment facilities, or of other nuclear capabilities, were inevitably interpreted in some countries as attempts by certain suppliers to prolong consumer dependence on foreign supplies and services.

THE INTERNATIONAL NUCLEAR MARKET

While all the present nuclear weapons powers developed their weapons capabilities primarily through their own efforts, there is no doubt that the actual and potential spread of nuclear capabilities is due largely to the expansion of international transfers of nuclear goods and services, and of technical cooperation and training under bilateral and multilateral nuclear cooperation agreements. The advanced nuclear states have been the major sources of this process of diffusion. Given their concern over the spread of nuclear capabilities, one might reasonably question the logic behind the encouragement given to the growth of this network. Leonard Beaton characterised US policies to promote the peaceful uses of atomic energy in other countries as "one of the most inexplicable political fantasies in history. Only a social psychologist could hope to explain why the possessor of the most terrible weapon in history should have sought to spread the necessary industry to produce them in the belief that this could make the world safer".[6] On closer examination, the question is perhaps less mystifying. The US, after all, could not prevent all other states from developing national capabilities. Neither abandonment of nuclear power nor full international control over sensitive facilities were real options; but the provision of nuclear assistance could be a source of influence. The development of international controls based on safeguarded transfers, in other words, was preferable to the development of uncontrolled national nuclear capabilities. Making nuclear assistance available would arguably make resort to indigenous development less attractive because it would be less necessary. The resulting links of dependence might also make a later weapons option more difficult to realise. Choice of an American light water reactor, for example, meant dependence on low-enriched uranium, and probably dependence on American enrichment services.

The international nuclear trade has thus been both a significant factor in the diffusion of nuclear technology, and also a primary mechanism of control in the non-proliferation regime. Nuclear transfers carry a safeguard burden as part of the purchase price; dependence on suppliers serves as a channel of influence; and vulnerability to the disruption of the international flow of nuclear goods and services imposes an immediate cost – in addition to any broader political costs that might follow – for a violation of political commitments. The ability and willingness of nuclear exporters to require assurances and to exert control, and of nuclear importers to give those assurances and accept some dependence in return for easier access to nuclear technology, have been the entering wedge and the key to the non-proliferation regime.

A number of trends have emerged during the last two decades, however, that together have serious implications for that regime. First, the concentration of supply has diminished. In the early 1960s, US companies came to dominate the world reactor market, and made the LWR virtually the standard power reactor. But now new competitors have arisen, even as older ones have disappeared. France and West Germany launched major attacks on the power reactor market in the 1970s, while Canada's CANDU had some small degree of inter- national success. Britain and France have become reprocessing and enrichment powers. And with the overlapping of nuclear equipment with some having other uses, other countries have been able to enter the market. Swiss companies, for example, were criticised by the US State Department in 1980 for allegedly continuing to provide technical assistance and equipment for a Pakistani centrifuge enrichment plant.[7] A handful of countries still dominate the supply of uranium, but other, smaller suppliers may be weak links, either through hijacking of shipments or by design. Links have been reported, for example, between Niger and Pakistan by way of Libya.[8] As the number of suppliers increases, the coordination of policy and the regulation of transfers become progressively more difficult.

Secondly, a corollary of this is that such countries as Argentina, Brazil or India might themselves become significant suppliers of nuclear assistance in the future. Argentina may be aiming for complete self-sufficiency in the nuclear fuel cycle by the mid-1980s, and for the development of a fuel cycle technology export capability by the end of the decade.[9] This kind of development would clearly add serious political divisions to an already somewhat strained supplier consensus.

Third, the reactor trade in particular is vulnerable to political decisions, and thus to shifts of opinion on the acceptability of nuclear power, the assessment of risks, appropriateness of different systems, and related matters. During the first half of the 1970s, the international nuclear trade expanded rapidly; but a falling off of demand appeared later as a result of tighter regulatory requirements, stiffer export controls, political opposition and high costs.[10] Falling domestic demand in supplier countries might initially enhance the attractiveness of export sales drives, but over the longer term seems more likely – because of its effects on national nuclear industries – to exert a depressing effect on international trade.

Finally, efforts to use supply as a means of influence over foreign nuclear programmes have not always met with success. Canada and the United States have threatened and used uranium embargoes in attempts to secure tighter safeguards commitments from European and other customers, leaving the frustrated purchasers to complain bitterly that broken contracts were a poor basis for an international regime. There emerged from the mid-1970s, then, "a growing realisation of the close connection between assurances of supply and successful non-proliferation policy; or, put conversely, of the fact that the failure to offer reasonable supply arrangements will lead to the development of multiple independent sources of supply, with consequent loss of control".[11] Threat of a supply disruption as a means of exerting influence has become steadily less credible and more and more likely to be counter-productive.

THE NON-PROLIFERATION REGIME UNDER FIRE

The formal parts of the non-proliferation regime in the 1970s included the inspection and verification powers of the IAEA for those countries which had signed agreements with it; the NPT, which entered into force in 1970; and the safeguards provisions of the various bilateral agreements on nuclear supply. At the root of Third World criticisms of the regime has been the charge that the NPT acted in effect to legitimise the existence of two categories of states, those with nuclear weapons and flourishing nuclear power industries, and those without either. A related charge was that the treaty's provisions constituted an unacceptable intrusion into sovereign rights. The nuclear "haves" were accused of failing to live up to the more positive aspects of the treaty, most notably in Article IV(1): "Nothing in this Treaty shall be interpreted as affecting the inalienable right of all the Parties to the Treaty to develop research, production and use of nuclear energy for peaceful purposes without discrimination and in conformity with Articles I and II of this Treaty" (which deal respectively with transfers of nuclear materials by nuclear weapon states and receipts of such materials by non-nuclear weapon states). Pakistani and other complaints of discrimination over the supply of peaceful nuclear technology[12] were echoed in a variety of forums during the decade, and found support among others from China.[13]

A rather different genre of criticism emerged from parts of the industrialised world after such developments as the 1974 Indian test, the expansion of French and German export capability, the appearance of full fuel-cycle agreements in the international nuclear trade, and the evident ability of a number of developing countries to secure nuclear-relevant equipment and materials by various methods, not all of them having the blessing of the governments of nuclear exporting states. The "trigger list" of equipment and materials that emerged from the London Club meetings of the latter in the mid-1970s constituted at first the main vehicle for this response. The French Government too was involved in this process. France was not a signatory of the NPT, an atomic energy official said in 1980, "not because it disagrees with the goals of the NPT but because it disagrees with the form. . . . In addition to the NPT there are the London guidelines and these we apply to the letter".[14] For the United States, the wide-ranging provisions of the Nuclear Non-proliferation Act of 1978, and the initiation of INFCE, were later, post-London, vehicles. Section 307 of the NNPA forbids nuclear exports to any nation or group of nations found by the President to:

> have assisted, encouraged or induced any non-nuclear weapon state to engage in activities involving source or special nuclear material and having direct significance for the manufacture or acquisition of nuclear explosive devices, and has failed to take steps which, in the President's judgment, represent sufficient progress toward terminating such assistance, encouragement, or inducement.

Together with Canada and Australia the US in the late 1970s also sought prior approval in decisions by recipient nations relating to the reprocessing, enrichment and subsequent storage of nuclear materials originating in these countries.[15] INFCE, proposed by President Carter in 1977 as a means of pausing to examine the basic assumptions of a plutonium economy, could be viewed by its participants at its close in 1980 in differing ways. On the one hand, parts of the exercise appeared to some to vindicate the argument that trends in the development of nuclear power, particularly at the back-end of the fuel cycle, contained major security risks. On the other hand, others took the results as supporting the proposition that for countries facing uranium shortages in the future, fast breeder reactors and spent fuel reprocessing represented urgently needed options, and as defeating the view that technical fixes could go a long way towards shielding nuclear power development from proliferation dangers.

THE NUCLEAR EXPORTERS: A COMPARATIVE PERSPECTIVE

Why concentrate in this volume on the policies and policy processes of the nuclear exporting states?

Firstly, while the ability of individual exporters and of exporters as a group to dominate the non-proliferation regime and the nuclear trade has been eroded, these states remain central to the control of nuclear weapons proliferation. They will continue to be crucial until such time as the very concept of supplier market power becomes meaningless. An exclusive emphasis on the regulatory potential and achievements of international institutions such as the IAEA, the NPT, and the OECD's Nuclear Energy Agency (NEA) can give only a partial picture of the character of the non-proliferation regime. Any assessment of the problems and potential of that regime must take due account of the approaches and activities of the exporting nations.

Secondly, nuclear policy in these states is growing in complexity as nuclear issues become more intractable and more firmly rooted in domestic politics. Non-proliferation has been a salient issue in domestic debates in some, though not all, of the nuclear exporting countries; but other issues have surfaced with some vigour, including the degree of dependence on nuclear power, the type of technology to be used, location of facilities, disposal and handling of wastes, costs and uranium exploration and mining. Export policy may be shaped in part by the manner in which such questions are dealt with, and as different bureaucratic and political interests are reconciled. Some of the exporting nations examined in this book – the United States, Canada, the Federal Republic of Germany and Australia – have an added layer of complexity arising out of divisions of jurisdiction in federal systems. It is not possible now – if it ever was – to take for granted the processes leading up to nuclear export decisions within a broader framework of nuclear policy-making and the working out of non-proliferation regime strategies. As the nature of the problem of proliferation dictates a continuing review of the policies of the nuclear exporting countries, so the nature of the policy processes in those states compels the analyst to probe more deeply into their workings.

Thirdly, while there exist a number of excellent single-country studies of the exporting states, broader comparative assessments of their policies and of the implications of these for the non-proliferation regime have been somewhat rarer. This has, after all, tended naturally to be a more policy-oriented literature, with emphasis placed accordingly on explorations of the character of technological change and its implications for policy choices; on the definition and extent of the proliferation problem, with particular attention to the issues posed for western governments and for international agencies by states in the Third World that may be approaching weapons paths; and on the contributions, constructive or otherwise, of the regime components of international bodies, treaties bilateral and multilateral, and the production of nuclear trade guidelines. Several western suppliers – the United States, Canada, France, West Germany, Britain and Australia – are discussed in the volume. Other countries, more particularly Japan and the Soviet Union, were excluded partly for reasons of length and partly to lend greater coherence to this bloc of chapters. Two additional chapters broaden this scope to encompass an evaluation of critical views from the countries of the South, and a discussion of persisting problems with the non-proliferation regime approached from a more theoretical perspective. Several related aspects, could not be included, such as nuclear terrorism or the implications for the conduct of hypothetical future wars, for example in Europe, of the existence of multiple centres of nuclear power production.

As far as the country chapters are concerned, the authors have aimed to tackle pertinent questions falling within three broad areas: (i) nuclear export policy, its relation to other foreign and domestic policy concerns, and the ways in which states have sought to reconcile their diverse interests in the nuclear export field; (ii) the policy process, including the interests and authority of and interactions between the various actors involved in the making of nuclear export policy, the significance of industry-government links, and the impact of public opinion and domestic politics; and (iii) approaches to the non-proliferation regime, including such questions as the nature of disagreements with other countries in the forging of common non-proliferation policies, the kinds of restrictions it would be willing to accept or interested in imposing, and the various solutions and recommendations for regime change or maintenance that it tends to favour. The controversial nature of many of the topics handled, however, in practice rules out an approach common to all chapters, and no attempt was made to restrict contributors exclusively to the confines of such a single framework.

NOTES

1. Arnold Kramish, "The Emergent Genie", in R. N. Rosecrance (ed.), *The Dispersion of Nuclear Weapons: Strategy and Politics* (New York: Columbia University Press, 1964) p. 264.
2. John Maddox, *Prospects for Nuclear Proliferation, Adelphi Papers*, no. 113 (Spring 1975) pp. 11–12, 16–17.
3. Enid Schoettle (SIPRI), *Postures for Non-proliferation: Arms Limitation and Security Policies to Minimise Nuclear Proliferation* (London: Francis & Taylor, 1979) p. 3.
4. Schoettle (ibid., p. 3) for example, notes 35, based on non-nuclear weapon states appearing twice on previous lists of nuclear weapon states by the end of this century: Argentina, Australia, Austria, Belgium, Brazil, Bulgaria, Canada, Chile, Czechoslovakia, East and West Germany, Finland, Greece, Hungary, Indonesia, Iran, Israel, Italy, Japan, Mexico, Netherlands, Pakistan, Philippines, Poland, Romania, South Africa, South Korea, Spain, Sweden, Switzerland, Taiwan, Thailand, Turkey, the UAR and Yugoslavia.
5. A. Wohlstetter *et al.*, *Swords from Plowshares: The Military Potential of Civilian Nuclear Technology* (University of Chicago Press, 1979) pp. 15, 16.
6. Leonard Beaton, *Must the Bomb Spread?* (Harmondsworth: Penguin, 1966) p. 88.
7. *Nuclear Fuel*, 29 Sept. 1980, p. 17.
8. *African Business*, June 1981, p. 18.
9. Ann MacLachlan, "Argentina: Tomorrow's Nuclear Exporter", *The Energy Daily*, 24 Sept. 1980.
10. *SIPRI Yearbook*, 1979, pp. 305–8.
11. B. Goldschmidt and M. B. Kratzer, *Peaceful Nuclear Relations: A Study of the Creation and the Erosion of Confidence*, International Consultative Group on Nuclear Energy, working papers (1978) pp. 51–2.
12. See for example "Pakistan Rejects Discrimination over Supply of Peaceful Nuclear Technology", *Dawn*, 20 Oct. 1978.
13. See "Every Country is Justified in Developing Nuclear Power Stations to Serve its Own Needs", report by Xinhua News Agency, Peking, 25 Mar. 1978.

14. *Nucleonics Week*, 16 Oct. 1980, pp. 9–10.
15. For these countries' positions on this set of questions, see below, Chapters 2, 5, 7.

Part II Policy Process in the Nuclear Exporting States

2 Four Decades of Living with the Genie: United States Nuclear Export Policy

Arnold Kramish

The complexity of international trade in nuclear materials is illustrated by the sagas of two consignments of uranium in 1980.[1] One batch of uranium was mined in Canada for a West German utility. The product was sent to the USSR for enrichment to fuel grade. That material then went to the United States for fabrication into fuel rods and finally found its destination in a West German power reactor.

Another consignment of uranium from Namibia to Austria never got there. It, too, was sent to the Soviet Union for enrichment, and then to West Germany for fabrication. By that time the Austrian reactor was cancelled by national referendum. The fabricated fuel found a purchaser, an American utility in Rochester, New York.

Both of the transactions were legal in all respects, violated no export–import regulations, and therefore became matters of public record. But the complexity of the transactions, involving many partners, suggests that were complicity intended, it might well be successful. And the end point might not be energy but nuclear weapons. This is particularly a possibility when the control or safeguard links are broken at any point of supply or processing.

President Seyni Kountche of Niger has boasted that "If the devil asks [me] to sell him uranium today, I'll sell it to him."[2] Apostate clients from Iraq, Libya, Pakistan and elsewhere have been making pilgrimages to Niamey to secure their shares of the devil's bounty. The same clients are finding eager vendors of machines, equipment and nuclear reactors, with which to feed the raw materials for research, power and/or bombs. Divining the ultimate use and controlling the use of materials and equipment is the task assigned to export policy.

NON-PROLIFERATION POLICY: THE BEGINNINGS

The problems of nuclear technology transfer are as old as the beginnings of the Second World War atomic bomb project. The race was against Germany acquiring the bomb first. As it turned out, the Germans lagged way behind the United States, which was co-operating in various degrees with the British and at arms length with the French ensconced in Canada. The first expressions of alarm uttered by President Roosevelt and his chief advisers were not in the context of other countries acquiring the bomb, but in terms of potential commercial competition from the British and from the French, who inconveniently held the first patents on nuclear reactors.

The concern that international atomic commercialism would deprive the United States of the peaceful fruits of the atom in the post-war period accounted for the tumultuous relationship with the British and Canadians during the Second World War.[3] By mid-1943, Anglo-American understandings on sharing nuclear data had completely broken down. The barriers were lifted partially when Churchill and Roosevelt signed the Quebec Agreement on 19 August 1943.[4] That was the first non-proliferation agreement.

The agreement provided that no information would be communicated to third parties and that the British Government would:

> recognize that any post-war advantages of an industrial or commercial character shall be dealt with . . . on terms to be specified by the President of the United States to the Prime Minister of Great Britain. The Prime Minister expressly disclaims any interest in these industrial and commercial aspects beyond what may be considered by the President of the United States to be fair and just and in harmony with the economic welfare of the world.

No concern was expressed that Britain or any other party might use information to build an atomic bomb; the emphasis was solely on preventing commercial nuclear trade.

The second non-proliferation treaty was more important because it reflected a dawning notion that if all the sources of nuclear raw materials could be controlled, then proliferation, not yet spelled out as such, might be contained. A fortnight after the invasion in Normandy, a "Declaration of Trust" was drawn up expressing the intent of the two governments "to control to the fullest extent practicable the supplies of uranium and thorium ores" within their boundaries and stating that the British would approach all Dominion Governments for the same purpose.[5]

Thus were conceived during wartime the dual themes that if commercialism and the sources of nuclear materials could be controlled, then the spread of dangerous nuclear activities might also be controlled. They were themes, logical enough in their simplicity, which would arise time and time again in the various schemes to curb nuclear proliferation.

The third British–American sharing agreement, without the force of a treaty, was an *aide-mémoire* of a conversation between Prime Minister Churchill and President Roosevelt at Hyde Park on 18 September 1944.[6] Its subsequent history is illustrative of statesmen's follies and lack of understanding of the proliferation process. The *aide-mémoire* was brief, containing three points. The first point rejected the notion that the world should be informed about the atomic project, "with a view to international agreement regarding its control and use". But when a bomb would be available it should be used against the Japanese who would be warned "that this bombardment will be repeated until they surrender". Thus should put to rest recent speculations on whether President Roosevelt would have used the bomb had he lived until it was ready.

The second point seemed to be an amelioration of the Quebec Agreement, for it provided that "Full collaboration . . . for military and commercial purposes should continue after the defeat of Japan." And finally, Allied concern about "leakage of information particularly to the Russians" was focussed curiously only on the activities of Professor Niels Bohr, who as "Nicolas Baker" had provided intellectual stimulus to the early bomb design work at Los Alamos. Thus the Hyde Park *aide-mémoire* focussed attention on the importance of security of information. The *aide-mémoire* itself was coded in such a way that it was misfiled by an American clerk who thought that "Tube Alloys", the British code for the bomb project, had something to do with ships' boiler tubes. The British had their copy in the right file, but the result was that the two Allies kept speaking past one another for about a year when they were discussing nuclear cooperation and control of the atom.

Thus the concepts of controlling exports of information and raw materials were in place before the end of the Second World War, and they have persisted, in one way or another, since. The third control idealism was related to the production of the new element not found in nature, plutonium. The basic atomic energy control document was, and still is in some respects, the Acheson–Lilienthal Report of 17 March 1946.[7] The document stressed that "any national or private effort to mine uranium will be illegal" and that only enough information would be provided a proposed International Atomic Development Authority to enable it to comprehend what it was to police. Then, a dramatic new technical method of control was revealed: "U-235 and plutonium can be denatured; such denatured materials do not readily lend themselves to the making of atomic explosives, but they can still be used with no essential loss of effectiveness for the peaceful applications of atomic energy." It was as if the atom had a benign soul which would make it good. And United States Presidents ever since have been lured and deceived by that fickle denaturant soul.

General Leslie R. Groves, head of the wartime atomic bomb project, was opposed to having an Acheson–Lilienthal panel in the first instance. When their report appeared, he assembled his own committee (on which some members overlapped with the Lilienthal committee) to issue a disclaimer on 9 April 1946[8] to emphasize two points. One, that "without uranium as a raw material there is no foreseeable method of releasing atomic energy", and that "denaturing, though valuable in adding to the flexibility of controls, cannot of itself eliminate the dangers of atomic warfare". Although some commercial versions of the published report appended the Groves Committee Statement, the official United States Government publications of the Acheson–Lilienthal Report did not. And concerned citizenry were impressed by statements from Nobel Laureates that denatured materials could be utilized in a safe way and that the operation of nuclear plants could "be left to private or national initiative".[9]

Meanwhile, the "McMahon Act", or the Atomic Energy Act of 1946, was being formulated.[10] Recast and amended several times since, it is the basic document on United States nuclear export policies.

THE NUCLEAR NON-PROLIFERATION ACT OF 1978

The Atomic Energy Act of 1946 was highly restrictive as regards nuclear cooperation, even with the wartime Allies. The Atomic

Energy Act of 1954 was less restrictive in order to allow the development of a domestic nuclear power industry and to permit the implementation of President Eisenhower's "atoms for peace" initiative of December 1953. The Nuclear Non-proliferation Act (NNPA) of 1978, otherwise known as Public Law 95–242,[11] was derived from congressional concern and hearings on the Indian nuclear explosion of 1974, second thoughts about the liberality of the Atomic Energy Act of 1954 (or at least unhappiness at the manner in which it had been interpreted), the election of a President (Carter) who had made nuclear proliferation a mainstay of his campaign platform (and who had forced his opponent, President Ford, to accelerate his own Administration's proliferation evaluations), and the enormous volume of publications which had proliferated into a veritable proliferation analysis industry.

Also, since early 1975 a Nuclear Suppliers' Group (NSG) had been meeting in London, rather quietly, to draw up export guidelines. The original conference consisted of the Soviet Union, France, West Germany, Canada, Britain, Japan and the United States. At the insistence of the Soviet Union the membership was later increased to fifteen nations: the French were beginning to demand that the group be terminated or be expanded. So it was problematical that what was really a council of the significant suppliers could have remained a viable forum of consensus. But by September 1977, the NSG had reached accord on a 16-point set of *Guidelines*[12] on specific materials and equipment to be restricted by the Suppliers. Also included were general criteria for physical protection of nuclear materials. Two weeks later, President Carter addressed the United Nations General Assembly, and in these words effectively killed the Suppliers' Group, although it survived – as a name, no more – for many years: "I believe that the London Suppliers Group must conclude its work as it is presently constituted so that world security will be safeguarded from the pressures of commercial competition. We have learned it is not enough to safeguard just some facilities or some materials. Full scope comprehensive safeguards are necessary."[13] Heralded as a bold initiative, it erased the non-proliferation policy slate clean and reverted to the commercial fears of President Roosevelt three decades earlier and the full-scope safeguards of the Acheson-Lilienthal report. Further, President Carter assured the General Assembly that "I believe from my own personal knowledge of this issue that there are ways to solve the problems we face. I believe that there are alternative fuel cycles that can be solved on a global basis." He thus returned to the fold of absolute belief in the efficacy of the denaturants of the original Acheson–Lilienthal report. Only a few (foreign) analysts dared comment that "the irony, of course, is that despite their illusory character, technical fixes have been a recurrent theme in American thinking about nuclear weapons spread since 1945".[14]

One would be remiss at this point to ignore the real lesson of the cycles of recurrence of the denaturant in United States proliferation policy. The value of denaturing is neither nil nor absolute, as the Groves Committee recognized in 1945. The problem is that it has been treated both as the ultimate technical "fix", as President Carter did (in his policy formulation years), and as of little value, as when the concept was deflated several times, including the recent past. Two active participants in the Carter policy wisely concluded that the policy "was flawed in important respects" and that the "plutonium produced from nuclear *power* reactors, though usable, is much less suitable for weapons".[15] This "denaturing" or "spiking" concept is so important in assessing the proliferation implications of international nuclear commerce, that the latter will continue to suffer or be dangerous if the subject continues to be treated in terms of extremes.

In another fortnight the representatives of thirty-six nations gathered in Washington to hear, with some puzzlement, the President remind them that he had studied the "peaceful use" of the atom in atomic submarines and that he had "a feeling that the need for atomic power itself for peaceful uses has perhaps been greatly exaggerated".[16] This was at the inaugural session of the International Nuclear Fuel Cycle Evaluation (INFCE), in which the President hoped that the community of nations would study together the perils of the atom and come to a common understanding on how to avoid them. Some two and a half years later the final INFCE conference, by now with a membership of 66 nations, showed that the exercise was a resounding success in helping to disseminate in a methodical way much of the information required to proliferate and to evade most of the safeguards. INFCE was a failure in that the technical experts rejected almost every expectation of the President, particularly his conviction that there were "alternative fuel cycles" that were safer.

None the less, it was at the beginning of the INFCE exercise that the formulation of the NNPA of 1978 occurred, and many congressional bodies attacked the problem of nuclear proliferation as fervently as did the President. The resulting Act was highly restrictive and gave precise, strict guidelines under which any materials which had been under United States control would remain under that control throughout in global commerce.

The NNPA of 1978 is not the only legislation defining limits on nuclear commerce. Three of the most important other measures are the Symington and Glenn amendments and the Export–Import Bank Act.

THE SYMINGTON AND GLENN AMENDMENTS

During the 94th Congress (1974–6), Senator Symington added a sanction provision to Public Law 94–329, whereby certain foreign nuclear actions would cut off non-nuclear military aid by the United States. In the next congress, through the amended Foreign Assistance Act of 1961 (now the International Assistance Act of 1977), Senator Glenn separated several legal aspects.[17] In this form, the amendments (known variously as the Glenn and/or Symington amendments) specified that no military aid could be rendered to any nation which delivers nuclear enrichment equipment, materials or technology, or to any country receiving enrichment-related technology, unless the equipment were put under international safeguards. A separate amendment specifies similar restrictions in respect to countries which deliver or receive reprocessing equipment.

The enrichment restriction could be overridden by the President if he determined and certified that the termination of military assistance would have a serious adverse effect on vital United States interests and that the country in question would not acquire or develop nuclear weapons or assist other nations in doing so. The reprocessing restriction could also be side-stepped if the President certified that vital United States interests would be adversely affected. No certification of a country's nuclear intent is required for the reprocessing waiver.

The Glenn amendment was soon to be tested by the Reagan Administration. Pakistan was engaging in the construction of a uranium isotope separation facility, something which inspired the Glenn amendment on enrichment. The perceived need to render conventional military assistance to Pakistan was the earliest test of the Reagan non-proliferation policy (point II), for as stated by Under-Secretary of State Buckley, "In place of the ineffective sanctions on Pakistan's nuclear programme imposed by the past Administration, we hope to address through conventional means the sources of insecurity that prompt a nation like Pakistan to seek a nuclear capability in the first place."[18] It remained to be seen whether Pakistan would foreswear any bomb-directed programme or whether she would end up with both conventional and nuclear armament, courtesy of the United States.

There is an odd assymetry in the amendments. Since Pakistan was believed to be reprocessing some fuel from her KANUPP reactor, her aid was in jeopardy on two issues. But for the President to override the reprocessing amendment, apparently the path is clearer to provide military aid to a country either providing or using reprocessing equipment.

THE EXPORT–IMPORT BANK ACT

Another legislative restriction involves the financing of exports through the Export–Import Bank Act.[19] Any loan or guarantee for any export involving enrichment, reprocessing, nuclear power or research, or heavy water production facilities must lie before the Congress for twenty-five days before it can be approved. Further, the Secretary of State must report to the Export–Import Bank if there are any related undesirable nuclear actions. If so, the President must determine that the loan is in the national interest. Certain actions can trigger a denial review. These include the explosion of a nuclear device by a non-nuclear weapon state or a violation of IAEA safeguards or of a bilateral agreement for nuclear cooperation.

THE NON-PROLIFERATION TREATY

The framers of the Treaty on the Non-proliferation of Nuclear Weapons (NPT) did not foresee categories of nations to which the treaty would not strictly apply. On the other hand, had the framers taken all possibilities into account, the treaty would not have been achieved. The Treaty does not guide relationships among states which are not yet signatories. The NPT does not foresee nuclear behaviour after a signatory state may have taken advantage of the privilege of withdrawing after three months advance notice (Article X), nor does it dictate what might be done if a state actually violates the NPT but desires to remain a signatory. There are no sanctions in the treaty.

The treaty does not require safeguards in non-nuclear weapon states for non-peaceful nuclear activities unrelated to nuclear weapons or nuclear explosive devices. Such facilities might include propulsion units for submarines or research reactors devoted to non-nuclear ordnance research. And, since the treaty defines a nuclear weapon state as a nation which has exploded a nuclear device prior to 1 January 1967, it has created a curious category of potential (or hoped for) signatories with whom it will be very difficult indeed to define any relationship before and after they sign the NPT. India is such a state since she exploded a nuclear device in 1974.

The problem of relating selective (i.e., troublesome) states to the NPT and to national export policies is not hypothetical. There is already the India problem. It is not inconceivable that once Pakistan detonates a nuclear explosive device, at that point another problem may complicate the situation – her seeking to adhere to the NPT, as India has not. Iraq, one of the earliest signatories of the NPT, could decide to pull out some day, with or without three months notice. The list of real possibilities and consequent problems, especially for nuclear suppliers, can be extended. It may not have been surprising that the delegates to the first NPT Review Conference (Revcon) in 1975 found nothing to discuss, but it seems that only sheer negligence can account for the same neglect at the 1980 Revcon.

It is mainly the problem of exports of nuclear materials and facilities which should be forcing nations to re-examine, separately and together, the NPT and the national laws which define and regulate nuclear behaviour. For the United States, the most vexing restriction is the self-imposed barrier against aid to nations not subject to safeguards on "*all* peaceful nuclear activities". If a state is party to the NPT, there would appear to be no problem, for under Article III it accepts such safeguards. For non-NPT states like Israel, India and Spain, their nuclear facilities are subject to different regulations (which some consider to be more strict) than those in nations accepting full-scope safeguards, and only some are under IAEA safeguards.

THE REAGAN POLICY

The Nuclear Non-proliferation Act of 1978 specifies that no "export shall be made unless IAEA safeguards are maintained with respect to all peaceful nuclear activities in, under the jurisdiction of, or carried out under the control of such state at the time of export" [Section 128 a.(1)]. And while the Administration of President Reagan had pledged to review all laws, regulations and procedures (such as those of the NNPA), the insistence on full-scope safeguards as a primary precondition for approval for nuclear-related exports remains. It is therefore important at this juncture to examine the seven-point policy of President Reagan which was enunciated on 16 July 1981[20] (the anniversary of the first atomic bomb test, a coincidence not noticed by the President):

The United States will:
I. Seek to prevent the spread of nuclear explosives to additional countries as a fundamental national security and foreign policy objective.

Here, the United States recognizes once again that the spread of nuclear explosive technology anywhere on the globe is a political and military destabilizing factor. Whether harsher means than demanding full-scope IAEA safeguards would ever be implemented awaited the test of a new proliferation crisis. Meanwhile, the existing restrictions of the NNPA of 1978 would be expected to be applied in full force. In this respect it must be recalled that the approval of new fuel for India's Tarapur reactor, strenuously pushed by President Carter in the waning days of his Administration, was opposed in the election platform statement of the Republican Party.

II. Strive to reduce the motivation for acquiring nuclear explosives by working to improve regional and global stability and to promote understanding of the legitimate security concerns of other states.

This second point was the first to arouse controversy for the new Administration. At issue were two legal restrictions not contained in the NNPA of 1978. The Glenn amendment states that no funds may be used for the purpose of providing economic or military assistance to any nation delivering or receiving assistance in nuclear enrichment technology and equipment and/or delivering or receiving assistance in nuclear reprocessing.

President Carter cut off military aid to Pakistan on this basis. The 1977 Act does allow the President to override these restrictions if the termination of such assistance "would be seriously prejudicial to the achievement of United States nonproliferation objectives or otherwise jeopardize the common defense and security". The Reagan Administration apparently believes that at least in the case of Pakistan, giving them military assistance would reduce their "motivation for acquiring nuclear explosives". That was a substantial wager, for there was no immediate signal that Pakistan was in any way reducing the pace of her enrichment or reprocessing ventures. It was this second premise of the new nuclear policy which was likely to be tested soonest.

III. Continue to support adherence to the Treaty on the Non-Proliferation of Nuclear Weapons and to the Treaty for the Prohibition of Nuclear Weapons in Latin America (Treaty of Tlatelolco) by countries that have not accepted those treaties.

Thus, because there is nothing better than a treaty-in-hand, the two basic non-proliferation treaties will be supported. The NPT may be sorely tested if, for example, a signatory like Iraq should be shown – without question – to be developing nuclear explosive devices. Already, a mystery explosion in the South Atlantic on 22 September 1979, may have tested the NPT.[21] The question was too embarrassing for the Carter Administration to pursue with any seriousness. It will be interesting to observe the reaction of the Reagan and future administrations to new "mysterious" events, should they occur.

The United States – like the People's Republic of China, France, the USSR, and the United Kingdom – is signatory to the second Protocol of the Treaty of Tlatelolco, whereby the nuclear weapons powers promise not to use nuclear weapons in Latin America. It was not so easy for the United States to agree not to deploy nuclear weapons in that area; the PRC and the USSR also desisted from signing the first Protocol of the Treaty of Tlatelolco. Now, however, the United States will seek to add its signature, the Senate permitting.

The significance of this third policy point for nuclear exports is that the NPT remains the principal external guideline for the United States. The regional Tlatelolco Treaty is less restrictive than the NPT. Article 1 prohibits nuclear weapons, but not nuclear explosive devices, and Article 18 allows their use. And Article 5 allows the possession of nuclear weapons delivery systems, if not the nuclear weapons themselves. Thus, parties to the Treaty can develop and/or acquire nuclear-capable weapons delivery systems indigenously or with outside help (conceivably even from the United States in view of the second policy point). The Protocols do not directly relate to nuclear exports, unless exports of entire weapons are considered. In this respect, it is interesting that Cuba, focus of the 1962 crisis, has not signed the Treaty of Tlatelolco and that the USSR has not signed Protocol I, signatories of which promise not to introduce nuclear weapons into the area.

IV. View a material violation of these treaties or an international safeguards agreement as having profound consequences for international order and United States bilateral relations and also view any nuclear explosion by a non-nuclear weapon state with grave concern.

This may be the most significant of the Reagan policy points. It appears to put the full force of United States diplomacy, at least, against any violation anywhere – even if the United States or its property is not involved in such a violation. This could be very meaningful in instances where the United States believes another nation is aiding the weapons capability of a third nation in violation of international treaties. On the other hand, this policy position would appear not to apply where two non-NPT signatory nations may be collaborating, as France and Pakistan once did. But it is the point to be most noticed, for example, by Italy in future aid policies toward Iraq, a signatory, or toward Pakistan, a non-signatory. This policy statement also seems to imply, as an example, that there will be increased effort toward identifying the perpetrators of future "mysterious" explosions.

V. Strongly support and continue to work with other nations to strengthen the International Atomic Energy Agency to provide for an improved international safeguards regime.

The fifth policy point is, essentially, a pledge of support to the IAEA, and a reaffirmation of faith in it. This means that the United States will support not only the maintenance and strengthening of IAEA safeguards, but most of the associated IAEA institutions – even those not directly identified with safeguards. The latter could include safety, waste management, physical protection of nuclear materials during use and transport and special regimes such as an international plutonium storage (IPS) system. The new IAEA Committee on Assurances of Supply would be supported as an adjunct to the effort to re-establish the United States as a reliable supplier of nuclear fuel.

The United States supports the continuing efforts of the IAEA to improve safeguards techniques. If there is increased confidence in such techniques, nuclear exports from many nations will benefit.

VI. Seek to work more effectively with other countries to forge agreement on measures for combating the risks of proliferation.

President Reagan's sixth point carries the message that the United States will not rely on IAEA safeguards exclusively. Presumably, the United States will not hesitate to enter into bilateral negotiations with the suppliers and the supplied and employ means to assure that certain transfers should not occur or that they be properly safeguarded – especially when it would appear that the nuclear material, equipment or technology might not be subject to IAEA safeguards.

Also, the Administration might seek to adopt uniform conditions of supply among supplier nations. There is more than a hint here that the new Administration would seek a safeguards ambience free from commercial competition. This is the dictum which set the Nuclear Suppliers' Group on its downward slide in 1977. Freedom from commercial competition is not necessarily good for non-proliferation, or indeed realistically achievable. It is quite possible that the vendor with the lowest price could be the most insistent on reliable safeguards. Conversely, if the buyer is determined to avoid safeguards he will pay any price. It would appear that the Reagan Administration should examine the broader effects of eliminating economic competition among nations before this hardy perennial is accepted as a fixed dictum of nuclear *non*-proliferation policy.

VII. Continue to inhibit the transfer of sensitive nuclear material, equipment, and technology, particularly where the danger of proliferation demands, and to seek agreement on requiring IAEA safeguards on all nuclear activities in a non-nuclear-weapon state as a condition for any significant new nuclear supply commitment.

As originally formulated, the seventh and final point was a subset of point six, the determination to work closely with other nations to seek measures to combat the risks of proliferation. It was later perceived to merit separation as a major policy point. For this point reaffirms the United States commitment to the full scope ("all") safeguards commitment of the NPT and the same conditions "for any significant new nuclear supply commitment" to nations which may not be NPT signatories. The policy seems to infer that for *sensitive* situations caution will be exercised even where full-scope safeguards apply. The adjective "new" appeared to give some flexibility in dealing with situations carried over from previous Administrations. And the full-scope safeguards requirement is in concert with the existing Nuclear Non-proliferation Act of 1978.

Thus, in several respects, President Reagan's "new" non-proliferation policy is on a continuum with those of his predecessors. In the instructions issued simultaneously with the policy, there were, however, some radical departures from previous thinking. Most dramatic were the changes in United States attitudes toward reprocessing and plutonium use.

The Administration announced that it would not oppose commercial civil reprocessing and breeder reactor development programmes in nations with *advanced* nuclear programmes and where such activities would not constitute increased risk of nuclear proliferation. Requests for the disposition or use of plutonium would be processed on the merits of each case pending development of general policy guidelines on reprocessing and the uses of plutonium in civil programmes like the breeder. For the first time, a broad policy was announced toward specific countries. Providing certain statutory requirements were met, the United States would approve requests for re-transfers of spent fuel elements for reprocessing in the United Kingdom, an NPT signatory, and in France, a non-NPT signatory state. As long as the ultimate use of nuclear materials is in reactors, where they are most easily safeguarded, the United States, normally at the time of issuing an export licence for nuclear materials, would authorize retransfers of those nuclear materials.

However, the United States would continue to oppose by non-licensing and other appropriate actions the introduction of sensitive facilities like reprocessing plants and breeder reactors in regions of political instability, and would seek to have other suppliers adhere to this same objective. Overall, the United States would seek to re-establish itself as a reliable supplier for legitimate nuclear needs and as a predictable partner in peaceful nuclear cooperation.

That same day, President Reagan instructed the Nuclear Regulatory Commission to act expeditiously on the new licensing philosophy, and the Department of State and appropriate agencies to initiate a review of revisions in law to implement the changes, particularly the new attitudes toward reprocessing and plutonium use. At the end of the summer of 1981 however, no significant changes seemed to be in train for United States non-proliferation policy. Many of these changes would hinge on changes in United States law, and therefore upon the Congress. So at least some of them were not preordained, for the Congress held and continued to hold strong independent views, particularly on reprocessing and plutonium use. It may be that the Administration's continued strong adherence to the principle of full-scope safeguards as a precondition to nuclear commerce would prove to be the touchstone in bringing the Congress to the Administration's views.

FUTURE PROSPECTS

Until 1972, United States reactor vendors dominated the world market with over ninety per cent of the sales. As industrial capabilities increased abroad through indigenous development and the licensing of American technology, the proportion of the world reactor market held by United States industry dipped to less than half by 1976. There were then eleven other reactor companies in seven other countries competing with two United States companies. In addition to the industrial competition, another major factor was that other governments began to protect their home markets as their nuclear capabilities increased.

Because nuclear export sales began to comprise a substantial fraction of national income, governments began to rely on other methods of support. As an example, the export of a standard size nuclear reactor contributed to West Germany's balance of payment the same amount as would the export of more than two hundred thousand Volkswagens. Thus, other governments indicated that their major, and perhaps only, export condition was simply that IAEA safeguards be applied to the reactors and to the fuel.

But in the United States the 1974 shock of the Indian nuclear detonation began to manifest itself in law and regulations. In February 1976, the United States government began to impose elaborate export licensing procedures, requiring the approval and coordination of several different agencies. With the passage of the Nuclear Non-proliferation Act of 1978, more rigorous export conditions had to be met. The domestic nuclear programmes began to wane, paradoxically, in a period of increasing dependence on foreign energy sources. The 1979 accident at Three Mile Island did not enhance the image of American nuclear reactors abroad. Foreign competition has increased dramatically; twelve US reactor projects were cancelled in 1980. As a result of all of these negative influences, the United States presently would be fortunate to capture in the world market about the same share it was losing in 1972. This, in less than a decade, is a dramatic reversal after four decades of nuclear leadership. A more important loss may prove to be the image of global technological leadership and the economic and political consequences of this. That need not be. The

Reagan non-proliferation policies are more flexible than the previous Administration's. It remained to be seen whether they would be wisely applied.

NOTES

1. "Russian Uranium Exported to United States", *New York Times*, 17 Aug. 1981, p. A8.
2. *Nuclear Fuel*, New York, 27 Apr. 1981, p. 13.
3. Margaret Gowing, *Britain and Atomic Energy 1939–1945* (London: Macmillan, 1964).
4. Ibid., pp. 439–40.
5. Ibid., pp. 444–6.
6. Ibid., p. 447.
7. United States Department of State, *A Report on the International Control of Atomic Energy*, Washington, D.C., 16 Mar. 1946.
8. United States Department of State, Press Release, no. 235, 9 Apr. 1946.
9. For example, Reference 7 (New York: Doubleday, 1946).
10. J. R. Newman and B. S. Miller, *The Control of Atomic Energy* (New York: McGraw-Hill, 1948).
11. Public Law 95–242, 10 Mar. 1978.
12. *Guidelines for Nuclear Transfers, 21 September 1977*, (*Survival*, Mar.– Apr. 1978, pp. 85–87).
13. The White House, press release, 4 Oct. 1977.
14. P. Lellouche, "International Nuclear Politics", *Foreign Affairs*, Winter 1979–80, pp. 336–50.
15. G. Smith and G. Rathjens, "Reassessing Nuclear Non-Proliferation Policy", *Foreign Affairs*, Spring 1981, pp. 875–94.
16. The White House, press release, 19 Oct. 1977.
17. Public Law 95–52, 4 Aug. 1977, sections 669 and 670.
18. "Why the United States Must Strengthen Pakistan", *New York Times*, 5 Aug. 1981.
19. The Export–Import Bank Act Extension of 1978, Public Law 95–143.
20. United States Department of State: President Reagan, *Nuclear Non-proliferation* Current Policy, no. 303 16 July 1981; The White House, fact sheet, 16 July 1981.
21. A. Kramish, "Nuclear Flashes in the Night", *The Washington Quaterly*, Summer 1980, pp. 3–11.

3 Giscard's Legacy: French Nuclear Policy and Non-proliferation, 1974–81*

Pierre Lellouche

Never has France's role in international nuclear politics been greater than since 1974. The period of Giscard's Presidency not only witnessed the first major successes of the French nuclear industry's export efforts and the launching of an ambitious domestic electro-nuclear programme, it also showed France's impressive technological advances in key areas such as fast breeder reactors and commercial spent fuel reprocessing. Moreover, whereas all other Western industrialised nations were severely hit by the nuclear recession of these years, France demonstrated a remarkable ability to insulate herself from both social (i.e., environmental) and economic difficulties associated with the development of a large nuclear programme. In fact France during the *septennat* increased her technological lead while carving out for herself an ever-growing role in the arena of international nuclear politics.

Towards the end of this period, however, domestic political protest over the siting of reactors indicated that France was not immune to this broader Western phenomenon. The Giscard era ended, moreover, with the election to the presidency of the leader of the Socialist Party, François Mitterrand. Shortly afterwards, in June 1981, the French-built nuclear power reactor in Iraq was destroyed by the Israeli armed forces. Giscard's term will remain in history as a nuclear one for

*Parts of this chapter have been adapted from sections of an earlier paper which appeared originally in volume 12 of the *Arbeitspapiere zur Internationalen Politik,* Forschungsinstitut der Deutschen Gesellschaft für Auswärtige Politik e.V., © 1980 Europa Union Verlag GmbH, Bonn.

France; it is less clear, in the early 1980s, that this will be the case under the Mitterrand administration. Do these kinds of developments presage change, perhaps even fundamental change, in French nuclear policy and nuclear export policy in particular? Not necessarily – though they do suggest that French policy during the present decade will be formulated in a more complex domestic and international environment than was the case in the 1970s. Continuity, rather, tends to be the hallmark of French nuclear policy. The aim of this chapter is to review the evolution of French thinking about nuclear energy and non-proliferation, with particular emphasis on the period 1974–81, in order to provide a better understanding of French policies in the past and a more adequate basis for discussion of possible changes in the future.

THE EVOLUTION OF THE FRENCH NUCLEAR-INDUSTRIAL COMPLEX

Perhaps more so than in other countries, atomic energy has always had in France considerable prestige value. This is in part due to history. French scientists brought an important contribution to the birth of nuclear science in the 1930s, and some even participated in the nuclear war effort in Canada. After the Second World War, France was the first nation to create an Atomic Energy Commission; and in the last four decades the atom has remained a political symbol of primary importance. It represents the scientific and economic modernisation of the country, a key condition for restoring to France her "rank" among the great world powers.[1] Under the Fifth Republic – until Giscard's election in 1974 – this symbolism manifested itself above all in the military field, with the creation of the *force de frappe* by de Gaulle, and its modernisation by Pompidou.[2] The new aspect contributed by Giscard's Presidency has been the vigorous effort to develop nuclear energy for *peaceful* purposes, with the aim of making France the leading "civilian" nuclear power while maintaining for it its position as the third-ranking military nuclear power.

This ambition has entailed a profound modification of the existing industrial structures. Until the early 1970s, the French nuclear-industrial complex offered a sharply contrasted picture: on the one hand, a very potent research apparatus largely geared to military applications and fully controlled by the state through the Commissariat à l'Energie Atomique (CEA); on the other hand, a weak and fragmented nuclear industry. This industry – strictly administered by the CEA as well as by the national electricity utility (Electricité de France – EDF), and deliberately anchored to the nationally developed graphite-gas reactor line (with natural uranium as fuel) while most other industrialised nations had long before opted for the American LWR – was unable to consolidate until after the early 1970s.[3] This explains the small number of exports of the French nuclear industry during that period, by comparison with the American giants. Domestically, the modest atomic power programme launched in 1964 materialised only partially and haltingly, largely because of economic uncertainties and hesitations on the part of the political authorities regarding the choice of a reactor line (graphite–gas versus LWR). Thus of the 4500 MW planned for 1975, only 2900 MW were installed by the end of 1976.[4]

It was only in the late 1960s, following the conclusion of the political and bureaucratic struggles over reactor line choice, that the industry began progressively to be reconstructed in order to take into account the new economic–energy imperatives facing the country. The new situation was characterised by a potentially dangerous dependence on oil imports. Between 1955–76, France's dependence on imported fossil fuel jumped from 36 per cent to 77 per cent.[5] This vulnerability prompted the need to develop a strong nuclear programme and to create for that purpose an efficient national industry, one able to compete with the large US companies in the world market. The experts of the PEON Commission, who had long supported the graphite–gas line largely in order to guarantee France's independence from US enriched uranium, were thus led to abandon their position. After 1968 the Commission recommended that France "follow the prevailing world trends" and switch to the LWR, which was viewed as a commercially proven and reliable technology.[6] Significantly, this decision was made by the Government in November 1969, after the resignation of de Gaulle, who had opposed the change.

President Pompidou then began the process of reinforcing the nuclear industry. Two manufacturers were selected, Framatome and Compagnie Générale d'Electricité. Each was the licensee of the two major American companies, respectively Westinghouse for the PWR and General Electric for the BWR. In the aftermath of the 1973 oil crisis, the domestic nuclear programme was accelerated. The "Messmer Plan" called for the construction of forty nuclear power plants in ten years at a cost, in 1975 terms, of 101 billion francs. The objective was to jump from 3000 MW nuclear in 1974 to 45 000 MW by

1985.[7] This was taken still further by Giscard after 1974. In February 1975, the nuclear programme was given an extremely ambitious goal: that of meeting one-quarter of the nation's energy needs by 1985 (i.e., 55 per cent of total electricity production). For 1976/7 alone, the new plan called for the construction of 1200 MW nuclear.

In keeping with these objectives, a further concentration of the industry was initiated. The BWR line was abandoned, and the Compagnie Générale d'Electricité was consequently forced to withdraw from the market. Framatome was given the monopoly of the manufacture of "conventional" nuclear reactors, producing the PWR type exclusively, with the objective of becoming a major actor in world markets.[8] The government also obtained a modification of the licensing agreement with Westinghouse. Under this the CEA became a shareholder in Framatome, while the American corporation agreed to a gradual reduction of its own participation.[9] The aim was gradually to change Framatome's licensee relationship with Westinghouse to one of equal cooperation by 1982, the date of expiry of the existing license agreements. Finally, agreements signed between the French and United States governments and between Framatome and Westinghouse in January 1981 effectively eliminated French dependence on American nuclear technology. Framatome thus became free to export reactors to any country subject only to the approval of the French Government, and was, in the words of the French Minister of Industry, a "full partner" with Westinghouse with "complete freedom of action in the industrial field".[10]

The Giscard Administration also undertook in its early years a profound transformation of the CEA itself. From a research-oriented enterprise, the CEA was to become, as its (then) General Director, André Giraud, put it, "a kind of scientific-industrial holding with specialised subsidiaries".[11] In addition to its partnership with Framatome, the CEA, through one of its subsidiaries (the COGEMA – Compagnie Générale des Matières Nucléaires), gained control over the entire commercial services of the fuel cycle, from uranium mining to enrichment and reprocessing and eventually attained a legal monopoly over the cycle.[12] These changes resulted in a complex mixture of private and public interests, prompting the left-oriented trade unions to denounce the "privatisation" of the CEA. This process of rationalisation and centralisation has affected all nuclear-related industries. Turbine generators for nuclear plants, for example, were provided from 1976 by Alsthom–Atlantique, created by a merger of two concerns and the takeover of another. In 1974, Creusot–Loire, the group which has overall industrial direction of Framatome, set up Framateg to handle general contracting for nuclear power plants sold to foreign customers; and in 1977 an EDF–Framateg subsidiary, Sofinel, was created to handle engineering for turnkey nuclear power plants in overseas contracts.[13]

A further important step was taken in December 1976, when the government of Prime Minister Barre decided to build the first commercial sized fast breeder reactor, in conjunction with West Germany and Italy. A new industrial venture was created for the Super-Phénix project, combining the CEA and the Novatome Corporation.

Even by 1976, then, France had become a veritable nuclear energy superpower. By 1979 the country had a total of fourteen nuclear power reactors in operation (not counting the Phénix–Marcoule fast breeder); a further thirty-one were then under construction or on order, and the Super-Phénix itself was scheduled to go into industrial operation in 1984.[14]

GISCARD'S FOREIGN NUCLEAR POLICY: THE NUCLEAR EXPORTS CONTROVERSY

These developments are intimately connected with France's position as a major nuclear exporter. The tie with Westinghouse, for example, remained a constraint; United States blessing had to be sought in 1979 when the possibility arose of French nuclear sales to China.[15] Nuclear export policy in turn was from 1974 closely linked to non-proliferation policy. The election of Giscard in May 1974 coincided with India's accession to the nuclear "club". The new President was thus immediately confronted with the issue of nuclear weapons proliferation. But the complexity of this issue, its relative novelty for French policy-makers, and the evolving domestic political setting, explain why more than two years elapsed before Giscard's new foreign nuclear policy was finally announced in September–October 1976. In all, four years were necessary before the President in May 1978 presented his own disarmament proposals to the UN.

Like many other areas of Giscard's diplomacy, the new policy reflected a delicate balance between "change and continuity", the key words of France's post-Gaullist political life. However, no "French non-proliferation doctrine" emerged. Rather, French policy appeared to be a mosaic of different attitudes adapted to each of the main problem areas of the nuclear issue. Particularly in the nuclear exports field, Giscard's diplomacy, when compared to that of de Gaulle and Pompidou, seemed to represent a change and even a rapprochement with the American position. In other areas, such as the debate about plutonium and fast breeders, it is clear that French policy under Giscard was more "neo-Gaullist" in substance.

The Gaullist legacy forms a crucial backcloth to Giscard's policies. Having itself "proliferated" in the name of national independence, Gaullist France always maintained a fundamental ambiguity with respect to the non-proliferation issue. While simultaneously defending the right of every state to build its own nuclear weapons – hence the French refusal to adhere to the NPT[16] – France also spoke out, in the name of international security, *against* a further spread of nuclear weapons. Paris for this latter reason promised in 1968 that France would conduct itself as if it were an NPT party. Underlying this ambiguity was the fatalistic Gaullist view of proliferation. In a world of inequity and aggression, the gradual spread of nuclear weapons seemed "natural" and unavoidable. American non-proliferation "strategies" that relied heavily on technical "fixes" and safeguards were thus seen by the Gaullists as doomed to failure over the long run.

However, this doctrinal ambivalence paired with an intellectual fatalism only related to the world-wide aspect of the proliferation issue. This was considered marginal in terms of France's security. What really counted for the Gaullists was the regional situation in Europe, and in particular the risk of the spread of nuclear weapons to a single country: the Federal Republic of Germany. In practice, therefore, Gaullist foreign nuclear policy was entirely focused on the "German problem". Fear of a nuclear-armed Germany accounts for the ambivalent French attitude towards EURATOM. It also explains the French proposals of 1962/63 in which de Gaulle apparently offered the protection of the *force de frappe* to the FRG as a counter to the American proposal for a "multilateral" nuclear force (MLF).[17]

In summary, the Gaullist attitude towards non-proliferation can be broken down into three main components: (i) rejection of the US position, in particular technical control and safeguards measures which were regarded as both ineffective and as incompatible with national sovereignty; (ii) acceptance in principle of the concept of non-proliferation, to the extent that this did not interfere with France's national nuclear programme in both the civilian and military sectors; and (iii) concentration on the problem of Germany, which was seen as directly linked to France's security.

By 1974/75, however, the proliferation issue had a number of new strategic and technological dimensions. These highlighted the limitations, indeed the irrelevance, of many of the Gaullist principles inherited from the 1960s; and led the presidency of Giscard to reassess France's attitude towards non-proliferation. Firstly, the problem of the "Nth country" no longer presented itself in European terms. Germany was not perceived as an immediate proliferation candidate. Instead, the danger was now seen to have shifted to the Third World. This new dimension made it easier for Giscard's France – which considered itself decidedly European – to improve relations with the Federal Republic and to erase many of the earlier suspicions and misunderstandings which had in the past prevented close cooperation between the two countries. Many influential Gaullists, however, retained their suspicions with regard to Germany. This fact constituted an important limitation on the President's freedom of action in the nuclear area. Moreover, elaboration of a French non-proliferation policy directly aimed at developing nations seemed inconsistent with the *mondialiste* destiny towards which the new President wished to orient his diplomacy. A double contradiction thus quickly became apparent. How would a new non-proliferation policy affect the traditional "German problem" in the context of a "European France"? And how would such a policy, which necessarily discriminates against the Third World, be compatible with the image of a "link" which Giscard's France intended to forge between the industrialised North and the underdeveloped South?

The second new dimension of the proliferation issue stemmed from France's own nuclear progress in the early 1970s. Whereas France had played only a marginal role in the international nuclear market in the 1950s and 1960s, she now became, through her ambitious export programme, directly drawn into the proliferation process.[18] Ironically, it was the very success of the President's nuclear industrial policy which suddenly forced Paris to show its political colours in the proliferation controversy. Having become, along with Germany, the most important exporter of nuclear technology, Giscard's France had to depart from the comfortable ambivalence with which the Gaullist Fifth Republic had previously been able to protect itself because of the weakness of its nuclear industry. This pressure to clarify its position on proliferation immediately raised the central political dilemma of the new Presidency. Implementation of a policy closer to the American arms control doctrine directly offended the Gaullist legacy still championed by the strongest elements within the government coalition. The contradiction was exacerbated, further, by the weight of the bureaucratic structures inherited from the Gaullist era – above all the CEA – which rendered any deviation from nationalistic principles even more difficult.

Thirdly, France in the 1970s was now committed to a large domestic nuclear programme. An effective non-proliferation policy could therefore entail important economic costs, including the loss of export revenues; uncertainties and threats to the fuel supply; delays in the construction of new installations as a result of increased safeguards; and above all a very real risk of losing the important technological advantage which France enjoyed in the area of fast breeder reactors and commercial reprocessing. Here lay a third contradiction: How could non-proliferation and energy independence be reconciled in a country which depended for 75 per cent of its energy needs on fossil fuels?[19]

It is against this background of diplomatic, domestic and economic considerations that Giscard's foreign nuclear policy was formulated and executed. The most significant change in this policy involved the question of nuclear exports to the Third World, an issue which mobilised much international attention in the period 1974–6. This period coincided in France with the first phase of the Giscardian presidency (May 1974–August 1976), a phase characterised by an increasingly difficult coexistence between a President advocating the development of new policies, and a Gaullist Prime Minister, Jacques Chirac, striving to preserve the principles of de Gaulle's Fifth Republic. In such a context, the proliferation controversy inevitably took on a symbolic value in the domestic political scene. The entire proliferation debate was perceived more as an internal political test of the new leadership than as a global issue affecting international security. From the perspective of French political elites, the handling of the nuclear issue by the new President would reveal the degree of his independence from or alignment with the United States; and Giscard was in any case already suspected of the sin of *Atlantisme*. Any deviation from Gaullist dogma would be considered sure proof of this. Giscard was thus caught in the crossfire between the United States, which had suddenly re-discovered the "spectre" of proliferation, and the vigilant Gaullists, who were always prepared to denounce any "collaboration" with Washington. In such a context, Giscard's policy fluctuated during this period between conciliation and conflict with the Ford Administration.

At first, Giscard tried to avoid taking a public stand in the controversy. He even made some conciliatory gestures towards Washington: as in the harmonious Martinique summit of 1974; the decision to participate in the London Suppliers Group – an important step since in 1974 France had refused to join the consultations of supplier nations in the Zangger Committee[20]; and discreet acquiescence in the veto by the United States of the French–South Korean reprocessing contract. At the same time, however, the Government of Prime Minister Chirac, through its policy of *grands contrats* with developing nations, encouraged the nuclear industry to expand its export activities not only of PWR power reactors (Iran, South Africa), but also of "sensitive" installations such as reprocessing plants (Pakistan, South Korea) and large research reactors (Iraq, Iran). Further gestures typical of the Gaullist sympathies of the Prime Minister were the long delay before joining the London Club – a move taken in order to obtain West Germany's ratification of the NPT[21] – and the spectacular public dispute, in the traditional Gaullist style, between Chirac and Kissinger over the French–Pakistani contract in August 1976.[22]

These contradictory signals from Paris dashed American hopes of a new rapprochement with France. To the US, France appeared determined to retain its traditional role as the main opponent of American arms control efforts. Chirac's resignation in August 1976 finally opened the way for a clarification of French nuclear policy in the manner hoped for by the Giscardians and other "moderates" within the French establishment, as well as by Washington. Only a few days after the resignation, the Elysée Palace imposed direct presidential control over all nuclear exports. It created on 1 September 1976 a Council on Foreign Nuclear Policy (CNPE) with special responsibility for non-proliferation questions.[23] The new policy was further established with two other steps. On 11 October a *Déclaration* was published explaining France's foreign nuclear doctrine; and on 16 December, there was announced a presidential order discontinuing until further notice the export of reprocessing facilities.[24] The moves appeared to signal a break with the Gaullist approach to non-proliferation, and were extremely well received in Washington. During the visit of Giscard to the US in September 1976 observers reported a clear French–American détente on the question of non-proliferation. On the other hand, the Gaullist press accused Giscard of having bowed to American pressure,[25] forcing the President's supporters to deny the accusation of *Atlantisme* and to insist that the new orientation of French policy did not amount to an "alignment with

Washington's views". "Is there really no other method of asserting the independence of our policy", they argued, "than placing it in opposition to another?"[26]

The immediate consequence of this Franco-American rapprochement on the nuclear exports issue was the breakdown of the French–German "front" which Chirac had helped to create during the previous two years. The "front" had been designed primarily to resist US non-proliferation pressures, and had proven to be quite effective during the London Suppliers Group's negotiations. In December 1976, the FRG thus was totally isolated in the nuclear exports controversy as the only country still willing to export reprocessing facilities. As a result, Bonn was now perceived in Washington as the chief obstacle to the development of a common non-proliferation approach by all nuclear supplier nations.[27]

In assessing the record of France in the nuclear exports area in the period 1976–81 three considerations must be borne in mind. First, there has been in the last few years a general crisis in the international nuclear market, with a particularly low number of orders from developing nations and a depression of markets in industrialised countries. The non-proliferation controversy took place in a context of a world-wide cycle of depression in nuclear energy development.[28] Secondly, the December 1976 order to "discontinue" exports of reprocessing plants – qualified in any case by the phrase "until further notice" – demanded no great sacrifice on the part of French industry. On the contrary, the reprocessing of spent fuel on French soil (La Hague) earns much more for French industry than the export of small installations at relatively low prices, an activity which has the additional drawback of weakening the French monopoly in this field. Reprocessing contracts for La Hague earned approximately 12 billion francs in 1977.[29] Many high officials of the CEA who opposed the embargo in 1976 on "national independence" grounds were later fully in favour of it, at least so long as France continued to enjoy a quasi-monopoly in commercial reprocessing services. Thirdly, the French nuclear industry was at the time less dependent than its German counterpart on nuclear exports. Framatome's order books are filled for many years to come by EDF's domestic contracts, a fact which considerably reduces export incentives and the willingness to transfer sensitive sweeteners. France thus enjoyed a unique position among western nations: her non-proliferation policy coincided with the economic interests of her nuclear industry. History has shown that such a coincidence of interests is crucial to the successful implementation of a state's foreign nuclear policy.

Whether this favourable situation can be preserved in the future is a difficult question. Much will depend on the evolution of the domestic nuclear programme during the 1980s. This potentially destabilising factor needs to be placed in the wider framework of France's diplomatic objectives. The contradiction between *mondialisme* and nuclear discrimination against the Third World was not resolved by Giscard. Up to a point the French Government did succeed, however, in preserving a delicate balance between non-proliferation (discreetly cancelling the Pakistani contract) and the establishment of France's image as the pioneer of the North-South dialogue. But in so doing, France endeavoured gradually to distinguish itself from other members of the London Group, going so far as to publicise differences of opinion among supplier nations. In various conferences, for example the Persepolis and Salzburg meetings of April–May 1977, a somewhat "neo-Gaullist" nuclear doctrine emerged which dubbed itself "moderate" and "Third World friendly" by opposition to Washington's "maximum confrontation" thesis.[30] The doctrine led France, along with West Germany, to oppose adoption of full-scope safeguards in the London Group Guidelines and to undertake several diplomatic initiatives aimed at reconciling non-proliferation and non-discrimination – with the ultimate goal of increasing France's technological prestige. At Salzburg in 1977 France presented a "peaceful" uranium enrichment process proclaimed as the solution to the proliferation issue; this "atoms for peace" *à la française* proved a bit premature, in that it was neither very new technically nor practically applicable for at least another ten years.[31]

France's non-proliferation doctrine, then, was capable of incorporating considerable change in the direction of full cooperation with developing nations. French officials have repeatedly denounced the discriminatory aspects of American non-proliferation policies and the traditional US tendency to rely on "technical fixes" in order to solve political problems. Decisions taken in Washington in the name of non-proliferation have been denounced in Paris as the cause of a "climate of mistrust" in international nuclear relations, a climate which itself accelerates proliferation. Yet the declaration of 11 October 1976 was so vaguely formulated as to encompass almost any future modification of nuclear export policy: Paris could choose to give priority either to the idea of an "understanding among the supplier nations" or to the principle that France "must remain master of its own nuclear export policy".[32]

Several of France's nuclear export agreements resulted in widespread controversy in the period after the formulation of the 1976 policy. Sales to Pakistan and Iraq in particular posed difficult issues for French nuclear policy-makers.

At the time of the French ban on export of reprocessing facilities in 1976, officials left it unclear whether France would continue with the reprocessing project in Pakistan or halt further work on it. In August 1978, after more than two years of hesitations and confusing public statements, Giscard apparently decided to cancel the contract.[33] However, in order to avoid further problems with the Gaullists at home and to limit the damage to France's image in the Third World, Paris chose not to announce the decision unequivocally. The French decision to "cancel" the deal was in fact announced by President Zia of Pakistan who cited a letter of 9 August 1978 from Giscard. Reports persisted, however, that aid to Pakistan was being continued through the Société Générale pour les Techniques Nouvelles (SGN), a COGEMA subsidiary. It appears, though, that despite Indian (and Israeli) claims, the French contention was correct that assistance was effectively terminated as of June 1979.[34] But the matter remained a sensitive one for French officials. In an October 1980 interview, a senior official of CEA, while defending the French non-proliferation record at some length, refused to talk about Pakistan on the grounds that his remarks could be misinterpreted.[35]

The still more sensitive Osirak reactor, using 93 per cent enriched uranium, was sold to Iraq by Chirac's government in 1974. It was sabotaged in La-Seyne-sur-Mer just one week before being shipped to Iraq, reportedly by a group of "French environmentalists". (The police stated that neither environmentalists nor Israeli or Palestinian commandoes had performed the acts; and officials noted that this was a "political action" in view of the fact that the perpetrators were certainly helped from the inside.[36]) Several observers said that whoever did the "job" did service to both the Israeli and the French Governments. Paris had earlier attempted, in vain, to convince Iraq to adopt France's new, low-enriched "caramel" fuel, which it was claimed presented minimal proliferation risks for the reactor.[37] The Iraqi connection continued to be plagued with disruption and intrigue. An Egyptian engineer working for the Iraqi atomic energy authorities was killed in Paris; and attacks were carried out on an engineering company in Rome involved in the deal. To official Israeli protests, Paris replied that all necessary precautions were being taken, that Baghdad had signed the NPT, that the contract would be supervised by the IAEA, and that France would supply only the fuel needed at a given moment.[38]

At the end of September 1980, eight days after the outbreak of the Iraq-Iran war, Phantom aircraft (presumably belonging to the Iranian air force, though this was not clearly established) carried out a raid on the Tamuz Research Centre containing the reactor; and on 7 June 1981, the Israeli air force made a successful direct attack on the installation, killing a French engineer. In the period between these two events, the leader of the Socialist Party, François Mitterrand, had become President with a background both of personal sympathy for Israel's security dilemmas, and of his party's criticism of the supply of enriched uranium to Iraq under the 1974 agreement on the grounds that this posed serious dangers for the security of Israel and for peace in the Middle East. Cultivation of improved relations with Israel was said at this time to be a goal of the new President, but officials did not hesitate to condemn Israel for its actions. Mitterrand himself insisted that the reactor had posed no threat to Israel, and repeated that French policy was to sign contracts only if Paris was assured that French technology would not be used for military purposes.[39] And Arab governments were assured that the new government was determined to honour contracts signed by the Giscard administration. France had still not, in other words, resolved the problems inherent in the conflict between the 1974 Iraq agreement and the 1976 non-proliferation policy; but it was evident that future sales of an alternative research reactor using only 20 per cent enriched uranium would go a long way towards easing further tensions on non-proliferation questions between Paris and Washington.

Indeed the criticism which France often met internationally for its nuclear export policies in the Giscard period conceals the degree to which France and the United States were reaching accommodation on various points. "One thing that really upsets us", a CEA official said in 1980, "is that France is routinely criticised, because it has an effective nuclear power programme, each time it makes a move abroad."[40] Cancellation of the Pakistan contract, and attempts to modify the proliferation aspects of the Iraq arrangement, combined with support for the London Club deliberations, meant that in practice France under Giscard in the late 1970s could capitalise politically on her "good behaviour" in the non-proliferation area. Paris could also criticise the US and other nuclear suppliers on this criterion. French officials were quick to note, following attempts by Pakistan to build a clandestine centrifuge enrichment plant, that US policy, by focusing exclusively on the commercial fuel cycle, had largely ignored the risks associated with small-scale facilities. Such events were seen to vindicate the French choice of gaseous diffusion as enrichment technology. Mention was also made of the special risks associated with CANDU reactors (which happen to be France's competitors in Third World markets), and of the particular eagerness of some nuclear suppliers to sell a heavy water plant to Argentina as a "sweetener" for a power plant order. Finally, such developments were also found to justify France's pioneer work in the area of proliferation-resistant fuel research reactors. French initiative in this field was extremely well received in the US.[41] The evolution of French nuclear export policy after 1976, then, turned out to be highly beneficial to France's overall diplomatic goals, while being of no cost (and even favourable) to her domestic nuclear industry and programme.

FRANCE AND THE INTERNATIONAL PLUTONIUM CONTROVERSY

The neo-Gaullist aspects of Giscard's foreign nuclear policy were most clearly evidenced by the positions taken by France in the transatlantic quarrel over the future of the plutonium economy. In effect, the quarrel sparked in April 1977 by the Carter Administration's decision to cancel the US Clinch River Fast Breeder Reactor and to forgo commercial reprocessing opened a *second* international proliferation debate, quite distinct from the earlier controversy about nuclear exports.

From a French perspective, the stake in the plutonium debate was a great deal more important than that in the ealier debate over nuclear transfers to the Third World. Stricter safeguards and export regulations, as set forth in the London Group Guidelines, were tolerable to French industry; but this was not true with respect to the vital technological, economic and energy damage threatened by the US anti-plutonium stand, which directly involved France's energy independence. Having for years spent 400 million francs annually for fast breeder research, and being committed to Super-Phénix, France had a leading position in the field to protect. Moreover, French officials were convinced of the absolute need for breeders and reprocessing as an essential means to preserve the country's energy future. Responding to Carter's policy, Foreign Minister Louis de Guiringaud declared in October 1977:

For a country like France which has no oil, no coal left, which has harnessed all the hydroelectric power it could, there is no other choice than to extract from every gram of uranium all the energy which it is possible with the present technology to extract. That is why we have decided to go for breeders.[42]

André Giraud, then head of the CEA, explained:

France owns estimated natural uranium reserves of 100,000 tons. While these reserves are not large, consumed in light water reactors they nonetheless represent 800 Mtoe, or one third of the North Sea oil reserves. Through the use of breeder reactors this uranium can produce 50,000 Mtoe, the equivalent of all the Middle East oil reserves.[43]

Giscard himself shared this analysis, and quickly announced his opposition to the Carter doctrine early in May 1977, a few weeks before the London summit.[44]

The Carter Administration thus ran into a firm and definite "no" from France with regard to the plutonium issue. But the novelty and the skilfulness of Giscard's diplomacy are indicated by the articulation of the "no", and by the fact that France went on to exploit the differences between Bonn and Washington to her own benefit. It is possible to distinguish two periods in which France seemed to adopt different attitudes. The first runs from the 7 April speech to the first stage of INFCE (summer 1978). This period saw France deliberately siding with Germany and EURATOM against the US. The second period began in autumn 1978 and covered the key negotiations towards the establishment of a new world nuclear order in the post-INFCE period. In this period the French seemed to adopt a more subtle approach closer to that of the US.

Thus instead of politicising the debate, as his predecessors would undoubtedly have done, Giscard favoured an emphasis upon the economic dimension of the problem. By stressing France's situation of special energy dependence, Giscard submitted that his country could not afford the "American luxury" of dispensing with the plutonium economy. In essence, the thrust of Giscard's demonstration was to dissociate non-proliferation from plutonium uses while isolating the Americans in their own attitude of denial. As a result the US had to face the reproach that it was repudiating its own time-honoured tradition by obstructing the economic and technological progress that fast breeders represent. As opposed to the 1974–6 dispute nuclear exports to the Third World, where Washington appeared to be in the right, Giscard was now showing that the sounder reasoning now lay with the French thesis.

The second step of this policy was to secure France's technological lead in the plutonium area through the enlistment of support from other parts of Europe, and above all from the FRG. In so doing Giscard renewed one of the traditional tenets of Gaullist diplomacy, namely the establishment of a French–German front against the US. This tendency, which surfaced in the 1962–3 responses to the MLF proposal, can be found in the 1977 French–German agreement on the Super-Phénix in which France reserved for herself the role of leading partner. The first front had been created in 1974–6 by Chirac so that France and Germany could better resist US non-proliferation pressures. Giscard broke this alliance in December 1976 by his reprocessing plant export moratorium. In 1977 Giscard proposed a new alliance to Bonn in the form of a more ambitious venture in which French breeder technology would be partnered with German industrial potential. In preparation since 1976[45], the fast breeder partnership assumed concrete form with the Paris Agreements of 5 July 1977. The main features were as follows: (i) agreement between Interatom (a subsidiary of KWU–Siemens in the advanced reactor field), Gesellschaft für Kernforschung Karlsruhe (GfK), and the CEA on the exchange of technical information and the coordination of future work by a joint liaison committee; and (ii) creation of a joint marketing company, SERENA (Société Européenne pour la Promotion des Systèmes de Réacteurs Rapides à Sodium), responsible for the exploitation of the joint know-how and the conclusion of licensing agreements with reactor manufacturers.

On the German side, participation in SERENA was to be limited initially to 35 per cent; this formula was to be revised to give France 51 per cent and West Germany (and its Dutch and Belgian partners) 49 per cent once the German side had completed construction of seven breeder reactors. This seemingly one-sided arrangement reflected France's technological and industrial lead in the area. However, the clauses giving the German side more of the fees after completion of the third, and then of the seventh, breeder were also intended, according to the drafters of the agreements, to provide an incentive for the Germans to move ahead with their breeder programme as rapidly as possible. The effect, from a French perspective, was thus to reinforce French leadership in breeder technology while protecting it from further American attacks. The "European breeder consortium" could possibly create some constraints for France, but the SERENA agreements did prevent Super-Phénix from becoming a "nuclear Concorde" at a time when the US strongly opposed plutonium reactors. For this reason France preferred to share its technological advantage with its European partners even at the cost of losing some freedom of action, rather than to retain a purely scientific monopoly with little capability to transform it into a commercially viable venture. "We are aware that French breeder technology must become as universal as possible", Giraud declared as early as May 1976. "As France cannot hope to retain a world-wide breeder monopoly, the best policy is to convince other manufacturers to adopt our technology."[46] Coming as they did three months after Carter's 7 April speech, the breeder cooperation agreements were enthusiastically received by the French nuclear community as "the spectacular answer by the European nations to American pressures".[47]

A similar policy of securing foreign support against the US was also successfully pursued in the reprocessing area. France obtained in 1977/8 an impressive series of contracts for La Hague from Germany, Japan, Austria, Belgium, the Netherlands, Sweden and Switzerland. These contracts, moreover, established France's *de facto* monopoly in this highly lucrative technology.[48]

Thus by the time the US launched INFCE in October 1977, France had in effect secured all the nuclear trump cards in her hands: (i) she enjoyed the control on her territory of the entire fuel cycle; (ii) she had established a clear leadership in breeder and reprocessing technology; (iii) she had reinforced this leadership by a policy of cooperation with most other industrialised nations, thereby shielding her breeder and reprocessing programmes from US as well as from domestic environmentalist pressures; (iii) she appeared to have a "good case" for breeders in view of her overall energy situation, and even played the role of *porte parole* for energy-starved Europe and Japan at the London summit of May 1977; and (iv) she also appeared "reasonable" in the non-proliferation debate, where she had earlier shown her good will to the US by adopting a nuclear export policy closer to that of the US than that of Germany.

The French readily agreed to join INFCE in August 1977, though not without some early suspicions as to US motives. Seen from Paris, INFCE was a US attempt to achieve two complementary objectives: to halt the growing technological gap between the US and its European competitors in the plutonium areas, and to retain control of world nuclear relations at a time when the US had lost its technological and commercial leadership. In the words of a revealing editorial in *Le Monde*:

> The US are acting just like children who want to stop the game when they are losing. To freeze the present situation amounts to forcing those countries which want to use nuclear energy to continue buying for a long time American enriched uranium, American nuclear power plants and power plants based on American technology.[49]

On the other hand, French nuclear officials understood that the US had already lost the battle against fast breeders. They made sure, however, that INFCE would not amount to a two-year freeze of the French programmes and hence allow the US to "catch up" by demanding two conditions: INFCE was not to interfere with European (i.e., French) enrichment, reprocessing and breeder programmes for its two-year duration; and the evaluation would only be "a technical exercise, not an international negotiation".[50] Earlier the French had insisted on the need to obtain Soviet participation. Moscow had accelerated its own plutonium programme, and its participation in INFCE would, it was thought, increase the isolation of the US anti-plutonium stand within industrialised nations from both East and West. Even so, the general feeling of the French nuclear community at the start of INFCE was that it would not only be meaningless in terms of practical outcomes, but that it would also deepen US isolation, particularly in view of the participation of several key developing nations. INFCE would moreover be valuable for French prestige, since it would be an ideal show-room for French advanced technology not only in breeders and reprocessing, but also in the area of proliferation-resistant uranium enrichment techniques which France was actively developing.

Initial French reactions to the US Nuclear Non-proliferation Act of 1978 were far less conciliatory. The extreme complexity of the Act, and the fact that it was not actually tested until the summer of 1978, made very difficult an analysis of its consequences in terms of French interests. The central point, however, was US insistence on "renegotiation" within two years of the 1958 US–EURATOM treaty which was supposed to run until 1995, and the threat of a US nuclear fuel supply embargo should negotiations fail to start within one month of the date of entry into force of the Act (10 March 1978). To the French, the NNPA came as a clear violation of international law. It was also viewed as a serious threat to the continuation of COGEMA's successful reprocessing activities. Indeed the early understanding of the Act was that the US demanded "prior approval" for reprocessing of all fuel of US origin, and that this involved at least half of the European and Japanese spent fuel reprocessed at La Hague. The French Government had traditionally been rather hostile to EURATOM, but these considerations propelled it to the forefront of a European crusade against American attempts to control the national nuclear energy programmes of EEC Member States. In a style recalling that of his Gaullist predecessors, Giscard obtained agreement from other EURATOM members that the NNPA initially be ignored. Indeed, the one-month time limit set by Congress was deliberately allowed to expire in the midst of a mounting press campaign against the US. Paris finally agreed in early July 1978 to a compromise formula whereby "discussions" would be held with the US, but not "negotiations". These "discussions", further, were to involve only those items not covered by INFCE: they could touch no subject of real importance, such as fuel supplies, breeders or reprocessing.

The French–American standstill of July 1978 on the NNPA–EURATOM issue was a first step towards a new rapprochement between the two countries on the entire plutonium-breeder question, a rapprochement which carried with it the beginnings of what threatened to become a dangerous rift between France and Germany.

There was movement on the American side. The State Department was quick to appreciate the extensive damage done to alliance relations by the Act. This led Carter to adopt a conciliatory attitude at the Bonn summit of July 1978. Here he committed the US to promote the "indispensible development of nuclear energy" as well as "to guarantee future supply of nuclear fuel in accordance with existing agreements".[51] Moreover, whereas in April 1977 the President had clearly indicated his desire that all industrialised nations follow the US example, Washington was now suggesting that it would take into account the "special needs" of its industrialised partners and, in effect, that they could go ahead with their fast breeder programmes. Joseph Nye stated in London in June 1978:

We ask who bet on breeders to include security costs which they impose on others, particularly safe fuel cycles, in their economic calculations. At the same time they can rightly ask us for greater assurance on fuel supplies. . . . Then each nation can bet as it wishes

on the economics of the breeder without imposing the political costs
of its actions on others.[52]

Particular measures called for were (i) avoidance of premature exports
of breeders, (ii) integration of proliferation resistant fuel technologies,
(iii) effort to minimise the flow of cold plutonium, and (iv) effort to
promote multinational solutions. Gradual US recognition of the
breeder was also confirmed by the launching in August 1978 of a $1.5
billion research and development programme.

Another crucial element in the evolution of Carter's policies was
interpretation of the NNPA in connection with the retransfer of US-
origin material for reprocessing in Britain and France during INFCE.
The problem arose over two shipments of spent fuel from Japan to be
reprocessed at Windscale and La Hague. Washington interpreted
section 131(B) (2) of the NNPA in a very liberal manner, with a view to
setting a precedent and to demonstrating its good will towards its
partners abroad.[53]

This evolving US policy was well received in Paris. The French
obtained confirmation that their essential interests would be preserved
in spite of the NNPA. France had no fundamental objections to the
four conditions in Nye's London speech; and the US itself appeared to
be moving progressively towards fast breeders. Further, interpretation
of the NNPA in the Japanese case preserved most of the commercial
interests of COGEMA, at least until the end of INFCE. With respect
to the post-INFCE world nuclear order as envisioned by the US, the
French also found that they could agree with most of the US
propositions, namely: (i) full scope safeguards; (ii) avoidance of
unnecessary sensitive facilities; (iii) use of diversion resistant
technologies; (iv) joint control of sensitive facilities; and (v) institutions to ensure the availability of the benefits of nuclear energy.[54]
Of the five, the only possible point of contention was the first. France
had been opposed in principle to full scope safeguards during the
earlier London Supplier Group's meetings. In practice, however, this
provision concerned only five nations (Egypt, Israel, India, South
Africa and Spain), which meant that there was clearly room for a *de
facto* compromise on this point between Paris and Washington.

Other areas of convergence appeared. Both countries were actively
cooperating in research on proliferation resistant fuel for research
reactors. Washington showed interest in the French chemical
exchange uranium enrichment process, while the French reacted
positively to the idea of an international fuel bank for enriched

uranium.[55] The French also declared their opposition to reprocessing for use in *thermal* reactors, much to the delight of American non-proliferation advocates. On top of the French decision to cancel the Pakistani contract, this all added up to a growing mutual understanding between the US and France at a crucial time in international nuclear politics.

Without doubt, this Franco-American rapprochement was increasingly perceived in Germany as a direct threat to the FRG's own nuclear programme, if not in certain circles as a clear anti-German alliance. Bonn began to feel that the post-INFCE compromise might well turn out to be another "deal" between nuclear weapon states discriminating against non-nuclear members of the Western industrialized world. Until May 1979, when the decision was taken to "freeze" the Gorleben project, German officials repeatedly insisted that they had to go ahead with their own commercial reprocessing plans. And unlike La Hague, the Gorleben project fell directly under the prohibition of the NNPA. Bonn was also opposed to the idea of an International Nuclear Fuel Authroity on the grounds that it would "mark the end of free market activities in the fuel cycle field",[56] and was committed to using reprocessed fuel in thermal reactors. Finally, the FRG stood firmly behind its commitment to sell to Brazil a reprocessing plant and an enrichment facility.

In certain respects, therefore, one could perceive an "objective" coincidence of interests between the US and France. Tensions between Bonn and Washington had existed since 1974/75, but this emerging Franco-German nuclear rift in 1978/79 came at a time when other areas of contention were appearing in their relations with each other, particularly over EEC agricultural and monetary issues. France was caught, in a sense, between the US on the one hand, with whom she shared the status of nuclear weapon state, and Germany on the other – which France needed for her European policy and yet at the same time feared because Germany was simply "too strong".[57] There is evidence that French officials were aware of the risks associated with a Franco-German nuclear rift. But a solution could not be isolated from domestic political struggles in France. At least the Gaullist and Communist Parties, who had favoured a "tough" nuclear foreign policy, were pleased with the freezing of the Gorleben project. At least in the short term, the decision consolidated France's quasi-monopolistic situation in the reprocessing field. For some, it also relieved anxieties about a potential German plutonium economy. One Gaullist deputy, for example, publicly accused Bonn of purposely undermining the WEU Treaty in order to acquire nuclear weapons; while according to the PCF France was helping Germany to build an atomic bomb by returning German plutonium reprocessed at La Hague.[58] Yet weaknesses in the French position were also apparent in 1979. After the Gorleben decision, France's position *vis-à-vis* the US was bound to be weakened. Appreciation of this may have played a part in the agreement reached between Bonn and Paris in the spring of 1979 on the conditions for the return to Germany of reprocessed fuel.[59]

France's relations with the US and the FRG were also affected by the progress of INFCE and by developments in the French Government's case against EURATOM.[60] In INFCE in 1978–80 the pattern of cautious Franco-American rapprochement continued to operate within the evolution of a broader consensus. This is despite the fact that the Harrisburg incident, in March 1979, appeared likely to precipitate a return on the part of the US to a much tougher stance on plutonium. The US in INFCE moved steadily towards a more moderate position on plutonium, with a gradual recognition of European breeder and reprocessing needs. This was matched on the French (and European) side by a similar recognition of legitimate US non-proliferation goals. Instead of the earlier "yes" and "no" battles, the question progressively became: "Where do you draw the line between those states which can have reprocessing facilities and those which cannot?" In his statement to the final plenary conference of INFCE in February 1980, the head of the French delegation expressed support for several propositions that had Washington's sympathy. France attached great importance, he stated, to scientific and technical work to establish processes more resistant to proliferation risks, for example in the area of moderately enriched fuel for research reactors hitherto using highly enriched uranium.[61]

French reservations about the EURATOM treaty are long-standing. Article 76 provides for an amendment procedure, and there had been three attempts at treaty revision in the period to 1975. The crux of the French (or more properly the Gaullist) case was that the arrangements set up by the treaty impinged too greatly on national sovereignty. The "integrationist" view was that only the Community had the right to negotiate supply agreements; indeed Britain's successfully negotiated agreement with Australia had already run into trouble with the Commission. Then in November 1978 the European Court of Justice ruled that only the EC could sign the IAEA convention on safeguards for the transport of nuclear materials. The decision caused a political furore in France, coming as it did a few months before the June 1979 elections to the European Parliament. It gave the Gaullists a perfect weapon against both the EEC and the pro-European Giscardians. Chirac claimed that as a result of the decision France had "lost her nuclear independence", while Michel Debré called the Court's intervention a "provocation" and a "truly criminal plot between the Commission, the Court, and Belgium"[62]. Giscard was thus compelled to take a firm stand on the modification of EURATOM. Moreover, France simply could not afford to lose her ability to procure nuclear fuel on a purely bilateral basis from non-EEC producers, or, even worse, to have her own stock of fissile materials open for "preemption" by any industrialist in the Community or the Supply Agency. France, too, remained the only country in the EEC maintaining and even accelerating a nuclear programme: the battle against EURATOM was thus also an attempt to insulate France from the nuclear depression which had hit everyone else in Europe.

A related clash – over the way in which the Community was represented at Vienna talks on nuclear protection standards – was averted in February 1979.[63] But the EURATOM issue presented Giscard with too many sensitive questions at a juncture in French domestic politics when opposition political parties were eager to grasp at any weapon with which to attack the Giscardians. The President discussed the matter at length in a Februry 1979 press conference, and the Elysée Palace announced early in March that France was going to seek "nouvelles dispositions" for the EURATOM treaty.[64] But as in 1965 and 1970, such ambitious schemes for major change in the powers given the EURATOM Supply Agency appeared doomed to failure because of lack of firm agreement on the need for revision on the part of EURATOM members.

FROM GISCARD TO MITTERRAND: PERSPECTIVES ON THE FRENCH NUCLEAR PROGRAMME

On the EURATOM question as on other aspects of foreign nuclear policy, then, French actions were conditioned by developments in internal French politics. And by the end of Giscard's presidency, the domestic electronuclear programme was beginning to feel some effects from a rise in political opposition to nuclear power. Until 1979/80, the programme seemed stronger than ever – even after reactions to Three Mile Island. In February 1979, just before this accident, the government decided on a slight acceleration of the programme; afterwards it was decided to increase the pace of new power plant orders by adding four units for 1980/81 on top of the five already scheduled.[65] The only apparently disturbing sign in this otherwise bright picture was that the nuclear plant programme was running behind schedule – by two years, according to the EDF President, Paul Delouvrier, in late 1978.[66]

For a long time public opinion stayed firm in its support of nuclear power. A poll taken after Harrisburg showed consistency with earlier findings, with 62 per cent of the population being in favour of the nuclear programme.[67] Giscard was himself a staunch defender of the nuclear option.

> To forego nuclear energy, for France means a lower standard of living and a lower employment level . . . because nuclear energy is produced by French technicians and workers, with very few imports of raw materials. If we get rid of this energy, and if we replace it with imported oil, we would have to pay for the full amount of our imports and this will be a levy on our standard of living and on our employment. Therefore, the nuclear choice is a vital choice for the employment and the standard of living of the French people.[68]

The other side of the picture, however, was represented by growing public doubts, first, about the adequacy of the information available on the French nuclear power programme, and, secondly, about the vigour with which the Government was pursuing the nuclear option. A Conseil d'Information Nucléaire was created in 1978, but such measures were largely cosmetic, despite promises on public information made in 1977 by the President. Polls taken in 1979 showed more than two-thirds of the public in favour of a referendum on nuclear power, and a wide consensus on the need for better information and for more direct popular participation in nuclear decisions.[69] In December 1980, moreover, the Government authorised EDF to build four reactors at Plogoff in Brittany, the scene of unprecedented public protests earlier in the year.[70] The authorisation conflicted, on the face of it, with public statements made previously by Giscard to the effect that nuclear units would not be sited among people who did not want them. Also in December, *Le Monde*, in a major editorial, warned the government of dire consequences if it continued to ignore public opinion in a flat-out pursuit of nuclear power.[71] Public discontent, then, was not a direct consequence of

Three Mile Island, but rather a spill-over of criticism of nuclear futures being voiced in other European countries, including the FRG. The sheer size of the programme, and the accelerating speed with which nuclear goals were being set, were also factors. In addition, the nuclear industry was itself by 1980 showing signs of strain. Technical difficulties appeared as well as financial ones, including cost over-runs of the order of at least one billion francs.[72] Finally, the fading political prestige of Giscard himself in the final months before the 1981 presidential elections robbed the pro-nuclear lobby of its most distinguished and powerful apologist.

Yet it must be emphasised that this changing domestic situation did not affect in any significant way either French technological achievements in the nuclear field, or the success with which France was able to challenge the US in the international nuclear trade. In November 1980, following a period of some uncertainty in the wake of the 1977 Iran deal and obstacles to a projected major sales package with China, South Korea placed an order for two 950-MW PWRs and fuel.[73] Further, the Marcoule vitrification plant for the treatment of radioactive wastes had its process adopted in 1981 by British Nuclear Fuels Limited over competition from the technique developed in Britain.

The essential objectives of French foreign nuclear policy under Giscard lay in the preservation of French technological and energy-economic interests. This emerged clearly in the breeder–plutonium controversy, where Giscard resorted to a firm "neo-Gaullist" posture. In pursuing this goal, Giscard played skilfully with the growing German–American quarrel, siding at times with Bonn, and at others with Washington. Commitment to the fast breeder remained an article of faith for Paris throughout INFCE. Indeed the US and Canadian uranium embargoes served to underscore for the French the urgent need to shift France away from dependence on imported uranium and in the direction of fast breeders, as well as develop uranium resources in countries like Niger.[74] Giscard's foreign nuclear policy also benefited immensely from France's unique situation as the one Western nation with a growing nuclear programme. French non-proliferation policy did not, however, find a distinctive doctrine. While refusing to adhere to the NPT, France had no alternative strategy to offer. Giscard's "disarmament plan", announced at the UN General Assembly Special Session in May 1978, barely touched the proliferation problem. On the other hand, French officials emphasised the commitment of Paris to the nuclear export guidelines that have emerged from the London Club.[75]

The traditional dilemma between change and continuity thus remained in 1981 for Mitterrand's presidency. Domestically, demands for change were evident from those frustrated by lack of information about the nuclear programme or those upon whom nuclear plants were being imposed. Dissatisfaction was by the end of Giscard's presidency widely shared among members of CFDT, the socialist trade union grouping, as well as by Socialist Party members who have traditionally been reluctant to endorse the nuclear programme. Following the election of Mitterrand, these currents began to be felt in nuclear policy. Plogoff was cancelled, following a campaign promise made by the new President, and in July 1981 a freeze on five nuclear power stations was announced. The second element of change involves non-proliferation policy and nuclear exports. The subject is of deep personal interest to Mitterrand, who has on several occasions voiced serious fears about the prospects of nuclear weapons spread. A tightening up of French nuclear exports and safeguards requirements was an early step taken by the new presidency in the case of Iraq. French adherence to the NPT thus emerged as a possible move of the Socialist Fifth Republic, a move which would break with a long Gaullist tradition.

Other factors, however, generate continuity. The French nuclear programme was no mere whim of Giscardians or of Gaullists. It was solidly grounded in a number of realities: France's global energy situation, the persisting need to diversify from oil, the existence in practice of a still strong nuclear establishment, and the presence of highly competitive companies and technologies. All of these factors will likely compel the governments of the 1980s at least to maintain the nuclear programme embarked upon by Giscard. This does not rule out a slowing down of the pace of nuclear development, nor the possibility that some nuclear reactors will not be constructed. But already 40 per cent of French electricity comes from nuclear power; it is probable that this proportion will increase, even if it does not reach the 55 per cent target set by Mitterrand's predecessor. There will also be powerful forces of continuity at work in the field of nuclear exports. In the same way that France continues to sell arms to the Third World, socialist ideology notwithstanding, she will continue to export nuclear reactors to the Third World. Mitterrand's acceptance of the need to rebuild the Iraqi reactor is a case in point.[76] Concern over the "German problem" is a further example of the continuity of the Gaullist heritage. Giscard's legacy in the field of nuclear exports and non-proliferation policy is thus of a measure of Gaullism qualified in certain key areas by an acceptance of the need for Franco- American rapprochement.

NOTES

1. Bertrand Goldschmidt, *Les Rivalités atomiques, 1939–66* (Paris: Fayard, 1967); Lawrence Scheinman, *Atomic Energy Policy in France under the Fourth Republic* (Princeton University Press, 1965); Pierre Papon, *Le Pouvoir et la Science en France* (Paris: Editions du Centurion, 1979) pp. 105–27.
2. Lothar Ruehl, *La Politique militaire de la Vème République* (Paris: FNSP, 1978) chs XI, XII.
3. Irvin C. Bupp and Jean-Claude Derian, *Light Water: How the Nuclear Dream Dissolved* (New York: Basic Books, 1978); and Philippe Simonnot, *Les Nucléocrates* (Grenoble: Presses Universitaires de Grenoble, 1978).
4. *PEON Report*, 1964, p. 17; *ibid.*, June 1977, annex 1, p. 83.
5. According to André Giraud in a Tokyo speech of March 1978 (CEA, *Notes d'Information*, no. 4, Apr. 1978). But this dependence was itself a result of the Fifth Republic's energy policy, which converted from a domestically supplied energy economy based on coal to an imported energy supply centred on petroleum.
6. *PEON Report*, 1964, pp. 14–17; *ibid.*, 1970–4, p. 10.
7. Syndicat CFDT de l'Energie Atomique, *L'Electro-nucléaire en France* (Paris: Seuil, 1975) p. 105; Simonnot, *op. cit.*, p. 269.
8. *Nuclear News*, Feb. 1977, p. 77.
9. *Enerpresse*, 2 Jan. 1976; *Le Monde*, 4 and 5 June 1976, and 10 Nov. 1976.
10. *Energy Daily*, 9, 17 (26 Jan. 1981); *Le Monde*, 24 Jan. 1981. The exchange of technical information was also provided for; together with an agreement by Paris to "consult" with Washington on any proposed nuclear sales of possible military significance or which constituted on the face of it serious proliferation risks.
11. *Enerpresse*, 14 Jan. 1976; *L'Expansion*, Jan. 1976.
12. CEA, *L'Industrie Nucléaire Française*, June 1977, pp. 42–90; *Revue Générale Nucléaire*, 1 (1978) pp. 43–5.
13. Ministère de l'Industrie, *The Energy Policy of France* (Paris, 1979) – p. 59.
14. Ibid., pp. 54–5.
15. *Energy Daily*, 9, 17 (26 Jan. 1981).
16. Wilfrid L. Kohl, *French Nuclear Diplomacy* (Princeton University Press, 1971) pp. 259–62.
17. Ibid., pp. 282–98.
18. In the earlier period France exported a research reactor to Israel (Dimona), but only one graphite–gas reactor in a joint venture with Spain, and one PWR in a joint venture with Belgium. See US General Accounting Office, *Overview of Nuclear Export Policies of Major Foreign Supplier Nations* (Washington, D.C.: GPO, 21 Oct. 1977). A reprocessing plant was sold to Japan following negotiations in 1966–70. See M. Lung and M. Coignaud, "L'Usine de Retraitement de Tokai Mura", *Revue*

Générale Nucléaire, 4 (1978) pp. 314–19.
19. *Revue Générale Nucléaire*, June 1977, p. 18.
20. SIPRI, *Safeguards against Nuclear Proliferation* (Stockholm: Almqvist and Wiksell, 1975) pp. 58–65.
21. Interviews with Gaullist officials.
22. *L'Express*, 16 Aug. 1976.
23. Decree No. 76–845, 1 Sep. 1976, *Journal Officiel de la République Française* 2 Sep. 1976) p. 5315.
24. Simone Courteix, *Exportations nucléaires et non-proliferation* (Paris: Economica, 1978) pp. 94–101.
25. *La Lettre de la Nation*, 17 Dec. 1976.
26. François de Rose, "Puissance nucléaire et responsabilité politique", *Le Figaro*, 17 Dec. 1976.
27. Interestingly, the German decision to discontinue exports of reprocessing plants was announced at the end of the German–French summit of 16–17 June 1977, and was formulated almost exactly like the French statement of 16 Dec. 1976. This followed a background of intense pressure from the Carter Administration for cancellation of the Brazil deal; like the French–Pakistani contract, however, the German–Brazilian deal was explicitly excluded from the embargo.
28. Pierre Lellouche and Richard K. Lester, "The Crisis of Nuclear Energy", *The Washington Quarterly*, Summer 1979, pp. 34–48.
29. *Le Monde*, 13 Apr. 1978.
30. See also Bertrand Goldschmidt, "Le Contrôle de l'énergie atomique et la non-proliferation", *Politique Etrangère*, 1977, p. 413; and *Revue Générale Nucléaire*, 4 (1977) pp. 205, 329.
31. François de Rose, "La Pierre philosophale", *Le Monde*, 13 May 1977; *Nucleonics Week*, 12 May 1977.
32. *Le Monde*, editorial, 13 Oct. 1976.
33. Interviews with French Government officials, autumn 1978.
34. *Nuclear Fuel*, 18 Aug. 1980, p. 8.
35. Jean Teillac, in *Nucleonics Week*, 16 Oct. 1980, pp. 9–10.
36. *Le Monde*, 15–16 Apr. 1979.
37. *Le Nouvel Observateur*, 16–22 Apr. 1979.
38. See further David White, "France's Nuclear Sales Prospects Brighten", *Financial Times*, 12 Nov. 1980.
39. Interview in the *Washington Post*, 18 June 1981.
40. Jean Teillac, cited in n. 35 above.
41. *Le Monde*, 3–4 and 6 Sept. 1978; *Le Matin*, 4 Sept. 1978; *International Herald Tribune*, 5 Sept. 1978.
42. *Le Monde*, 27 Oct. 1977.
43. Speech in Tokyo of 8 May 1978, reprinted in CEA, *Notes d'Information*, no. 4 (Apr. 1978).
44. Interview, *Le Monde*, 7 May 1977.
45. Guidelines were agreed in May 1976. See *Les Echos du CEA*, 3 (1977) pp. 5–7; *Revue Générale Nucléaire*, 3 (1977) pp. 221–3; and SIPRI, *Yearbook 1978*, pp. 23–4.
46. Interview, *Le Monde*, 20 May 1976.
47. *Revue Générale Nucléaire*, 3 (1977) p. 221.

48. F. Sorin, "La COGEMA: Réalisations et Projets", *Revue Générale Nucléaire*, l (1978) pp. 43–6; *Nuclear News*, Nov. 1978.
49. *Le Monde*, 2–3 Oct. 1977.
50. Statement by André Jacomet at the INFCE Organising Conference, 19 Oct. 1977 (Conf. Doc. 7).
51. *Le Monde*, 19 July 1978.
52. *Proceedings of the Third International Symposium held by the Uranium Institute, London, 12–14 June, 1978* (London: Mining Journal Books, 1978) pp. 325–7.
53. Interviews with US officials.
54. Nye, cited in n. 52 above.
55. Interviews with French Government officials.
56. Günter Hildenbrand, "A German Reaction to US Non-Proliferation Policy", *International Security*, 3, 2 (Fall 1978).
57. André Fontaine, "Que faire de l'Allemagne?", *Le Monde*, 22 Nov. 1978.
58. *Le Monde*, 22 and 24 Nov. 1978; *L'Humanité*, 17 May 1978.
59. *Financial Times*, 17 May 1979.
60. On the background to the latter question see Guy de Jonquières, "French Designs on EURATOM Strain Relations with Bonn", *Financial Times*, 3 Aug. 1979.
61. "Discours de M. de Commines representant de la France à la conférence finale de l'Infce", Feb. 1980, p. 3.
62. *Le Monde*, 25 Jan. 1979, and 11 Apr. 1979.
63. *Financial Times*, 7 Feb. 1979.
64. *Le Monde*, 15 and 17 Feb. 1979; 7 Mar. and 6 Apr. 1979.
65. *Le Figaro*, 7 Feb. 1979; *L'Express*, 7–13 Apr. 1979.
66. Pressure was cited from environmental groups, as well as new safety regulations; longer administrative procedures were also a factor (*Le Monde*, 17 Oct. 1978; and Giraud, in *Le Monde*, 17 Apr. 1979).
67. *Le Monde*, 4 May 1979.
68. Television interview published in *Le Monde*, 18 Apr. 1979.
69. *Le Monde*, 4 May 1979.
70. *Nucleonics Week*, 4 Dec. 1980, p. 2.
71. Ibid.
72. Bruno Dethomas, "Qui paiera le surcoût du Programme Nucléaire?", *Le Monde*, 10 Jan. 1979.
73. *Nucleonics Week*, 13 Nov. 1980, p. 3.
74. Jean Renon, president of Foratom, in *The Times*, 27 May 1978. On the search for supplies, see Bertrand Goldschmidt, *Le Complexe atomique: histoire politique de l'énergie nucléaire* (Paris: Fayard, 1980) pp. 439 ff.
75. Jean Teillac, of CEA, interview in *Nucleonics Week*, 16 Oct. 1980, pp. 9–10.
76. Jim Hoagland, "Mitterrand's Terms for Repairing Plant", *Washington Post* article republished in the *Manchester Guardian Weekly*, 28 June 1981, pp. 15–16.

4 The Politics of Nuclear Exports in West Germany

Erwin Häckel

NUCLEAR ENERGY AND POLICY MAKING IN WEST GERMANY

The development of nuclear energy in Germany has a long and twisted history. It was not until ten years after the Second World War that a programme of nuclear research was initiated (or rather, re-installed) in the country where the fission of atomic nuclei had first been discovered in 1938. When the Federal Republic of Germany attained sovereignty in 1955, it was lagging far behind many countries in its capacity for the scientific and industrial utilization of nuclear energy. Two decades later West Germany's nuclear programme ranked among the most ambitious and the West German nuclear industry among the most expansive in the world. Half a decade later again, the industry stood at the brink of collapse and the country's nuclear programme had ground almost to a standstill.

The ups and downs of nuclear development reflect the intricacies and interactions of political and economic decision-making processes in West Germany. When the Federal Government set up its first programme of nuclear research and development in the mid-1950s it was supported by virtually all segments of the political spectrum: parties of the right and left, public opinion, the scientific community, labour unions and business associations. The only sceptics at that time were vested interests in competing energy-producing industries (coal, hydrocarbons) and a majority of electric utility companies who were wary about an unknown and unproven technology.[1]

By the mid-1960s the utilities, impressed by the performance of experimental power stations in Germany and abroad, swung around in favour of nuclear energy and began to place orders for nuclear power plants in rapid succession. Significantly, their choice fell on the light water reactor of American design which had shown its merits as a reliable working horse in US submarines and civilian nuclear installations. While this choice was viewed with some dismay by the Government and the scientific community, who had put their stakes on a variety of indigenously developed reactor designs, the manufacturing industry seized the opportunity and concentrated its efforts henceforth on the perfection of light water reactors. This strategy was pursued most successfully by Siemens, Germany's largest electric manufacturer and the holder of a Westinghouse licence for pressurized water reactors. Its subsidiary company, Kraftwerk Union (KWU), subsequently branched out into various activities of the nuclear fuel cycle and captured an increasing share of nuclear power plant orders, finally leaving only BBR (a subsidiary of BBC, the Swiss–German electric manufacturer) as a minor competitor in the domestic market.

By the mid-1970s, the spectacular growth of the German nuclear industry reached its pinnacle. More nuclear power plants had been ordered in West Germany than in any other country save the United States.[2] Official estimates anticipated a tenfold increase of nuclear electric capacity for the next decade. The Federal Government proclaimed nuclear power as the major source of alternative energy for West Germany in the coming "post-petroleum age".[3]

Then, suddenly, the heyday came to an end. Construction of nuclear power plants was now blocked, interrupted, suspended, or interminably slowed down almost everywhere in the country. Less than half the nuclear electric capacity that had been projected for 1980 came actually into operation. Not a single nuclear power plant was newly ordered by German utility companies in the latter part of the seventies.[4] Inexorably, the life of West Germany's nuclear industry seemed to be drying up.

A variety of independent factors – political, economic, cultural – has contributed to this situation. Not any one of these factors, but their combination and interaction is responsible for the current deadlock of the German nuclear programme.

Most obvious, of course, is the role of the anti-nuclear movement of ecological activists, alienated and rebellious youths, social drop-outs and anti-modern romantics – the "green" movement, as it is called in Germany. This is not a German speciality, indeed it appeared there somewhat later than in countries like the US or Sweden; but its impact was magnified by particular German circumstances. The mass media endorsed much of its argument, and the public at large, although still predominantly in favour of nuclear power, displayed an increasing sense of indecision and uncertainty about the issue.[5]

Indecision and uncertainty have marked the process of nuclear energy policy in West Germany ever since the middle of the seventies. The Federal Government continued to argue in support of rapid nuclear expansion but appeared to have lost the initiative. The Federal Parliament (*Bundestag*), previously a rubber-stamp for nuclear programmes, adopted a wavering attitude. The political parties were affected by "green" ideas in varying degrees: the ruling Social Democrats and Free Democrats waxed hesitant toward nuclear energy on the federal level and increasingly hostile on the state and local levels; the Christian Democrats remained staunchly pro-nuclear in their role of federal opposition but appeared inconclusive in positions of governmental responsibility at lower levels. A majority of state governments of either persuasion dragged their feet deliberately in the process of issuing licenses for the construction and operation of nuclear facilities. The growing complexity of nuclear regulatory procedures contributed to bureaucratic overhead and administrative procrastination. Accumulation of unresolved policy choices such as nuclear siting and waste disposal inflated the role of law courts in the scrutinization and adjudication of nuclear controversies. Two-thirds of nuclear construction sites in the country lay idle in late 1978 as a result of legal challenges. Regulatory uncertainties, rising cost overruns, pending law suits and unfilled orders, as well as a general downturn of economic activity discouraged utility companies from filing applications for new nuclear plants. Germany's ambitious nuclear programme had become bogged down in a maze of fuzzy responsibilities, red tape, tactical manoeuvring, and disorientation in the face of incompatible priorities.[6]

Under conditions of fragmented authority and massive politicization, the role of the Federal Government in the determination of domestic nuclear policy was reduced in the late 1970s to a modest act among a host of actors. Not so, however, in the field of external nuclear policy. The debate about nuclear energy in West Germany, as in most other countries, is essentially an inward-looking preoccupation of parochial interests; international aspects are scarcely noted. Hence, the making of external nuclear relations was left almost entirely to the parties immediately concerned, i.e., the Federal Government and the nuclear industry. Both have interacted closely in their policy pursuits and moved relatively free from third-party interference. It is obvious, however, that their foreign activities were heavily influenced by the pace of nuclear developments in the domestic arena.

THE SIGNIFICANCE OF NUCLEAR EXPORTS FOR WEST GERMANY

Nuclear exports figure as a mere trifle in Germany's foreign trade balance. Statistical data available for the period 1977–1979 show an average annual amount of DM 750 million worth of nuclear exports, of which nuclear reactors and fuel elements accounted for some DM 330 million, i.e., about one thousandth of West Germany's total export earnings.[7]

These figures are, of course, misleading. Experts agree that nuclear exports have a key role to fulfil for the German economy. Among many reasons the direct effect on industrial employment, though cited most frequently in public discussions, is probably the least compelling.[8] More pertinent is the effect on industrial growth and development. The construction of a nuclear power reactor at home or abroad involves some 700 subcontracting firms besides the contractor himself. Most of them are small or medium-sized industrial enterprises with a labour force of less than 200. These firms are holders of that type of highly specialized industrial skills and expertise which are an essential prerequisite for Germany's capacity to hold its position as the leading vendor of advanced industrial products on the world market. The German economy depends on this capacity more than any other major industrial economy.

Due to the lack of domestic orders for nuclear power plants the nuclear industry in West Germany can now utilize less than half of its production capacity. There is an imminent danger of idle production facilities being dismantled and qualified personnel being laid off or running away into more promising trades. The industry faces the risk of a critical and possibly irreversible loss of technological know-how, innovative momentum, and productive capability.[9]

In this situation it is the foreign market that could give vital relief to the hard-pressed industry. There is some reason to expect that domestic demand for nuclear power plants will pick up again later in the 1980s. The nuclear industry therefore depends essentially on foreign demand if it is to survive long enough for the anticipated recovery. Given the existing production capacity of completing some four to six nuclear reactors per year, there is a requirement then for at least two reactors per year ordered from abroad. The record shows that the German nuclear industry has since the mid-1970s never been able to meet this goal. Over the last decade, an average number of less than one reactor has been exported from Germany (see Table 4.1).

The list of countries receiving German nuclear power plants is revealing. There are two distinct groups of clients: neighbouring countries in Western Europe (Netherlands, Austria, Switzerland, Spain) and newly industrializing countries in the Third World (Argentina, Iran, Brazil). Each of these countries has maintained close economic relations (and in some cases close political ones, too) of long standing with West Germany; in each of them, the German industry is traditionally one of the most important commercial partners. Siemens, the parent company of KWU (Germany's leading reactor manufacturer), holds a strong market position in each of these countries.

Risks as well as opportunites for nuclear exports are revealed in this

TABLE 4.1   *Nuclear power reactors exported from West Germany*

Importing country	Power station	Type of reactor	Net electric power (MW)	Construction started	Commercial operation started
Argentina	Atucha-1	PHWR	345	1968	1974
Netherlands	Borssele	PWR	447	1969	1973
Austria	Tullnerfeld	BWR	692	1971	x
Switzerland	Goesgen	PWR	920	1973	1979
Iran	Iran-1	PWR	1200	1975	xx
Iran	Iran-2	PWR	1200	1975	xx
Brazil	Angra-2	PWR	1245	1976	1985?
Brazil	Angra-3	PWR	1245	1976	1986?
Spain	Trillo-1	PWR	990	1976	1985?
Argentina	Atucha-2	PHWR	692	1981	1987?

NOTES
Table includes power reactors in operation or under construction.
PHWR = pressurized heavy water reactor
PWR = pressurized (light) water reactor
BWR = boiling (light) water reactor
x = construction completed, operation suspended
xx = construction discontinued

SOURCE   *Power Reactors in Member States* (Vienna: IAEA, 1979, 1980, 1981).

pattern. The foreign market for German nuclear reactors is limited to a small number of countries with certain characteristics. Among these characteristics is the economic and technological capability of the recipient country to commission and operate a nuclear power plant, though not to construct it on its own, and the willingness of its government to enter into a comprehensive, complex, and long-lasting relationship with the exporting country. The European countries that have opted for German reactors are mostly small, wealthy and politically stable, but they cannot be counted on as an expansive market. Prospects for nuclear energy in the Netherlands, Switzerland and Austria are subdued by domestic disputes no less than in West Germany. Austria is in fact the only country in the world where a completed nuclear power plant – a boiling water reactor from KWU – has been barred from operation by parliamentary fiat.

Newly industrializing countries, on the other hand, do have expansive potential for nuclear sales. These countries are held to be the most rapidly growing market for German industrial products.[10] German banks have not hesitated to provide sizable loans to finance the bulk of nuclear power plant orders from these countries. But again, the inherent risks are considerable. In Iran, the Islamic revolution has overthrown not only the Shah's regime but also his ambitious nuclear programme (six reactors from KWU).[11] In Brazil, the largest nuclear export project ever concluded (eight reactors from KWU and a complete nuclear fuel cycle) has been called into question from two sides. On the one hand, domestic critics charge that the project is over-ambitious, wasteful, ill-conceived, and detrimental to Brazil's national interests.[12] On the other hand, the build-up of nuclear industrial capacity in Brazil, based on the transfer of German technology, proceeds at such a brisk pace that the share of domestic firms in reactor construction is likely to grow rapidly in the coming years while the share of components imported from Germany is bound to diminish correspondingly.[13] In Argentina, the situation is similar. The two Latin American countries have done away with the purchase of turn-key nuclear power plants from abroad; their governments are determined to seek national self-sufficiency in the nuclear field as far as possible and to substitute indigenous production of nuclear facilities for dependence on foreign supplies as soon as possible. To this end, Argentina and Brazil have recently come together to put aside their rivalries and join efforts and resources for an accelerated development of their fledgling nuclear industries.[14]

For the Germans it is no surprise to find their major nuclear clients striving for more self-reliance. This trend has been anticipated and is in fact encouraged by German suppliers. The transfer of nuclear technology to customer countries holds a particular appeal to Third World states with ambitious industrialization programmes, and the German nuclear industry has deliberately used this appeal in its competition with contractors from other countries. To transform bilateral relations from simple trade into a complex and continuous pattern of cooperative project management and transnational division of labour may be the only realistic as well as profitable business strategy for the German nuclear industry. There remains a significant and multiple role for KWU to play for many years in the growth and development of "national" nuclear industries in Argentina and Brazil. The company, in contrast to French, Canadian and some American competitors specializing in the manufacture of nuclear reactors, can draw strength from the fact that it operates as an affiliate and integral part of Siemens, one of Germany's most diversified and expansive multinational corporations.

It is true, however, that the world market for nuclear reactors is likely to shrink rather than grow as a result of these developments. Industrializing countries of the Third World may then no longer be available as an outlet for nuclear exports, they will possibly enter the export market as competitors themselves. If nuclear power programmes continue to be bogged down in Western industrial countries, then the scramble for international market shares among reactor manufacturers is bound to become more intense.[15] The industry's outlook in several countries appears not better than in Germany or even worse. Some companies are drifting nearer the brink of disaster and seek desperately to win foreign contracts for their under-utilized production lines.[16]

Table 4.2 shows that German reactor manufacturers hold a modest third place among nuclear supplier countries in terms of power plants exported. In terms of export shares in a country's total production, however, the German nuclear industry exceeds all other countries by a wide margin. No less than one-third of the total capacity of nuclear power plants manufactured in West Germany has been exported; if the number of power plants were counted, the corresponding figure would be as high as 43 per cent. No other Western country comes close to this figure. The Soviet Union, although nearest to the German case, is in an entirely different situation; its nuclear industry can rely on a large and safe domestic market where a shortage of supply, not of demand, is the major problem.

Thus, the German nuclear industry is far more dependent on the world market than any other country's industry. This is reflected in the willingness to go farther than its foreign competitors in catering to the specific wishes of customers abroad. For instance, KWU continues to manufacture heavy water reactors for the export market (where it has been successful with this product twice in Argentina) even though the company specializes in light water reactors and discourages use of the heavy water variety as being uneconomical. KWU has also pursued (inconclusively to date) the development of smaller reactor units tailored specially to the needs of developing countries. The company also goes out of its way to offer fuel supply assurances and a variety of auxiliary services to foreign customers as part of its reactor sales package. On the financial side, KWU has arranged export loans and guarantees by German private and public banks to cover most of the expenditure incurred by foreign reactor purchasers.[17]

Due to its dependence on the foreign market the German nuclear industry is particularly sensitive to political restrictions or competitive disparities in international nuclear trade. Foreign sales are a necessity for survival rather than a source of large profits for the industry. Prices are calculated at a minimal margin, so there is little flexibility to offer discounts to prospective customers. If other countries succeeded in their effort to capture larger shares of the nuclear export market, the stakes would grow even higher for the German nuclear industry. Increased competition might then result in increased pressure on the German Government to assure more favourable political conditions for foreign nuclear commerce.

THE SIGNIFICANCE OF THE GERMAN ROLE IN INTERNATIONAL NUCLEAR COMMERCE

International trade in nuclear power plants is more than an ordinary business transaction; it is a highly political process involving the participation of many actors and institutions in an intricate pattern of private, governmental, public and semi-public exchanges, arrangements and commitments across a wide range of national and international concerns.[18] Many factors contribute to the political sensitivity of nuclear commerce: domestic controversies about nuclear power, massive vested interests, the extraordinary complexity, size, financial volume and duration of individual projects, and of course the ever-present danger of a possible misuse of nuclear technology for other than peaceful purposes. International trade in nuclear materials and facilities, not unlike the arms trade, is a quasi-political activity that calls for and is subject to political control and regulation.[19] Any country engaged in nuclear commerce is engaged in a delicate game of world politics.

West Germany is one of the major actors in this game. In the world market for nuclear power plants the German industry has come to be the major competitor for American companies (see Table 4.2). The Soviet nuclear industry holds a monopoly in the *chasse gardée* of Comecon countries but is almost absent as a competitor in the world market. The French company Framatome, while highly successful at home, has yet to accomplish its huge sales projects with Mexico and China. Among competitors from other countries only the Canadian firm AECL has managed to survive in the international market for nuclear reactors.

More than any other single export project it was the agreement for nuclear cooperation between West Germany and Brazil, concluded in June 1975, that has highlighted the explosive political character of international nuclear commerce. The agreement created misgivings and misunderstandings on many sides, strained diplomatic relations between West Germany and the United States, played a prominent

TABLE 4.2   *National shares in world nuclear exports*

Country   Nuclear power plant production by 31 December 1980

	total production (MW)	total exports (MW)	share of production exported (%)	share of total world exports (%)
USA	228 888	36 442	15.9	51.6
France	56 124	3 644	7.0	5.2
USSR	55 975	15 470	27.6	21.9
West Germany	36 239	11 192	33.7	15.8
Canada	17 926	2 354	13.1	3.3
UK	15 682	200	1.3	0.3
Sweden	8 160	1 320	16.2	1.9
other	31 045	—	—	—
world	450 039	70 622	15.7	100.0

NOTE   Table shows total net capacity in electric MW for nuclear power plants in operation, under construction, or ordered; percentages rounded.

SOURCE   *Atomwirtschaft-Atomtechnik*, 26 (1981) table 8, p. 217.

role in national and international discussions about nuclear weapons proliferation for several years, and continues to serve as a reference case (whether as a model to copy or as a blunder to avoid) for subsequent nuclear trade accords.

The German-Brazilian nuclear deal aroused so much attention not for its sheer volume alone (which comprised, after all, the largest export project in the history of German industry, amounting to at least DM 16 billion) but for its specific circumstances. The agreement was concluded at a time when several countries, notably the United States and Canada, were agitated in the aftermath of India's "peaceful nuclear explosion" by discussions about the imminent danger of nuclear proliferation in developing countries. While the public mood in these countries called for international nuclear trade to be curtailed for the sake of non-proliferation, the German-Brazilian deal seemed to fly offensively in the face of these aspirations. In the agreement the German contractors undertook to supply up to eight large power reactors and, in adddition, to set up within two decades a complete and advanced nuclear industry in Brazil.[20] Not only materials, products and facilities were to be supplied, but also technological know-how, training, production capabilities, skills and blueprints. Included was the transfer of demonstration-size plants for uranium enrichment and reprocessing. For the first time in the history of nuclear commerce a developing country was to be given access to the technology of producing nuclear explosive material.

For the German industry the Brazilian deal was an exemplary advance towards a new pattern of long-term and comprehensive cooperation with a rising Third World country.[21] For its critics it was an irresponsible gamble with international security.[22] The fact that Brazil has consistently refused to join the Non-proliferation Treaty was regarded as a particularly disturbing and ǒminous circumstance.

There can be no doubt that the German offer to enter into a comprehensive transfer of nuclear technology was decisive for the Brazilians who turned down the more restricted tender from Westinghouse, the American firm that had previously been favoured over KWU. It is a moot point whether or not the controversial supply of "sensitive" enrichment and reprocessing technology was deliberately added to the deal to "sweeten" the purchase of KWU reactors. The fact remains that no company beside KWU has ever been willing to share its knowledge so generously with a developing country and to stake its prestige so firmly on a partnership of unprecedented duration, breadth and ambition.

It is evident that such a boldly conceived scheme has a special appeal to countries of the Third World whose interest in nuclear technology stems not merely from an assessment of national energy needs but more importantly (and perhaps erroneously) from the significance of nuclear energy as a source and symbol of modernity and innovative capacity, of national pride and achievement.[23] Such countries seek to play a role in international nuclear commerce not only as purchasers of turn-key power plants but also as trusted partners and respected collaborators in an enterprise of mutual interest and benefit.

The business strategy of German nuclear exporters seems to meet this desire particularly well. It is probably not accidental that KWU has in recent years prevailed over competing tenders in those countries – Brazil, Argentina, Spain – where the company could assure "national" industries (including, of course, local Siemens subsidiaries) a large and growing share in nuclear power plant construction.

There is an additional factor that may give the German industry some competitive advantage in international nuclear commerce. Reactor manufacturers from a non-nuclear weapon state such as the Federal Republic of Germany are beyond the suspicion that they might withhold from their foreign clients certain items of technology which would be used for nuclear purposes in their home country. An industrial nation that is itself among the underdogs of the international non-proliferation regime can enjoy some natural sympathy among Third World countries where resentment about an alleged discriminatory denial of "sensitive" nuclear technology under the pretext of non-proliferation runs high. It is, however, an embarrassing fact for the German nuclear industry that its preferred partner countries – Brazil, Argentina, Spain – continue to stay aloof from the Non-proliferation Treaty.

It is this fact which puts an effective rein on the German nuclear industry's export zeal. The industry, pleading at home for the "political acceptance" of its product, cannot afford to cast a shade of doubt on its responsible behaviour in the context of non-proliferation policy. Lingering reminiscences of an earlier episode of technical cooperation with South Africa continue to tarnish the industry's image abroad.[24] More recently the industry has adjusted its previously care-free attitude about possible connections between peaceful nuclear energy and nuclear weapons technology (an attitude, to be sure, that was shared by nuclear industries and policy makers of many countries in the aftermath of the NPT) and is now taking pains to follow and fulfil minutely the policies prescribed or suggested by Bonn.[25]

THE EXPORT POLICY OF THE FEDERAL GOVERNMENT

German nuclear export policy is basically defined by the Federal Republic's role as a signatory of the Non-proliferation Treaty. Careful execution of the Treaty's obligations has never been questioned inside or outside the Federal Government. All exports of nuclear materials, facilities and technologies are subject to governmental scrutiny and licencing; export licenses are granted only on assurance of IAEA safeguards. Otherwise the Federal Government holds that the free flow of international nuclear commerce, properly safeguarded, is permitted and guaranteed and, indeed, encouraged by the NPT to further the worldwide use of nuclear energy for peaceful purposes.[26]

As it turned out, however, this unambiguous and legally incontrovertible position needs to be refined and readjusted in ambiguous and politically controversial situations. Such situations arise from two problems: firstly, the limited efficacy of IAEA safeguards and, secondly, the imperfect universality of NPT adherence.

IAEA safeguards are designed not to prevent the diversion of nuclear material but to expose it. The misuse of safeguarded material is prevented only to the extent that the risk of detection serves as a political deterrent. Some governments, notably the US Administrations since 1974, have maintained that there should be additional precautions, going beyond NPT safeguards, to improve the reliability of the non-proliferation regime by deliberately barring national governments, and in particular non-NPT states, from having access to "sensitive" nuclear technology. Against this position the German Government insisted originally on the unabridged principle of free nuclear commerce. Hence it authorized the German nuclear industry's controversial export deal with Brazil, including the supply of "sensitive" equipment for enrichment and reprocessing, and has continued to stand firmly by its commitment in spite of repeated remonstrances from Washington.[27]

In the latter part of the 1970s, however, the German Government has gradually revised its position. As a member of the "London Club" of nuclear supplier countries it agreed to act in conformity with the group's guidelines and to exercise "restraint" in authorizing "sensitive" exports.[28] In 1977 the Federal Government, following a policy reversal by the French Government, took one step further to announce its determination (unilaterally and without binding force) to grant no more licenses for the export of reprocessing facilities and reprocessing technology "until further notice".[29] It was not expressly stated, although implied for practical purposes, that this declaration of self-restraint applied to the export of enrichment facilities as well. Still another step away from the principle of free nuclear trade was taken in 1980 when the Federal Government withheld an export license for delivery of a heavy water reactor to Argentina until finally the German suppliers ceded to a Swiss company the contract for simultaneous delivery of a heavy water manufacturing plant, which had been part of the original tender to Argentina.

In effect, then, the German Government has joined, albeit grudgingly, the front of nuclear supplier countries imposing a worldwide embargo on the export of "sensitive" nuclear merchandise. It should be noted, however, that this is a result of the Government's susceptibility to American political pressure and of its desire to avoid an isolated policy position among allies rather than of being persuaded by the ultimate wisdom of a policy of technology denial. There can be little doubt that West Germany would quickly readjust its position on "sensitive" exports if France or any of the nuclear supplier countries decided to loosen theirs.

In regard to the imperfect universality of NPT adherence the Federal Government has been confronted for many years with the dilemma that major recipient countries of German nuclear exports remained adamant in their rejection of the NPT. The German Government has not come around to impose on these countries (either bilaterally or within the framework of the nuclear suppliers' group) the legal requirement of having all their nuclear facilities placed under IAEA safeguards ("de iure full-scope safeguards"). In effect, however, the Government has again moved more and more towards the American position. It has successfully persuaded the governments of recipient countries to accept IAEA controls that cover practically all their nuclear activities of significance ("de facto full-scope safeguards").

Some of these controls over German-supplied nuclear goods go beyond the normal scope of NPT safeguards. In the trilateral agreement between the Federal Republic of Germany, Brazil, and the IAEA it is stipulated that international safeguards shall apply not only to fissile material but also to nuclear technologies (including, of course, the "sensitive" ones) supplied by German contractors. All facilities based on such a technology are subject to safeguards, regardless of whether they are built in Germany, Brazil or elsewhere. Plutonium separated from spent fuel in Brazil shall be put into special storage under international custody. In a similar vein it was agreed with Iran (a member of the NPT) that IAEA safeguards over German-built reactors would remain in force even if Iran abrogated the Treaty.

Over the years Germany has consistently pursued a policy course that sought to maintain a pragmatic balance between the requirements of nuclear non-proliferation and export promotion. The Federal Government has always rejected the idea that these requirements entailed a necessary conflict of interests, let alone an insurmountable contradiction of ends.[30] Rather, it is the Government's position that non-proliferation policy and nuclear export policy can and should be combined in a mutually beneficial relationship.

The basic philosophy of this approach is enshrined in the formula "Non-proliferation by Co-operation". It argues that nuclear exports to Third World countries, including those that reject the NPT, need not contribute to the proliferation of nuclear weapons but may indeed help to discourage or prevent it. Close and extensive collaboration in nuclear programmes and a permanent transfer of nuclear technology can, according to this view, render the "German connection" so attractive for industrializing countries that any misuse of civilian nuclear technology for military purposes would be deterred by the political and economic risk of a sudden rupture of that privileged relationship. It is in the view of the German Government that a network of bilateral or multilateral cooperation based on mutual trust and tangible interests and reinforced by freely agreed safeguards is a more effective and more reliable non-proliferation measure than would be any attempt at technology denial and political intimidation.[31]

This view does have some persuasive strength. It is shared by many governments, whether opponents or adherents of the NPT, and is supported by the experience of many years of smooth cooperation among industrial countries, notably EURATOM. The German position is also corroborated by the importance attached by the Brazilian and Argentinian Governments to the association of their national nuclear programmes with Germany and by their outspoken commitment to the non-proliferation of nuclear weapons in Latin America.[32]

The German policy position is, however, not without shortcomings and pitfalls. It may be borne out in the cases of Brazil and Argentina and yet be fallacious as a general policy prescription for any country. It assumes that international cooperation could increase the economic benefit of a peaceful nuclear programme for industrializing countries so dramatically, and strengthen their political interest in its continuation so decisively, as to outweigh any interest in a nuclear weapons programme. A policy placing such emphasis on economic priorities over considerations of ideology, national security or power politics may be predicated on an assumption that cannot hold for a country which is interested in nuclear weapons. It is perhaps unduly influenced by West Germany's particular outlook and experience as a country that has renounced nuclear weapons of its own only to rely on the nuclear weapons of its allies. Finally, there is still the possibility that a faltering nuclear programme at home will inflict lasting damage on the competitive stature of the German nuclear industry abroad. A breakdown of nuclear exports would jeopardize the survival of the industry in West Germany, destroy its role as a valued partner in international nuclear commerce and cooperation, and void its potential contribution to the development of peaceful nuclear programmes in the world.

NOTES

1. For a concise well-documented analysis of the early phase of nuclear energy development see Otto Keck, "Government Policy and Technical Choice in the West German Reactor Programme", *Research Policy*, 9 (1980) pp. 302–56.
2. Hans Michaelis, *Kernenergie* (Munich: DTV, 1977) pp. 188–9.
3. *Energieprogramm der Bundesregierung: Erste Fortschreibung vom 23. Oktober 1974* (Bonn: Bundesministerium für Wirtschaft, 1974).
4. The first new domestic order after a spell of five years was placed in Aug. 1980, for the nuclear power station Isar–2.
5. Public opinion polls on nuclear energy are reported in *Die Zeit*, 13 Apr. and 30 Nov. 1979; *Süddeutsche Zeitung*, 19 Sept. 1979; *Kernenergie und Umwelt*, Nov. 1978, p. iii, and July 1980, p. iii; *Der Spiegel*, 24 Mar. 1980, p.30, and 23 Feb. 1981, p. 32.
6. See Herbert Kitschelt, *Kernenergiepolitik – Arena eines gesellschaftlichen Konflikts* (Frankfurt: Campus, 1980).
7. "Der kerntechnische Außenhandel der BRD 1977–79", *Jahrbuch der Atomwirtschaft 1981* (Düsseldorf: Handelsblatt, 1981) p. B 58.
8. The immediate employment effect resulting from construction of a 1300 MW light water reactor nuclear power plant in Germany has been estimated in the range of 35,000 man years; see Martin Bald, "Beschäftigungseffekte durch Bau und Betrieb von Kraftwerken", *Atomwirtschaft-Atomtechnik*, 22 (1977) pp. 518–19.
9. O.H. Schiele, "Die Situation der kerntechnischen Industrie in der Bundesrepublik", *Atomwirtschaft-Atomtechnik*, 25 (1980) pp. 434–9; "Die Kraftwerk Union muß die Kapazitäten kürzen", *Frankfurter Allgemeine Zeitung*, 12 Mar. 1981.
10. For an authoritative analysis by Institut der deutschen Wirtschaft see

Frankfurter Allgemeine Zeitung, 26 Aug. 1980; see also Klaus Eßer and Jürgen Wiemann, *Schwerpunktländer in der Dritten Welt: Konsequenzen für die Südbeziehungen der Bundesrepublik Deutschland* (Berlin: Deutsches Institut für Entwicklungspolitik, 1981).

11. Bijan Mossavar-Rahmani, "Iran's Nuclear Power Programme Revisited", *Energy Policy*, 8 (1980) pp. 189–202.
12. Kurt Rudolf Mirow, *Das Atomgeschäft mit Brasilien – Ein Milliarden-fiasko* (Frankfurt: Campus, 1980); Hartmut Krugmann, "The German-Brazilian Nuclear Deal", *Bulletin of the Atomic Scientists*, 37 (Feb. 1981) pp. 32–6.
13. *Frankfurter Allgemeine Zeitung*, 7 May 1981; see also Rüdiger Hossner, "Brasilienabkommen – Quo Vadis?", *Atomwirtschaft–Atomtechnik*, 26 (1981) pp. 314–15.
14. See Günter Fahl, "Zum argentinisch-brasilianischen Kernenergieab-kommen von 1980", *Atomwirtschaft–Atomtechnik*, 25 (1980) pp. 623–4.
15. For assessments of nuclear sales prospects see W. Bohmann and O. Fickel, "Der Kernkraftwerksmarkt mit Leichtwasserreaktoren in den 70er und 80er Jahren", *Atomwirtschaft–Atomtechnik*, 26 (1981) pp. 19–26; Irwin C. Bupp, "The Actual Growth and Probable Future of the Worldwide Nuclear Industry", *International Organization*, 35 (1981) pp. 59–75.
16. Mans Lönnroth and William Walker, *The Viability of the Civil Nuclear Industry*, ICGNE Working Paper (New York and London: Rockefeller Foundation and Royal Institute of International Affairs, 1979).
17. For details of financial arrangements for Argentina see *Frankfurter Allgemeine Zeitung*, 9 Aug. 1980.
18. Hans-Hilger Haunschild, "Technologietransfer im Bereich der Kern-energie: Eine gemeinsame Aufgabe von Staat, Wirtschaft und Wissen-chaft", *Atomwirtschaft-Atomtechnik*, 22 (1977) pp. 66–8.
19. Cf. Steven J. Baker, "Export atomarer Energie – auch ein Handel mit Waffen?", *Technologie und Politik*, 4 (1976) pp. 86–103.
20. "Das Abkommen über friedliche Nutzung der Kernenergie zwischen der Bundesrepublik Deutschland und Brasilien", *Europa-Archiv*, 30 (1975) pp. D 485–9; "Brasiliens Option für die friedliche Nutzung der Kernener-gie: Das Kernenergieprogramm vom 10. März 1977", *ibid.*, 32 (1977) pp. D 387–93.
21. "Die nukleare Kooperation: Bundesrepublik liefert Brasilien nukleare Infrastruktur", *KWU-Report*, no. 19 (1975) pp. 1–9; Hans Frewer, "Aufgaben und Probleme beim nuklearen Technologietransfer", *Atomwirtschaft–Atomtechnik*, 22 (1977) pp. 412–18.
22. See, e.g., Norman Gall, "Atoms for Brazil, Dangers for All", *Foreign Policy*, no. 23 (1976) pp. 155–201.
23. Jorge Sabato and Jairam Ramesh, "Atoms for the Third World", *Bulletin of the Atomic Scientists*, 36 (Mar. 1980) pp. 36–43.
24. Arguments have focussed mainly on the brief period of cooperation between STEAG, a West German mining and engineering firm holding licenses for the experimental jet-nozzle uranium enrichment process, and the Atomic Energy Board of South Africa in the late 1960s. A comprehensive review of the alleged involvement of German corporations in the South African nuclear programme is attempted by Zdenek

Cervenka and Barbara Rogers, *The Nuclear Axis: Secret Collaboration between West Germany and South Africa* (London: Heinemann, 1978); for a critical rejoinder see *Survival*, 21 (1979) pp. 141–2.

25. For an authoritative view from a KWU manager see Günter Hildenbrand, "Nuklearexport, Technologietransfer und Nichtverbreitung von Kernsprengkörpern", *Sicherheitsüberwachung und Nichtverbreitung* (Bonn: Deutsches Atomforum, 1979) pp. 170–87.
26. Gerhard Meyer-Wöbse, *Rechtsfragen des Exports von Kernanlagen in Nichtkernwaffenstaaten* (Cologne: Heymanns, 1979).
27. For the background and evolution of German-American dissent over nuclear export policy see Karl Kaiser, "Auf der Suche nach einer Weltnuklearordnung: Zum Hintergrund deutschamerikanischer Divergenzen", *Europa-Archiv*, 33 (1978) pp. 153–72; and Helga Haftendorn, *The Nuclear Triangle: Washington, Bonn and Brasilia – National Nuclear Policies and International Proliferation*, Occasional Paper no. 2 (Washington: Georgetown University School of Foreign Service, 1978).
28. "Richtlinien der Gruppe der Nuklearlieferländer für den Nuklearexport", *Europa-Archiv*, 33 (1978) pp. D 171–81.
29. "Erklärung der deutschen Bundesregierung, vom 17. Juni 1977 zur Nuklearexportpolitik", *Europa-Archiv*, 32 (1977) pp. D 698–9.
30. For this view see, e.g., Lothar Wilker, "Nuklearexport – und Nichtverbreitungspolitik – ein Prioritätenkonflikt für die Bundesrepublik?", *Nuklearpolitik im Zielkonflikt: Verbreitung der Kernenergie zwischen nationalem Interesse und internationaler Kontrolle*, ed. Lothar Wilker (Cologne: Wissenschaft und Politik, 1980) pp. 77–105; and Harald Müller, *Energie-politik, Nuklearexport und die Weiterverbreitung von Kernwaffen: Analyse und Dokumentation* (Frankfurt: Haag & Herchen, 1978).
31. Heinz Dittmann, "Die Nichtverbreitungspolitik der Bundesregierung", *Sicherheitsüberwachung und Nichtverbreitung* (Bonn: Deutsches Atomforum, 1979) pp. 157–69. The author, a long-time department head in the German foreign office, carried primary responsibility for the formulation of the Federal Government's non-proliferation policy in the 1970s.
32. See the statements by Paulo Nogueiro Batista and Carlos Castro Madero, presidents of the nuclear energy establishments of Brazil and Argentina, in *Reconciling Energy Needs and Non-Proliferation*, ed. Karl Kaiser (Bonn: Europa Union, 1980) pp. 55–9 and 175–7, respectively. For recent statements by President Figueiredo of Brazil see *Frankfurter Allgemeine Zeitung*, 21 May 1981.

5 Canada and the Quest for International Nuclear Security

P. R. Johannson

India's detonation of a nuclear explosive device in May 1974 created shock waves that were felt through the world's nuclear community. One place where the shock waves registered a particularly strong effect was in Canada, the source of the technology which India had used to develop the explosive. Canadian nuclear policies underwent a series of changes throughout the remainder of the decade, reverberating to the diminishing echoes of India's explosion. In the eyes of many Canadians, existing policy had been shown to be inadequate. This led to a determined search for new ways to prevent, or at least delay, future nuclear proliferation. Canadian nuclear policy had placed great emphasis on the need to prevent nuclear prolifcration; but the Indian explosion upset earler assumptions about the security of existing non-proliferation efforts.

In the aftermath of the Indian explosion, an effort was made to make others accept Canada's definition of appropriate safeguards. As the 1970s drew to a close, tough Canadian nuclear export policies led to disputes with the country's major trading partners in Europe and Japan. Canadian officials had tried to force them to accept the stricter safeguards which were developed in response to India's explosion. The effort failed. Because of several factors, including concerns about sovereignty raised by other countries, the lack of the same sense of urgency felt by the Canadians, and the lack of sufficient international 'clout', Canada was unable to convince others to accept the strict safeguards. The defeat does not mean the end of the effort to develop a more stringent safeguards regime, however; it merely means that a new international regime will develop through consensus. The initiative now rests elsewhere than Ottawa.

The purpose of this chapter is to review the issues which explain Canada's efforts in the 1970s, so as to forecast how Canada will approach the evolution of a new non-proliferation regime. To understand the complex mix of international and domestic influences which have shaped Canadian nuclear policies, it is necessary to review several elements: the process by which nuclear policy is made, the present policies, and the important variables which have affected these policies. This permits a projection of the type of international nuclear regime which will be favoured by the Canadian government.

CANADIAN LEGISLATION

Canada is a Parliamentary democracy, with its federal (and provincial) governments patterned on the British model. Cabinet is responsible for the actions taken by the government, in things nuclear, as in other matters. But governments rarely concern themselves with detail; rather, Acts of Parliament, which outline the broad organizing philosophy of the government, set parameters of appropriate activity by the civil service. Thus, central to nuclear policy is the legislation governing the subject.

The 1946 Atomic Energy Control Act lies at the heart of Canada's nuclear programme and policies. Many of the wartime arrangements which had been undertaken in secret as part of the effort to develop the atomic bomb were formalized in the Act. The preamble contains the philosophical statement which has guided nuclear energy in Canada since 1946:

> Whereas it is essential in the national interest to make provision for the control and supervision of the development, application and use of atomic energy, and to enable Canada to participate effectively in measures of international control of atomic energy which may hereinafter be agreed upon;[1]

Two important points should be noted here. First, by declaring the subject to be in the "national interest", the government placed atomic matters within the jurisdiction of the federal government. Second, an important rationalization for this claim of authority was to permit Ottawa to make international commitments in Canada's name for the control of atomic power. Thus concern for the international aspects of atomic power – known today as "nuclear proliferation" – has long been present in Canadian thinking on the subject.

The Act created the Atomic Energy Control Board to supervise, regulate and promote the atomic industry in Canada. The Board was given wide authority to regulate nuclear affairs; it could facilitate research, license production of atomic energy, uranium prospecting and mining, as well as regulate the production, import, export, transport, possession, ownership, use or sale of "prescribed substances." In short, the Atomic Energy Control Board *was* the fledgling Canadian nuclear industry. Authority over all aspects of nuclear development was vested in the appointed Board, which reported to a single Minister in Cabinet. Despite changes in the nuclear industry and the world since 1946, this structure continues at present.

Changes to the legislation governing nuclear energy in Canada are forthcoming. (A draft Nuclear Regulatory Act was introduced in the House of Commons in 1978, but it did not proceed past first reading.) The intended changes are straightforward, though not without controversy. Provincial governments have complained that federal authority over nuclear matters has invaded other areas of provincial jurisdiction, such as mining, health and the ownership of natural resources.[2] A more coordinated approach to jurisdiction can be expected in a forthcoming re-introduction of the Nuclear Regulatory Act. Another complaint, that the Atomic Energy Control Board is insufficiently separate from the nuclear industry, may be dealt with in the new act.[3] Greater distinction between the regulation and promotion of nuclear power may be expected. But there will be few changes regarding the manner in which the Canadian government manages the export of nuclear materials; that procedure will remain largely unchanged, as it rests partially on other federal statutes.

A second piece of legislation affecting Canadian nuclear commerce is the Export and Import Permits Act of 1953/54. This statute establishes controls over the trade of particular commodities. (It is a Canadian equivalent of the US "Trading with the Enemy Act".) In order to export a product that is named on a control list (which can be modified by regulation), a potential exporter must first obtain a permit from the federal government. Nuclear materials are on the list, so that control over such exports is readily available. The combined effect of the powers of the Atomic Energy Control Act and the Export and Import Permits Act is that the federal government can restrict any nuclear transaction. Cabinet thus enjoys the authority to vet any individual transaction and to deny any sale which does not contain appropriate safeguards conditions.

THE CANADIAN POLICY PROCESS

Policy is made within the confines of this broad legislative authority. In the thirty-five years that Canada has had nuclear policies, two quite different approaches to policy-making can be seen. In the first, experts had control of policy, harmonizing it with other important foreign policy subjects. In the second approach, the policy-making procedure was opened up to include various perspectives within the government.

Thus in the earlier stages of Canada's nuclear history, the Advisory Panel on Atomic Energy was formed to advise the government on appropriate policy. This was a small group of very senior Ottawa officials, chosen for their expertise in nuclear and foreign affairs.[4] Policy was arrived at after informal consultations among members of the Panel; recommendations were forwarded to Cabinet, and generally were adopted as offered. This process – which downplayed the influence of political actors – ensured that Canadian policies were consistent internally, and were "in line" with prevailing foreign policy. By the late 1960s, however, the Panel's influence over nuclear policy-making had been weakened. Three reasons for the decline were the rapid expansion of the size of government in Canada, the increased complexity of nuclear affairs, and the development of a new, formalized procedure to make policy decisions. Today, the Panel continues to meet, although its main function is to coordinate the policy objectives of various bureaucratic interests in Ottawa. The dominance of "experts" in setting nuclear policy in Canada has waned.

The development of a more formal procedure for making policy decisions has permitted an increased access of different interests to Canadian nuclear policy.[5] Under the revised procedure, which was introduced by the Trudeau government in the late 1960s, all policy proposals are subject to review by a wide cross-section of interested parties in the federal government. (The procedure applies to all government policies, not just nuclear issues.) A department wishing to make a change must first obtain approval from its Minister, and then submit the proposal to Cabinet, which then assigns the proposal to a Cabinet Committee for further consideration. At the level of the Cabinet Committee, the proposal is examined by representatives of other ministries. If revisions are required, the document is then returned to the originating department, and the process begins anew. Having finally cleared the Cabinet Committee process, the document is returned to Cabinet for discussion and approval. Once initialled by the Prime Minister, the document is given public announcement as government policy.

The point to note in this procedure is that at various stages of the process, there is scope to permit the influence of various interests. Policy – at either the domestic or foreign level – is the product of political consensus within Cabinet. In terms of foreign policy, the government's intention was to ensure that policy "is the extension abroad of national policies".[6] This new procedure has permitted domestic concerns to affect nuclear export policy. Where once "experts" controlled the options available, and offered their considered opinions to Cabinet for approval, the new procedure downplays their influence. The opinions of the experts, while still heard, must now compete with the priorities of politicians. By opening up the policy-making procedure, the Trudeau government provided the means to make policy defendable by Cabinet. The effect of the new system has been to introduce bureaucratic "pulling and hauling" over policy, and this has proven a complicating factor when setting nuclear export policy.[7]

CANADA'S NUCLEAR POLICIES

Before dealing with the variables which have affected past Canadian nuclear policies, and likely will in the future, some attention needs to be given to present realities. This section is concerned with reviewing the development of Canada's nuclear industry, as well as the domestic and foreign policies which have brought it to this point.

Domestic applications of nuclear power have long been an important feature of Canada's nuclear efforts. Canada's nuclear industry (which includes both reactors and uranium production) can trace its lineage back to the Second World War. The dominant features of the present industry reflect the continuation of procedures set down in wartime, particularly regarding the role played by crown corporations. The first of these firms was the Eldorado Gold Mining and Refining Company, which was purchased by the Canadian government in 1943 at the urging of the Americans and British.[8] The 1946 Atomic Energy Control Act permitted the use of crown corporations to develop nuclear energy. In 1952, nuclear research being done by the National Research Council was turned over to a new crown firm, Atomic Energy of Canada Limited (AECL). Today, these two firms – Eldorado Nuclear and AECL – are the backbone of Canada's nuclear industry.

To a very large extent, the nuclear business in Canada is a government business. In the reactor field, AECL set out to do original research on the heavy-water process which had been inherited from the wartime effort. It was intended that private firms would be responsible for the production and sale of commercial systems, but this plan did not work out. The one private company which did try to market the CANDU, Canadian General Electric, dropped the effort in the 1960s when few orders were forthcoming.[9] Canada's domestic programme began to develop with the Pickering station (near Toronto), which was begun in the 1960s. Today, there are many small firms that produce components for the CANDU. AECL has become the proprietor of the CANDU technology, and thus a *de facto* reactor producer.

A similar governmental influence is apparent in the uranium industry. Spurred on by the quest for uranium for the weapons programmes in the US and Britain, the Canadian industry grew at a frantic rate during the 1940s and 1950s. But the 1959 decision by the Americans to cancel their purchase order, which was followed soon afterwards by a similar British decision, sent the industry into a deep slump. Various efforts were initiated by the government to assist the industry, including a stockpiling of uranium to maintain production levels and various efforts to arrange long-term contracts with purchasing countries. This effort culminated in the government's active promotion of an "orderly marketing arrangement" (or cartel) which attempted to improve the price structure of uranium.[10] When the uranium market did take off, early in the 1970s, as part of the global energy crisis, the Canadian government set reserve requirements for uranium producers, to ensure that reactors in Canada would have assured supplies.[11]

Today's Canadian uranium industry is dominated by private firms, though the government influence remains vital. The two largest producers, Denison Mines and Rio Algom (a subsidiary of RTZ of London) together provide some 80% of uranium production in Canada. Eldorado Nuclear operates Canada's only uranium refinery, maintaining a government presence above and beyond Eldorado's mining operations. A trend which is increasing is the establishment of joint-venture operations, involving a Canadian government-related firm (such as Eldorado Nuclear) and state-oriented energy companies in France (AMOK) and West Germany (URANERZ). This is in part due to the long-threatened (but not yet implemented) federal government plan to restrict foreign ownership of uranium properties to 30 per cent. Thus nuclear activities in Canada are strongly affected by the presence of government-owned operations.

Nuclear energy has an important role in Canada's energy strategy which will continue until the turn of the century and beyond. Nuclear power presently provides some 8 per cent of the country's electricity, although this is concentrated in central Canada, principally in Ontario, where nuclear power provides 23 per cent of that Province's electricity.[12] 4800 MW are currently "on-line" in Canada; some 15 200 MW are projected by 1988, which would be 15 per cent of Canadian electricity generation. Few cost-effective options are available to the nation's industrial heartland, and more stations will be built.[13] It is not clear yet how much other regions will rely on nuclear power. The point to note is that nuclear power has an accepted place in the energy strategy being pursued by the Canadian government.

Decisions regarding the future direction of nuclear development in Canada have yet to be made. The industry is anxious to proceed with the development of the thorium-cycle CANDU, a mid-point between traditional reactors and the fast breeder. However, costs of the research required are not insubstantial, and as AECL does over 90 per cent of nuclear research in Canada, this will be a government decision. For the time being, continued development of the CANDU system will be all that is expected, effectively eliminating the fast breeder from active consideration.

Canada's nuclear export policies have developed in three stages since 1945. The first phase saw Canadian policy set in accordance with US and British efforts, as part of western alliance policy to prevent nuclear proliferation. The second phase emerged in 1965 in reaction to French efforts to arrange long-term supply contracts for Canadian uranium. When France objected to Canadian requirements for safeguards on such sales as being discriminatory – which, when compared to the lack of such stipulations on Canadian sales to the US and the UK, it was – Canadian policy was changed. After 1965, Canadian nuclear materials could be used only for peaceful purposes by any importing country, thus making the safeguards universal in application.[14] The third phase of Canadian policies emerged from the reaction to India's detonation of an atomic device in May 1974; it is this third period of Canadian policies which is of principal interest here.

Through a series of policy statements, Canadian policy after 1974 became increasingly stringent in nature; by the end of 1976, Canadian policy was perhaps the toughest of any western supplier country.

There are five main elements to Canadian nuclear export policy; these can be summarized in point form:

(i) there is no such thing as a "peaceful nuclear explosion"; any nuclear device is warlike in intent; any non-nuclear weapon state which explodes a nuclear device will have all Canadian nuclear shipments terminated;

(ii) all states should accept international supervision of nuclear materials; the IAEA is the appropriate agency;

(iii) all states should adopt the "trigger list" of materials which was developed by the Nuclear Suppliers Group (NSG);

(iv) all Canadian-supplied materials and technology will be safeguarded for their life *as well as* the future generations of fissile materials that are produced from that material or technology;

(v) Canadian exports must be covered by full-scope safeguards; recipient countries must either sign the NPT or accept the same coverage by the IAEA.[15]

The acceptance of such strong standards by all states could have done much to prevent future nuclear proliferation. However, the manner in which Canadian officials chose to pursue their policies in part prevented such a development.

The main contention between Canada and other countries arose from the fourth point in the above list. Acceptance of the "contamination principle" by an importing country gave Canada effective control over the disposition of materials originally supplied by Canada. In practical terms, this requirement meant that importing countries could not reprocess spent fuel that had originated in Canada without Canadian approval. The new policy required that existing export contracts be re-negotiated to provide this coverage. Major customers were the first to be affected. When negotiations with the European Community and Japan dragged on over two years without success, the Canadian government placed an embargo on uranium shipments to those countries in an effort to force their acceptance of the "contamination principle." Negotiations continued throughout 1977, but neither side was prepared to back down.

INFCE (International Nuclear Fuel Cycle Evaluation) was used as a means of ending the embargo; hopes in Canada were that INFCE would identify reprocessing as a dangerous undertaking, and thus require supplier controls. But the results of INFCE were quite the opposite to what the Canadians (and the US) had hoped. Instead of condemning reprocessing, the multilateral enquiry concluded that interruptions of supply were equally dangerous, putting the Canadian embargo in an unfriendly light. The ramifications of the INFCE findings have yet to be seen in a revised Canadian statement of policy, although some recognition of the changed circumstances can be expected. This is discussed in greater detail below.

In summary, Canadian nuclear policies are reasonably consistent in terms of domestic policy objectives. The domestic nuclear programme accepts international proliferation concerns; Canada has signed and ratified the NPT, which provides full-scope coverage of Canadian nuclear facilities. Because the country has abundant uranium supplies, there is little sympathy for the fast-breeder option; Canadian policy is thus unenthusiastic about reprocessing spent fuel. Canadian nuclear export policy reflects these domestic realities. There is an important policy inconsistency that has appeared in Canadian foreign policy however. This results from the use of an embargo on fuel supplies to important trading partners in Europe and Japan, while at the same time pursuing other foreign policies calling for improved economic ties between Canada and these same two economic units. This inconsistency, and its implications, is explored in greater detail elsewhere.[16]

THE POLICY VARIABLES

Keeping in mind the process and legislative structure which governs nuclear affairs in Canada, it is now possible to turn attention to the factors which have influenced Canadian policies. Of interest here are the salient features of the political and economic environment which affected Canadian nuclear policies in the 1970s, some of which may be expected to be relevant policy variables in the coming decades. For the most part, these influences are domestic in nature, although attention is given to those international influences that may prove to be important.

There are several different types of domestic variables that have affected Canadian policy. These may be grouped into two large categories: those which result from the existence of a Canadian nuclear industry, and those which stem from a history of political confrontation over things nuclear. Each category deserves attention.

The continued existence of a Canadian nuclear industry is the most obvious of the domestic variables that will affect future Canadian policies. As noted earlier, the federal government has been closely involved with the industry's development, and has taken steps on several occasions to protect the industry when threatened. Of interest in this regard are: the stockpiling programme for uranium, which began after export markets collapsed in the early 1960s; the support given to AECL when private firms left the reactor-building effort; the continued opposition to foreign ownership of uranium reserves; and, of course, the active assistance given to the formation of the international uranium cartel. Having already invested considerable effort and money in support of the Canadian nuclear industry, the government may be expected to provide similar support in the future. Indeed, Prime Minister Trudeau is on record as describing the industry as the kind of "future" industry which the government intends to support.[17] Thus an important domestic influence over future Canadian nuclear policies will result from the continued well-being of the nuclear industry.

On a global scale, the Canadian capacity to produce CANDU reactors is modest.[18] To date, 14 CANDU generating stations are built or under construction; 9 of these are in Canada, 5 in other countries (India, Pakistan, Argentina, South Korea and Romania.) The industry has the capacity to produce 3000 MW per year, but present orders leave this capacity only about 50 per cent utilized. While some domestic growth is to be expected, the need to find export markets for the CANDU is apparent.

The uranium industry's future is more secure than the reactor industry, though it too is dependent on exports. Less than 10 per cent of production is destined for Canadian end-use.[19] The government's requirement that domestic reactors have a committed supply of uranium will increase the share of uranium produced for domestic use to about 17 per cent by 1988. Canada presently produces about 20 per cent of the world's uranium. Production peaked in 1959 at 12 300 tonnes in 1959, but slumped until the 1970s; in 1977, 5800 tonnes were produced. Exploration and development of new deposits is continuing, and the six present producers are expected to increase to ten in this decade. The importance of the export market should be noted, as Canadian production of uranium is geared towards global demand figures.

In summary, the well-being of Canada's nuclear industry is dependent on continued access to world markets. This is a domestic reality which will affect nuclear export policy. Canadian dependence on foreign markets to maintain efficient levels of production – for both reactors and uranium – may be expected to continue in the future.

The second category of domestic variables that have had an influence on policy developments stems from the political atmosphere surrounding nuclear topics in Canada. There are four elements to be considered in this category: a tradition of strong opposition to nuclear weapons, difficulties experienced in completing export sales of uranium and reactors, the public and political outcry over the Indian explosion, and the efforts of the opponents of nuclear energy. These four elements have all played a part in affecting the political environment within which nuclear policies are made.

Despite its dependence on the American nuclear arsenal for its security, Canada has a strong political tradition which opposes nuclear weapons. (A case can be made about the hypocrisy this involves, but such is not the objective here.) This anti-nuclear weapons stance has enjoyed considerable support for some two decades. During the 1960s, debate over acquisition of nuclear weapons for the Canadian armed forces was an important issue in two federal elections. While the (Pearson) Liberals, who favoured acceptance of the weapons, were elected, the (Diefenbaker) Progressive Conservatives found considerable support in opposing the acquisition. The social democrats in the New Democratic Party have consistently opposed nuclear weapons for Canada. Thus there is an historic place in Canadian politics for things nuclear.

The Trudeau governments have reflected their leader's personal opposition to nuclear weapons. (Trudeau severely criticised the Liberal Party's nuclear weapons policy in 1963.) Since first assuming office in 1968, Trudeau has ended the nuclear role for the armed forces in Europe and announced plans to end the use of nuclear warheads in anti-bomber defences in Canada. Moreover, Trudeau has called for a "strategy of suffocation" to bring an end to the spiral of weapons development among the world's nuclear weapons states.[20] Regardless of the fact that it may have been hypocritical, the Canadian political tradition reflects a sense of political morality regarding nuclear weapons.

India's development of a nuclear device from Canadian technology tied together nuclear power and nuclear weapons in the Canadian political marketplace. It produced a first-magnitude political furore. Trudeau was reportedly furious with the explosion, and released copies of 1971 correspondence between himself and Prime Minister Gandhi which had discussed reports of India's intentions to develop a bomb.[21] Anger with the Indians after the explosion led to a termination of all but food-aid programmes between Canada and India. But the political uproar was only beginning. The media indulged in an orgy of self-righteous breast-beating about the Indian explosion.[22] The

Opposition hammered at the government in the House of Commons. If the Indian explosion itself had not caused problems for the government, the manner and extent of the political repercussions were considerable in themselves. The tradition of a self-righteous pose on nuclear topics had come home to roost for the government, creating pressures for the development of much tougher nuclear safeguards.

To muddy the political waters even more, news of some considerable embarrassment to the government regarding nuclear sales became known soon after the explosion. First there was the fact that AECL had reached agreement to sell CANDU systems to Argentina and South Korea. To critics of the nuclear sales efforts, both customers were potential proliferators. Future "Indias" were foreseen as the end product of such sales. Then it became known that international sales agents (i.e. middlemen) had been employed by AECL to assist with making the sales. Once again the self-righteous enjoyed an opportunity to condemn the government, this time for paying bribes to assist the sales effort. Finally, it became known that Canada had been involved in the planning and development of an international uranium cartel during the early 1970s. More than just crown-owned firms were involved; the government had been fully informed of the cartel, and had used the powers of the Atomic Energy Control Act to facilitate Canadian membership in the cartel.[23] Once more, the self-righteous had room to crow about the government's actions.

Coming soon after the Indian explosion and the agents' fees scandal, the cartel unleashed political furies. The floodgates of opposition to Canada's nuclear programme were opened. The dispute was emotional, hotly partisan and difficult for the government. There were few, if any spokesmen prepared to defend the nuclear industry. All the pressures on the government pointed in one direction: towards the establishment of a tough, effective and non-compromising set of standards that would guide the conduct of future Canadian exports of nuclear materials.

Given the uproar surrounding the government's actions, the antinuclear movement found well-fertilized ground in which to work. The premise of much of their opposition was environmental in nature, and the movement was able to command considerable media attention for its efforts. The Atomic Energy Control Board was attacked as being unduly secretive in its practices and inappropriately close to the nuclear industry to provide effective regulation. A sit-in was held outside the Board's headquarters, demanding the release of classified information. Other protestors organized invasions of existing nuclear facilities and protested plans to build new plants. The events at Three Mile Island provided nuclear opponents with new material to justify their cause. Throughout all their efforts, however, it is difficult to conclude that the anti-nuclear movement has had a significant effect on Canadian policies. Undoubtedly their presence posed additional worries for the government, but given the prevailing climate of opinion on Canada's nuclear programme, it is hard to measure the direct effects of the opponents. The future influence of the opponents is equally hard to predict, although public attention seems to be turning to the problems associated with waste disposal, rather than to the merits of nuclear energy *per se*.

At this point the effects of the changed decision-making procedure, which was described earlier, can be seen as affecting past policies. The reader will recall that the new procedure forced new policies to run a gauntlet within the Cabinet committee system before gaining approval. What is of interest in this case is that the resounding public outcry over nuclear embarrassments provided a potent political force that demanded attention. The new decision-making procedure permitted domestic political concerns to shape the range of options available to the government. The resulting nuclear export policies were designed to be beyond reproach in domestic political terms. In particular, the adoption of the "contamination" principle, which was being demanded in the House of Commons, can be seen as resulting from the strident commentary arising out of India's use of Canadian technology to develop an explosive device. A more dispassionate approach to setting policy might have led to a less stringent set of controls; but the reverberations of the Indian explosion through the Canadian polity seemed to require such a hard-line position. Whether or not the policy was a well-advised one is discussed in greater detail below. The point to note here is that the changed procedure for setting government policy provided the means for transmitting the political demands for stronger non-proliferation policies into action.

In summary, the important domestic variables which have affected Canadian policies result from the existence of the nuclear industry and the atmosphere surrounding nuclear issues in Canada. Because there was an industry – which was government controlled – the government sought to make its future existence secure. Because of the political tradition of self-righteousness regarding nuclear topics, the government was forced to adopt tough standards to facilitate future nuclear commerce. Because of the changed procedure by which Cabinet made policy, the policies adopted were perhaps tougher than they might or should have been. These domestic variables explain much of the motivation for Canadian policies during the 1970s.

There are also important international factors which have shaped Canadian policies. In particular, there is the role played by the United States in Canada's nuclear activities. In many important ways, Canadian thinking about nuclear proliferation has been affected by the US. This is not to say that Canada has been slavishly loyal to US leadership; it is rather to suggest that in important ways, Canadians have tended to view developments and priorities in much the same light as Americans. This tendency – and it is really nothing more than that – will likely continue in the future. On the one occasion that Canada did set out to provide leadership to the international nuclear community, in the attempt to get Europe and Japan to accept controls over reprocessing, the effort proved unsuccessful. Moreover, the Canadian initiative ran counter to US efforts, for the effects of a fuel embargo are to reinforce national prejudices against "internationalizing" the nuclear fuel cycle. In other words, Canada's embargo on uranium could have had the effect of *furthering* the autonomous national fuel cycle, at the very time that President Carter was speaking out against the "plutonium economy". Despite the fact that the appearance of accepting US leadership is a difficult domestic problem, it may be expected that in the immediate future, Canada will follow the American lead.

Indeed, this may be termed a "North American" variable which will affect Canadian policies. From a North American perspective, secure with large supplies of uranium, the issues facing a new international non-proliferation regime are viewed in much the same way. Both Canada and the United States have abundant energy alternatives that could be developed instead of nuclear power. Both countries have large coal reserves, extensive tar sands and shale oil deposits as well as access to more exotic alternatives, such as solar, wind and wave power. The presence of these options, despite the likely expense of effective development, affects the political environment in both countries. North American opponents of nuclear energy can suggest using such alternatives and command considerable public sympathy. In the same way, the relatively abundant uranium supplies in each country lead government officials to sincerely question the need or importance of pursuing the "plutonium economy". In each country, there is considerable time available yet before decisions regarding reprocessing spent fuel or development of a fast-breeder technology have to be made. Moreover, there is a general dependence in North America on technical solutions to the proliferation problem. Although Canadian spokesmen suggest a more flexible approach than the US (for example, Canada claims to be "agnostic" on reprocessing questions), the fact remains that technical measures to prevent proliferation have long been at the base of both American and Canadian policies. Thus the realities of viewing the world from a North American perspective will shape Canadian policy developments in the coming decade and beyond.

There are other international variables which can be indicated as well. The position adopted by Canada's major trading partners in Europe and Japan will have a bearing on Canadian options and perspectives. We might term this a foreign policy variable. The use of the uranium embargo against Europe and Japan in 1977 was a decision which had important implications for foreign policy. Seen in this light, the embargo was poorly-advised for a number of reasons. It didn't work. The Europeans and Japanese did not accept Canadian demands for controls over reprocessing of Canadian-supplied fuel. It implied that Canada did not want to sell nuclear commodities. But the exact opposite is the case, as noted earlier. The embargo was in direct contradiction to an important foreign policy goal, the pursuit of the "Third Option", which involves the development of close commercial and social ties between Canada and Europe and Japan.[24] The embargo was applied soon after negotiations on establishing "contractual links" with Europe and Japan had been completed, thereby suggesting that the Third Option was only rhetorical in objective. If nothing else, the embargo decision suggested that there was very little effective coordination of foreign policy planning in Canada. Finally, the uranium embargo damaged Canada's reputation as a reliable supplier of raw materials; the consequences of this effect will likely be felt for many years to come. Canada's retreat from the embargo decision revealed an understanding of these realities. The way that Europe and Japan respond to the effort to build a new non-proliferation consensus will thus have an important effect on Canada and Canadian foreign policy.

The final international variable will be the nature of the emerging non-proliferation regime. Canadian thinking on non-proliferation topics has, from the earliest days, placed great emphasis on multilateral solutions to the problem. Indeed, given Canadian diplomatic traditions in supporting international agencies as an article of faith, the way that the regime develops will have a great bearing on future Canadian nuclear developments. For this reason, it is apparent that Canada will be closely involved with the emergence of a new regime. Thus it is possible to turn attention to the future, and give some consideration to the way Canada is likely to approach the formation of the new regime.

CANADA AND A NEW INTERNATIONAL REGIME

A more realistic approach to a new international non-proliferation regime by Canada may be expected to evolve. Future Canadian nuclear export policy likely will not be as strongly affected by domestic variables as was the case in the 1970s. The fact that Canada's effort to force acceptance of the contamination principle was unsuccessful may be expected to weigh heavily on Canadian policies in the 1980s. Moreover, as the use of the uranium embargo ran counter to other important Canadian foreign policy goals, and revealed the need for a more comprehensive approach to policy, it is reasonable to assume that less demanding conditions will be set in the coming decade. But this is not to suggest that Canada will abandon the effort to build a more effective international non-proliferation regime. Far from it. Rather, it is to suggest that future Canadian policies will be developed as part of a consensus, rather than by the effort of individual countries. From the discussion of the important domestic and international variables on the preceding pages, it is possible to glean some indications about how Canada will approach the evolution of a new regime.

Two of the domestic variables stand out as being particularly important for the coming decade. The first is the political tradition opposing nuclear weapons proliferation. This factor will make it almost impossible for a Canadian government to retreat very far from the standards set in the 1970s. The second factor that will be important is the need to develop export markets for CANDU reactors and uranium. This variable pulls in a different direction that the first; it is likely to provide a more balanced approach to safeguards policies than was apparent in the 1970s. But because the Indian explosion inextricably linked together the pursuit of peaceful nuclear power with nuclear proliferation, it will not be possible to go too far in favouring the needs of the Canadian nuclear industry. If only because there is a perception in the government that continued acceptance of the domestic nuclear industry is tied to strong export conditions, Canadian policies will be broadly similar to those set down in the 1970s.

Nor is Canada likely to be passive about the emergence of a new regime; in all likelihood, Canada will be actively involved in the process, as it has been in the past. The development of the Nuclear Suppliers Group emerged in part from a Canadian effort in 1974 to gain support from other suppliers for a "model contract" which would be used in all export sales. That initiative was not successful, although its relationship to the "trigger list" concept should be noted.[25] Canada was active in the NSG, seeking the adoption of full-scope safeguards by all exporters. In the same vein, Canada was actively involved in the INFCE negotiations, co-chairing Working Group 1 (Fuel and Heavy Water Availability) with India and Egypt. Thus an active participation by Canada in the evolution of a new non-proliferation regime can safely be projected.

An overview of the broad outlines of present Canadian export policies permits some insight into the nature of a new safeguards regime which Canadian negotiators will support. From a Canadian perspective, the new regime must rest on some basic points: on the continued expansion of the NPT system of full-scope safeguards; on continued support for the IAEA as the appropriate agency to carry out safeguards inspections; (for countries that reject the NPT, some new full-scope system will be required;) finally, some form of continuing relationship between suppliers and consumers over future generations of fuel and technology will be sought. This last point will obviously be of major importance to importing countries, in light of the loss of sovereignty and control of domestic energy policy it implies. The negotiations between Canada and EURATOM over the implications of the contamination principle will prove to be the keystone of future Canadian policy, if not the new regime as well.

From the foregoing, it should be apparent that Canada will continue to press for a tough international safeguards regime. The domestic variables which forced the escalation of Canadian policy in the 1970s will still be present. The self-righteous stance regarding nuclear weapons, the process by which policy decisions are made in Ottawa and the nuclear opposition will all continue to be present, regardless of the role played by individual politicians. If there are to be modifications to Canadian policies, they will likely be tempered by other important variables which have been identified: the need to export CANDU reactors and uranium; the reaction of Europe and Japan to Canadian efforts to gain acceptance of the contamination principle; the role played by the United States in the evolving regime. Perhaps the best that can be hoped for is a more balanced Canadian appreciation of the real Canadian interest, which is the establishment of an effective, workable, and thus globally acceptable nuclear non-proliferation regime.

NOTES

1. Canada, *Atomic Energy Control Act*, RS c11, s1.
2. Sasketchewan, "A Brief Summarizing Comments and Concerns of the Provinces with Respect to Bill C-14", (mimeo), Federal Provincial Conference of Mines Ministers, Ottawa, 2 Nov. 1978.
3. P. Roff Johannson and J. C. Thomas, "A Dilemma of Nuclear Regulation in Canada: Political Control and Public Confidence", *Canadian Public Policy*, vol. VII, 3 (Summer 1981), and Ontario, Royal Commission on Electric Power Planning, *Report*, vol. 1 (Toronto: Queen's Printer, 1980) pp. 77–8.
4. P. R. Johannson, *Nuclear Exports and Canadian Foreign Policy*, (forthcoming) esp. ch. 6.
5. For a discussion of the increasingly formalized decision-making process, see Canada, Privy Council Office, "Policy Planning and Support for Ministerial Decision-Making in Canada"; Michael Pitfield, "The Shape of Government in the 1980s: Techniques and Instruments for Policy Formulation at the Federal Level"; Hon. Mitchell Sharp, "Decision-Making in the Federal Cabinet," in Thomas A. Hocking (ed.), *Apex of Power*, 2nd edn. (Scarborough: Prentice-Hall of Canada, 1977).
6. Canada, Department of External Affairs, *Foreign Policy for Canadians*, (Ottawa: Queen's Printer, 1970) p. 9.
7. The concept of "pulling and hauling" comes from Graham T. Allison, *Essence of Decision: Explaining the Cuban Missile Crisis* (Boston: Little, Brown, 1971). For a Canadian interpretation of this approach, see Kim Richard Nossal, "Allison Through the (Ottawa) Looking Glass: Bureaucratic Politics and Foreign Policy in a Parliamentary System", *Canadian Public Administration*, 22, 4 (Winter 1979).
8. Wilfrid Eggleston, *Canada's Nuclear Story* (Toronto: Clarke, Irwin, 1965).
9. One international sale was made to Pakistan by CGE.
10. John Christopher Thomas, "The International Uranium Cartel Affair", (unpublished M.A. thesis, University of Sussex, 1978) and June H. Taylor and Michael D. Yokell, *Yellowcake: The International Uranium Cartel* (New York: Pergamon Press, 1979).
11. Hon. Donald S. Macdonald, Minister of Energy, Mines and Resources, "Statement on Uranium Policy, September 4, 1974", as reproduced in Canada, Energy Mines and Resources, *1976 Review of Uranium Enrichment Prospects in Canada* (mimeo).
12. Leonard and Partners Ltd, *Economic Impact of Nuclear Energy Industry in Canada,* vol I: *Executive Summary* (Ottawa: for the Canadian Nuclear Association, 1978) p. 2.
13. Though noting the existence of a strong debate over future demand projections, Ontario's Royal Commission on Electric Power Planning

recommended that the nuclear option be kept open. *Report*, vol. 1, p. 37.
14. P. R. Johannson, "Politics, Parliament and Foreign Policy: The 1965 Uranium Debate", paper presented to the Annual Meeting of the Canadian Political Science Association, Montreal, June 1980 (mimeo).
15. This list is a condensation of a number of policy statements made by various Canadian ministers between 1974 and 1980. For contextual detail, see Johannson, *Nuclear Exports and Canadian Foreign Policy*.
16. Ibid.
17. Pierre Elliott Trudeau, "Canada's Obligations as a Nuclear Power" (Speech to the Canadian Nuclear Association, Ottawa, 17 July 1975), *Statements and Speeches* (75/22).
18. Leonard & Partners, *Economic Impact of Nuclear Energy Industry in Canada*, vol. I: *Executive Summary*, p. 10.
19. Ibid., p. 8.
20. Toronto *Globe and Mail*, 27 May 1978, p. 1.
21. Letter from Prime Minister, P. E. Trudeau to Srimati Indira Gandhi, Prime Minister of India, 1 Oct. 1971. Copy supplied by Prime Minister's Office, Ottawa.
22. See Walter Stewart, "How We Learned to Stop Worrying and Sell the Bomb", *Maclean's* (Nov. 1974).
23. Johannson and Thomas, "A Dilemma of Nuclear Regulation in Canada".
24. Hon. Mitchell Sharp, "Canada–U.S. Relations: Options for the Future", *International Perspectives* (Autumn 1972). See further R. Boardman, "Canadian Resources and the Contractual Link: The Case of Uranium", *Journal of European Integration*, 4 (1981).
25. Johannson, *Nuclear Exports and Canadian Foreign Policy*, ch. 4.

6 The Politics of Fading Dreams: Britain and the Nuclear Export Business

Robert Boardman and Malcolm Grieve

Britain's nuclear programme has not on the whole enjoyed a good press. A world leader in the field in the 1950s, the country was struck early in the game by a sense of malaise that it has proved impossible to eradicate. Older criticisms of poor industrial and governmental organisation, of failure in the world's export markets, and of errors of judgement in reactor choice were joined in the 1970s by the charge that in a crowded island the nuclear option was not a safe energy strategy. A former leading member of the Friends of the Earth (FOE), a group which took the key role in fighting plans for the Windscale reprocessing facility, has spoken of "the nuclear industry's track record of over-optimism and misjudgment",[1] while *The Times*, from a somewhat different angle, has commented (in 1981) that "the history of the development of nuclear power in Britain over the past decade and a half has been a sorry tale of wrong decisions, missed opportunities and wasted money".[2] The author of a recent study sees the nuclear power question as part of a wider phenomenon: "Britain has settled for handling too many twentieth-century problems with nineteenth-century political and administrative attitudes and machinery, and this is one of the major reasons for her continuing decline".[3]

Our aim in this chapter is rather more limited than the dissection and evaluation of such judgements. Attention is focused for the most part on the politics of Britain's foreign nuclear trade. At the beginning of the 1980s this trade, with certain exceptions, seemed to have come to the end of a rather short road. With the proposed, and long-awaited, addition of the PWR to the reactors around which Britain's nuclear programme has centred since the mid-1950s, hopes of a major export market developing on the basis of distinctively British nuclear technology had been virtually extinguished. The proliferation issue aside, this failure to become a leading world nuclear exporting country raises some intriguing questions. Britain, after all, has had vast experience with nuclear power. The safety and performance record has been good. Until the early 1970s Britain produced more nuclear power than the rest of the world, including the United States, combined; and the cheapest electricity then being produced for the Central Electricity Generating Board (CEGB) network came from a nuclear power station.[4] Even in the environmentalist atmosphere of the later 1970s no significant public pressure emerged to limit even marginally the capacity of the British nuclear industry to sell its products abroad. The first part of the chapter looks at the evolution of British nuclear policies with a view to identifying the importance within the overall nuclear power programme of the pursuit of export sales, and then at the character of the overseas trade. A second part examines the interplay between this activity and British policies on nuclear weapons proliferation. We turn finally to a brief consideration of the wider public debate in Britain on nuclear power.

EXPORT GOALS AND THE NUCLEAR PROGRAMME

While the civilian nuclear power programme is the object of study here, it should not of course be forgotten that Britain is a nuclear weapon state. And as its official biographer has noted, "many aspects of the history of British nuclear power . . . cannot be fully understood if they are isolated from the military programme".[5] At the outset, it was clearly the latter that had priority. In wartime exchanges of the 1940s with the United States, Britain maintained consistently that the military potential of nuclear research came first. Given a vacillating, cautious and sporadically hostile attitude on the part of Washington after 1946, the British Government saw no alternative to the creation of a separate British nuclear fuel plant as a matter of national interest to provide the military programme with weapons-grade fissile material. Opting for production of plutonium, rather than of highly enriched uranium, then constrained early decisions on power reactors. By 1955 Britain was firmly committed to a nuclear future, both in military and civilian terms. A White Paper on the nuclear power programme looked forward to the construction in the period to 1965 of twelve Magnox reactors, by which time it was forecast that nuclear stations could be producing one-quarter of the nation's electricity. Also in 1955 the *Statement on Defence* renewed with vigour the British goal of developing a major strategic nuclear force.[6]

From the start, then, the nuclear power programme enjoyed a measure of politically exploitable prestige that went considerably beyond what would have been available to one designed solely to meet energy needs. On the other hand, the inflated claims and rhetoric that often accompanied official statements also served eventually the interests of critics. In the 1950s atomic energy officials tended to take it for granted that Britain's technological leadership – Calder Hall was delivering electrical power in 1956, the Shippingport plant in the United States not until the following year – would generate overseas sales. More considered appraisals of export possibilities had to await the protracted debates of the 1960s and 1970s on reactor choice. Export potential was not the sole criterion in these debates, but it remained an important one. The drive for exports thus overshadowed nuclear policy in Britain as it did many other areas of domestic and foreign policy during these decades.

Sales of Magnox reactors to Japan and Italy in 1959 did not, however, create a momentum of success in foreign markets. Hope that a valuable export trade could be established, once Britain's nuclear industry had a surer foundation, had been voiced in the 1955 White Paper, but the Magnox reactor's limited growth potential and the appearance of technical problems – notably corrosion difficulties – restricted British competitiveness in the early 1960s. Ironically the reactor itself later became something of a symbol of nuclear mismanagement in Britain. "We know now that the decision on Magnox was made without any proper appraisal", one MP said in a 1974 Commons debate. "It was made with inflated ideas of export potential, which were never realised, and an unwarranted, almost absurd, lack of attention to foreign expertise."[7] There were some extenuating circumstances. Pioneering systems in any new field have bugs; and export sales of Magnox reactors were viewed not so much as a long-term strategy, as a means of recovering some of the investment costs while the next generation of reactors was being developed. (Reports of the death of Magnox exports may, too, have been exaggerated – in 1980/81 there was again talk of the system finding Third World buyers because of its relatively small size.) But the successor to Magnox in the gas-cooled tradition, the advanced gas-cooled reactor (AGR), likewise failed to take off in world markets. The decisive factors in the 1964 decision to move to this reactor were its greater development potential, safety and higher thermal efficiency; but the official fanfare which greeted the start of the AGR construction programme in 1964/65, the launching of an overseas sales drive, and interpretation of the AGR "breakthrough" as a victory over United States nuclear technology,[8] are all indicative of the optimistic export atmosphere of the time. Unexpected cost increases, construction delays, the appearance of persistent technical problems, and the difficulties associated with on-site construction methods, however, soon made it clear that Britain had not yet found an internationally competitive reactor design.

Cheap electricity, though, was the crux of the AGR rationale. As far as exports to smaller European or to developing countries were concerned, a broader measure of agreement was possible that an alternative 1960s design might be preferable. This was the steam-generating heavy water reactor (SGHWR), the Winfrith prototype of which was opened in 1968.[9] When the new Labour government announced its preference for the SGHWR over other reactors in 1974, one weakness of Magnox was said to be that it had no export potential; the same was thought to be true of the AGR. The SGHWR thus exploited British technology (adopting the LWR would make for exports, but would put Britain in a position of dependence on American technology), gave scope for collaboration with Canada, and because of its modular construction it could be produced in smaller sizes for export.[10] This argument had been developed by the AEA since 1972. A member of the Authority's staff wrote in 1974 that the SGHWR was "particularly suitable for the requirements of developing countries". Winfrith showed it to be a dependable reactor; it was safe (a criterion on which PWRs were generally criticised in Britain); it used one-third the quantity of heavy water of competing systems; it was suitable for desalination plants; and, given oil price rises, developing countries would over the next decade be turning increasingly to nuclear power, which could be providing more than 70 per cent of the energy needs of some by 1983.[11]

But the SGHWR in turn proved to be a stop gap measure as far as Britain's nuclear power programme was concerned, and a non-starter in terms of foreign sales. As the decade wore on the international rush to light-water systems came to seem inevitable, and supporters of alternatives more and more like latter-day Canutes. Transition to a mixed programme including the PWR, however, did not come quickly. Some of the nuclear actors in Britain were converted early. The CEGB, attracted by the PWR's cheapness and the rapidity with which it could be brought into operation, had been adding up the points in its favour since 1973; the National Nuclear Corporation (NNC), of which GEC, the Westinghouse PWR licencee in Britain, was principal shareholder, was also a PWR advocate. The government, though, reflecting internal agonising within the AEA, still had doubts about the PWR's safety, and for a long time the conviction that selection of the PWR would be another nail in the coffin of British high technology was decisive. It did, however, recognise the "considerable world export potential" of the PWR and accept that overseas business was "an important factor that must be taken into account in decisions on nuclear policy".[12]

Yet the proven export record of the United States based on LWRs could not be ignored. Walter Marshall, later AEA Chairman, told a 1976 conference that "for some years we nurtured hopes of exporting gas reactors against strong competition, and we were not realistic enough to recognise that we could not compete with LWRs on the large US market. For this reason we have become somewhat disillusioned with the whole business of reactor exporting".[13] His predecessor, Sir John Hill, summarised AEA thinking in a document presented the same year to the Energy Secretary. The SGHWR was costly, would be subject to a potentially slow installation programme, and could not compete with established systems abroad. The PWR, on the other hand, was a world reactor. Germany and France had recently won export orders for PWRs even though no such system was operating at the time in France. Immediate export business was therefore "likely to be based, worldwide, on light water reactors of the PWR type". AGRs could not be exported against LWR competition.

> We must accept that it will not be easy to break into this worldwide business. . . . We must accept that, in the short term, export orders in the nuclear field will be for ancillary equipment, fuel and components for light water reactors. . . . Any thermal reactors we do build should be PWRs built under licence and therefore using components identical to those we want to try to sell to the rest of the world.[14]

There was, the NNC stated more bluntly in 1977, no case for the SGHWR; the choice was between the AGR and the PWR. The former allowed Britain to build on its gas experience;

> but we would be turning our backs on exports of nuclear power

stations and on the expansion of exports of certain components, with potentially damaging consequences for the future export of British power plant. . . . We have ascertained no advantages in the AGR system which are so certain that they would justify the rejection of the opportunities for export, which the PWR has and the AGR has not. . . . Amongst the countries that are expected to require power reactors in the 1980s there are a number where circumstances favourable to the UK as vendor should exist. The PWR is the system giving the best prospects in this respect and also in improving the export position of UK suppliers of individual PWR components.[15]

This accumulated case for shifting towards the PWR did not, however, vindicate scrapping the AGR. Critics continued to raise doubts about the viability of PWR reactor or component exports, in the light of growing world industrial capacity to produce it and reduced demand projections. Tony Benn, Energy Secretary from 1975–9, said at one point that he was "fed up" with reading that British gas reactor technology had no export value.[16] Support was expressed – likewise on export grounds – for adoption, in conjunction with the AGR programme, of the DRAGON high-temperature gas-cooled reactor (HTR), an international project with which Britain had been closely involved for several years. The upshot of the 1970s debates on Britain's nuclear future, then, was that the AGR survived but allied with a 1980s commitment to the PWR. The way ahead for the AGR programme was cleared in 1978, though major construction orders in connection with the proposed Heysham and Torness AGRs did not finally appear until 1981.[17] In 1979 the new Conservative government announced a 15 000-MW nuclear expansion programme in the decade from 1982, and a public inquiry into the CEGB's planned Sizewell PWR was later scheduled for 1983.[18]

THE PURSUIT OF EXPORTS

The pursuit of nuclear exports was thus an integral, if not overwhelmingly successful, part of Britain's nuclear programme from the 1950s. Forecasts of possible overseas sales were an important feature of the arguments of the 1960s and 1970s about the kind of reactor on which the programme should be based, and were crucial to the political acceptability of the case for both the SGHWR and, later, the PWR. The exports dimension also had implications for the long-standing problem of how best to organise the nuclear industry.

Various forms of government-industry collaboration emerged from time to time to promote nuclear exports. The AEA itself did not for the most part engage directly in this activity, but took the role rather of paving the way for selling efforts by firms and consortia. In recent years, for example, it has had a small section the officials of which travel regularly to sound out export possibilities. In one or two cases only has the Authority been involved in tendering directly overseas for nuclear power contracts.[19] A short-lived arrangement was set up in 1966 with the aim of coordinating foreign sales activities. The members of this British Nuclear Export Executive were the AEA together with the three nuclear industrial consortia of the day. Its role was defined broadly as being to promote the export of nuclear power stations of British design. Little was achieved – nothing at all if this goal is taken as the criterion.[20] The government also had for a time in the late 1960s a Reactor Export Policy Committee.[21]

In general, though, export orders were sought chiefly by the companies themselves, with background support from the government's trade promotion bodies in cooperation with various industrial groups. Typical of the preparation for British participation in the international nuclear industries fairs held at Basle, for example, was collaboration between the various British firms and consortia, the Commercial Department of the British Embassy in Berne, the British Nuclear Forum, the AEA, and the Department of Trade.[22] This interaction produced over the years a degree of official expertise in British government on matters of international nuclear sales, and involved some government-industry exchanges of personnel – one British Nuclear Fuels Ltd. (BNFL) official, for example, serving at one time as a First Secretary (Atomic Energy) in the British Embassy in Tokyo.[23] But these kinds of promotional endeavours reached their peak in the late 1960s and shortly afterwards, especially following the major nuclear industry reorganisation which took place in 1968.

Internationally, Britain had to keep face: to maintain a presence in the hope of dispelling commonly held assumptions about industrial weakness, indecision in nuclear policy, and reactor failings. The British Embassy in Washington described the objective of the British presence at the 1970 Atomfair as being:

to correct an all too common ignorance amongst some sectors of American industry of Britain's experience and capabilities in the nuclear power field, an ignorance summed up aptly by the question that one American engineer . . . put to a representative of a British firm earlier this year – 'from which US company does the UK buy all her nuclear power equipment and fuel?'[24]

Similarly, a report from the Embassy in Berne saw British participation in the Nuclex fairs as "an irrefutable sign of Britain's resolve to sell nuclear reactors and equipment overseas in the face of the most intense international competition".[25] Part of the reason for the disillusionment with reactor exporting which Marshall remarked on in 1976 was that all this was not just sales talk. In 1970 a several billion dollar nuclear expansion programme was under way in the United States; even before the energy crisis of 1973/74 it could reasonably be argued that developing countries would become increasingly reliant on nuclear power in the 1970s and 1980s – and Britain in 1974 had in the SGHWR a reactor which the AEA thought particularly well suited for this market; electricity from nuclear power stations in Britain was relatively cheap; the AEA had some justification for referring to itself as "the world's leading nuclear research and development organisation";[26] Britain had long experience with nuclear power, had pioneered and developed a sequence of gas-cooled systems, and was producing more nuclear power than any other country; and sales of fuel, reprocessed fuel and of radioactive materials were substantial. Failure to sell reactors, then, meant not only lost income. It had a crushing effect on morale both in the nuclear industry in Britain and in the AEA. By the late 1970s the final defence of the PWR option had come to be not that it would facilitate British re-entry into world reactor markets, but, less grandly, that it would help British industry expand its overseas sales of equipment, materials and components related to this kind of system.

From car manufacturer to gas-pump attendant: the change in Britain's fortunes was far from being as extreme as this, but it sometimes seemed like it. "The over-optimism of ten years ago", Hill said in 1975, "coupled with a totally unsatisfactory industrial structure have left us with more problems and disappointments than we would have wished in the last few years."[27] The question of industrial structure was a nagging one for many years. Fragmentation helped to set a pattern of lost orders in the 1960s. As one of the AEA's publications noted, "With too many consortia chasing too few contracts the result was inevitable."[28] Competitiveness in world markets demanded rationalisation and more effective industrial organisation; to complete the circle, one reason for pursuing exports was the boost that this would give, if successful, to the British power plant industry generally. In 1968 the Government ushered in a reorganisation which resulted in the creation of two nuclear design and construction companies. The change represented, Benn said:

> a balanced proposal designed to get the best out of the AEA combined with the greatest possible prospects of selling reactors abroad, which is the only way in which we shall get a return on the many hundreds of millions of pounds which we have spent on atomic energy in the last few years. . . . We have not sold a reactor abroad for some years . . . we want to get the maximum concentration of effort and the minimum of wasteful competition or design competition in a field in which this could be decisive in selling reactors abroad.[29]

It was not until 1973 that a single company, the National Nuclear Corporation (NNC), was formed in place of the seemingly endless process of industrial alliance formation and break-up that characterised the British nuclear programme in the 1960s.

Problems of industrial organisation tended to get most of the blame for export failures and weaknesses in the domestic programme (though industry in turn tended to point the finger at interdepartmental in-fighting and lack of policy coherence on the government side). Yet clearly other factors were at work – the export situation has not changed radically since 1973. Nor could industry or the AEA be faulted for the assiduity with which foreign sales were sought in the late 1960s and early 1970s. A case in point, one that achieved some notoriety, was the proposed reactor sale to Greece in 1969. The AEA signed an agreement with the Public Power Corporation of Greece for the sale of a 450-MW SGHWR due to achieve full power by 1974. The terms of the deal, however, also included sale by the Greek Tobacco Board of some 40 000 tons of tobacco to Britain.[30] British cigarette manufacturers, inadequately consulted, then protested that Greek tobacco was unsuitable for blending for sales in the British market. The deal eventually fell through, though not before Opposition MPs had had their share of amusement at the Government's expense.

In practice nuclear exports tended to be based on uranium sales and radio isotopes. Exports of equipment for reactors hovered around £1–2m annually in the 1960s and 1970s.[31] No more power reactors were exported after the two sold in 1959, though there have been occasional sales of various kinds of small research and training reactors – ten, for example, were sold in the period 1966–9 to Switzerland, Romania, Chile and Brazil.[32] On the other hand, natural uranium sales during the first half of the 1970s ranged from £4.7 m to £29.6 m annually, while sales of artificial radio isotopes totalled £25.1 m and £24.6 m respectively in the years 1974 and 1975.[33] Growth on the fuels side can be seen by the yearly expansion of exports by BNFL since its creation. From 1971–80 export sales of the company in succeeding years amounted to £6 m, £6.3 m, £8.4 m, £5.9 m, £12.4 m, £11.1 m, £23.2 m, £30.0 m, and £40.7 m.[34]

NUCLEAR EXPORTS AND PROLIFERATION

Compared to the export sales figures achieved by the United States, France or West Germany over the same period all this does not add up to a very significant dent in the world nuclear trade. Officials have been able to boast wryly at international conferences that for this reason Britain's record on proliferation was a good one. It was this question – together with the altered domestic environment of nuclear policy-making – that increasingly occupied the attention of the AEA and the Government's atomic energy officials in the second half of the 1970s. It produced what Hill in 1978 called a "very different environment" for the British nuclear programme.[35] In the early 1970s government policy was to keep trade and politics separate, with civilian nuclear issues being handled as far as possible on a technical level without the intervention of such complicating factors;[36] but later in the decade this was impossible. There was no immediate shift in official perceptions following the Indian test of 1974, however. Indeed one school of thought was that it remained the British interest to maintain good relations with the Indian Government – and, further afield, with other Third World Commonwelth countries – and that this interest ruled out precipitate measures designed to tighten the international trade in nuclear goods.

In the event Britain was closely involved with this process. Her status as a nuclear exporting nation was one contributing factor. But a seat was also guaranteed by two other circumstances. First, as a nuclear weapon state Britain also had a long background of participation in talks in overlapping arms control areas. But secondly, the Government was committed to nuclear power options at the back-end of the nuclear fuel cycle, notably the reprocessing of nuclear fuels and research and development in the field of commercial fast breeder reactors. When the Carter Administration's non-proliferation policies came to focus in the spring of 1977 on the emergence of a plutonium economy Britain was among the leading European protagonists speaking out for what was seen as the nuclear future of the 1980s and 1990s. London's aim was thus to protect the essentials of Britain's nuclear programme and ensure the continuity of the export drive while checking the risks of weapons spread. Or, in the formula used in parliamentary statements, government policy was "to enable all countries to share in the benefits of nuclear science through trade in equipment and technology, wherever this can be done in conformity with the Nuclear Non-proliferation Treaty and without giving rise to the danger of proliferation of nuclear explosive technology."[37]

Fast breeder reactors had long been part of the visionary future of the British nuclear programme. Export prospects, in addition to fears about the feasibility of nuclear power in a world of depleted uranium stocks, were again a key part of the rationale. Marshall was himself in the mid-1970s one of the chief proponents of this link. Other countries were not so well placed for energy supplies as was Britain, he argued in 1976.

> It follows therefore that there will be a large export market for fast reactors and fast reactor components, and that this represents a large opportunity for British industry to capitalise on our present position in this technology. I do not think this point can be overstated. . . . This seems to me to be a point of such simplicity and significance that I am surprised that it is not being pressed by people other than myself. Perhaps it is because the nuclear and power engineering industries are too worried about the problems of surviving next year to give much thought to prospects a decade or more hence.[38]

According to AEA thinking in the mid-1970s the implication was that United States domination of the world nuclear market might turn out to be a transitory phenomenon. Fast reactor development, its Director stated in 1976, would increasingly centre on the sodium-cooled system pioneered in Britain.

> In considering overseas markets for our industry, we should therefore anticipate that fast reactors will gradually break into the near monopoly held by light water reactors. . . . Here is a technology

we have pioneered which is technically accepted and will be needed by the rest of the world and where, therefore, we are in a relatively good position to meet our domestic needs and export reactors, fuel and components.[39]

Looked at from the early 1980s, this perspective on fast reactor development in Britain appears over-optimistic. In 1973 projections envisaged a lead station coming on line in 1981 or thereabouts with further stations planned for the mid-1980s; by 1981 Marshall was hoping for a decision by 1985 leading to a commercial fast reactor constructed by the early 1990s.[40] Work on the fast reactor concept, begun in 1953, has had a number of problems to contend with, both technical and political. The Dounreay Fast Reactor (DFR) was in operation from the late 1950s and produced electricity mostly for the Scottish grid; the next stage, construction of a Prototype Fast Reactor (PFR), also at Dounreay, was completed in 1974, and this reactor was generating 60 per cent of its full power output by the end of 1976. The mid-1970s, however, were taken up with wider public and scientific debate about the future of the fast reactor in the British nuclear programme, the main casualty of which was postponement of the decision on when (rather than if) to go ahead with the building of a commercial demonstration fast reactor (CDFR). In 1979 Prime Minister Thatcher publicly praised the PFR effort, and said that a decision on CDFR would have to be reached within two years;[41] but in practice the decision process proved less amenable to the imposition of deadlines.

Production of plutonium was similarly no novelty in Britain in the 1970s, having been the original motive for the country having a nuclear programme in the 1940s and an important factor shaping the character of the civilian power programme in the 1950s In the late 1960s irradiated nuclear fuel from the Garigliano and Latina power stations of ENEL, the Italian electricity authority, was being reprocessed at Windscale, and the resulting plutonium and uranium shipped back.[42] In 1971 BNFL joined with French and German groups to establish United Reprocessors GmbH with the aim of marketing irradiated oxide fuel reprocessing and the arrangement of associated transport and ancillary services based, at least initially, on the Windscale and La Hague reprocessing plants. In line with the government's general policy of separating as far as possible commercial nuclear development from political factors, reprocessing was put on a strictly commercial footing from 1968; but it was BNFL's reprocessing plans for the

Windscale facility in 1976 which eventually generated perhaps the most intense and heated public political battle to have taken place in connection with the British nuclear programme. This point will be taken up later.

Thus by 1977 a vital sector of British nuclear power planning was under attack from two fronts: from a new Administration in Washington intent on taking a fresh lead against nuclear weapons proliferation and determined to seize on plutonium as a culprit; and from groups and news media at home alleging that the government was mindlessly taking the country into a nuclear future of extreme hazard. The previous September the AEA's journal *Atom* published its first piece on proliferation. In it Hill anticipated the general line taken by Britain later in INFCE. Many countries, he said, had the skill to develop nuclear weapons or peaceful nuclear power programmes.

> Furthermore they will be more likely to do so if they are denied nuclear power by the countries that have it today. There is no way that this knowledge, which is now worldwide, can be uninvented. . . . The problem of proliferation of nuclear weapons is in my view far and away the most worrying aspect of nuclear power . . . [but] the solution to this problem is political and international.[43]

Lying behind British participation in INFCE sessions in 1978–80 were several assumptions. First, the nature of the problem as this had been defined in Washington was contested. The root problem of the non-proliferation regime was seen to be not plutonium production, reprocessing or technological failings, but rather a lack of adequate assurances of supply. The point was made with particular force in the light of the Canadian and United States embargoes. The "capriciousness" of uranium suppliers, said the head of the British delegation, constituted in itself good reason why countries like Britain had to opt for reprocessing; an "effective non-proliferation policy", the Foreign Secretary had maintained earlier, "must go hand-in-hand with a viable energy strategy".[44]

Secondly, the view that there were technical solutions to the problem of proliferation – during INFCE a caricature rather than an accurate picture of American thinking – was denied. The only viable solutions, as Hill had stated, were political. The argument was developed by an AEA staff member in a 1981 paper. The construction of power reactors, J. G. Collier argued, did not represent the most direct or attractive route to the acquisition of fissile material for nuclear weapons, although if these or other civil nuclear facilities already existed in a country their misuse for the production of such material was possible. But any country with the technological skills and know-how to build and operate nuclear power facilities on a commercial scale would also have the technical capability of constructing the rather less complex facilities needed to prepare fissile materials by the more direct route. "In this situation", he concluded, "the only real barrier to a country producing nuclear weapons is the commitment by the government of that country to the principles of non-proliferation."[45] Technical methods of diminishing proliferation risks from research reactors or civilian nuclear power programmes were, however, actively explored by British and other INFCE participants – those designed to reduce the presence of plutonium in separated form in the fuel cycle, for example, to use radioactivity to protect fissile materials from diversion, and to protect fissile materials by the use of physical barriers. Marshall, for example, together with Chauncey Starr of the Electric Power Research Institute, California, presented to INFCE the Civex concept, a method of making plutonium lethal by retaining radioactivity, though this was put forward as a possible technique for the 1990s rather than for the immediate future.[46] The more ambitious United States arguments concerning the merits of thorium fuel cycles, though, tended to be discounted; they stemmed from excessive emphasis on plutonium, discussion of which, Hill had said in 1976, was "far more emotive than rational".[47] It followed also that it was not possible, in the British view, to compare different fuel cycles and technologies and give each a measure on a proliferation scale; any such "league tables" would simply provide information on the best ways to make nuclear weapons.

Thirdly, a British approach to INFCE was to criticise the thinking underlying policies of denial. This non-proliferation strategy, it was argued, was ultimately self-defeating. Selling nuclear power plant in developing countries implied encouragement of the skills necessary to operate such plant, but denying this technology would tend to put a premium on the development from scratch of a more extensive range of fuel cycle capabilities.

The conclusions of INFCE in early 1980 were on the whole welcomed as vindicating these kinds of arguments. The head of the British delegation to the final plenary session again stressed the importance of uncertainties in the supply of uranium and the role political factors were playing on the supply side, and linked the need for fast reactors to such considerations. Proliferation, he went on, had been shown by INFCE to be a political and not a technical problem. "Misapplication of the civil nuclear fuel cycle is not in our view the only, or even the most likely, route for a nation to follow if it wanted to develop nuclear weapons." Moreover, systems were difficult to compare. "We therefore endorse the conclusion that it is not possible . . . to put fuel cycles in ranking order of proliferation risk." There were two main messages of INFCE: "first the need for measures to reduce the uncertainty in the medium and long term availability of uranium; and secondly the need for institutional measures to lessen the risks of proliferation given that technical measures or the use of any particular fuel cycle do not provide answers". Stability in the nuclear trade was the crucial point. It was

> only by providing such stability that we can reduce the incentive for countries to become independent in the fuel cycle and avert the fear and risk of proliferation that such development entails. We need, too, to rebuild confidence that non-proliferation does not mean interference in supply arrangements and that commercial contracts will be fulfilled subject to agreed non-proliferation conditions.[48]

Britain, though, was not a central opponent of United States views in INFCE. The British role was seen to be one rather of broker between Washington on the one hand, and Bonn and Tokyo on the other on the issues of reprocessing, use of plutonium in thermal reactors and the fast reactor future. And in practice, officials have pointed out, the United States accepted that Britain was among the countries which needed fast reactors eventually; the argument tended to be more one of timetables, with the United States emphasising that in the 1980s and after there was likely to be more uranium around than the British had earlier thought. In the interim between the termination of INFCE and the 1980 Presidential elections talks were held between AEA and United States officials on the prospects for collaborative programmes on fast reactor development,[49] but before the incoming Administration had pronounced on the matter as far as the United States domestic programme was concerned the future remained uncertain. Thus a degree of wider international acceptance of fast reactor needs was combined with an acknowledgement that this and other nuclear policy areas had been proceeding earlier in the 1970s with an excessive zeal. As Marshall observed in 1981 on Britain's situation, the cutback of thermal reactor programmes throughout the world meant that the cost of uranium was not going up as fast as had been expected. Given this fact, in conjunction with Britain's oil and gas resources, "I think it's true that in retrospect we can say we started on fast reactors rather sooner than we needed."[50]

The INFCE cooling off period was an important factor making for what British atomic energy officials saw in 1981 as the much less dangerously competitive character of the relations between the nuclear exporting countries compared with the situation five years earlier. The progressive tightening of export regulations, in part as a result of exchanges in the Nuclear Suppliers Group, pointed in the same direction. The relative ease with which Pakistan had been able to acquire for its nuclear programme items which enhanced weapons production potential, for example, led to the British Government's clamping down in late 1979 on equipment exports for use in uranium hexafluoride conversion plants and equipment that could be used in the manufacture of gas centrifuges.[51] It became an aim of policy also to reduce eventually the level of enrichment in reactor fuel to 10–15 per cent. Liaison at the international level, moreover, was matched by a similar process of concertation at the interdepartmental level in government and with industry. The British team at INFCE included officials from the AEA, the Department of Energy, the Foreign and Commonwealth Office, the Ministry of Defence and BNFL.[52]

The other part of Britain's foreign nuclear policy, that of encouraging – within non-proliferation guidelines – the spread of nuclear power in developing countries, was edged aside somewhat in the security-oriented atmosphere of the 1970s. The aspects that surfaced were generally marginal to the main thrust of policy. Additional financial assistance, though, was offered by the government in 1980 to NPT-signatory developing countries over the next four years to support nuclear energy projects.[53] This side of government policy was sustained by three main kinds of considerations. First, as we saw earlier, Britain never fully relinquished the hope that its reactors and nuclear technology might one day find significant Third World markets. But secondly, from a political and diplomatic perspective, the FCO in particular was sensitive – as it had been in the aftermath of the 1974 Indian test – to the wider costs of a refusal to accommodate legitimate developing country needs for nuclear power in the face of spiralling imported oil prices; and, thirdly, from a security point of view, a non-proliferation strategy based on a policy of denial was thought inherently contradictory and one resting on the constraints likely to be set by technological dependence ultimately more effective.

PUBLIC OPINION, NUCLEAR POWER AND EXPORTS

Even before Harrisburg in 1979 the domestic political environment in which British nuclear policy was formulated had changed. A variety of pro- and anti-nuclear groups emerged. Nuclear power was out of the closet: low-profile nuclear policies were no longer feasible.[54] Even so, little in the way of a substantial debate on nuclear exports and proliferation questions arose, and the significance of this widened arena of nuclear politics in Britain in the middle and late 1970s for such issues lies more in the broader challenges it posed to the British nuclear power programme itself. Indeed in some respects public interest in exports as such tended to wane as a natural consequence of the uncertainties and policy shifts that marked the 1960s and 1970s. Until the mid-1970s nuclear exports was an issue periodically taken up by Opposition M.P.s or editorial writers. The overseas sales potential of different reactors was raised, the government criticised for failing to promote exports and to reverse the declining morale of the nuclear industry, British gas-cooled technology defended, or else proposed nuclear sales to regimes considered disreputable by the left were condemned. By the second half of the decade, other issues predominated: the siting of reactors, safety and environmental health questions, alternatives to nuclear power, radioactive waste disposal, the transportation of nuclear materials, uranium exploration, and reprocessing. Exports and proliferation risks tended to fall last, if at all, on lists of policy changes demanded by anti-nuclear groups. An Energy minister provoked no response when, in a television discussion in 1981 on nuclear power, he dismissed the question of proliferation as unimportant.

Reprocessing, however, was a question that straddled both domestic and international politics because of the foreign business being done and planned at Windscale. The 1977 public inquiry is a useful example of the limits of pressure group influence in the nuclear policy area in Britain. The development of British reprocessing facilities to serve foreign firms had been from 1975 the object of intense media attention. The *Daily Mirror*'s famous headline "Plan to Make Britain World's Nuclear Dustbin" set a trend of journalistic phrase-making that included the *Guardian*'s reference to plutonium "swilling about the seas" and even the Women's Institute journal *Home and Country*'s "deadly necklace around our coast".[55] But the case prepared for the inquiry by FOE and other groups was ultimately unsuccessful. More particularly, although the well-publicised Royal

Commission on Environmental Pollution had concluded in 1976 that
the spread of nuclear power "will inevitably facilitate the spread of the
ability to make nuclear weapons and, we fear, the construction of these
weapons", FOE's argument linking proliferation dangers to
reprocessing activity was systematically demolished in Mr Justice
Parker's report on the Windscale inquiry.[56]

In general, though, the proliferation issue has not figured
prominently in anti-nuclear arguments. The FOE representative at
one 1977 meeting, for example, maintained simply that there was no
export market for nuclear equipment or materials anywhere at that
time, or that in any event a lot of government-financed export credit
would be required and that there were better uses for this money;[57] the
intriguing implication – that profitability was the key to the political
acceptability of the nuclear trade – was not, however, drawn. Further,
an anti-nuclear case which stressed proliferation risks has tended to
run up against certain dilemmas, in that the general argument against
nuclear power has usually been best – or at least most vehemently –
developed by individuals or groups attracted also to pro-South
advocacy. More broadly based criticism of Britain's nuclear power
programme was, however, continuing to mount in the late 1970s and
early 1980s. One 1980 opinion poll appeared to show that two-thirds of
the public did not want more nuclear power stations to be constructed;
the annual conference of the Liberal Party approved the same year an
amendment calling for the scrapping of all stations; and in 1981 the first
report of the Commons' energy committee criticised what it saw as
persistent and unjustifiable government optimism on nuclear matters
and, more especially, the assumptions underlying CEGB policy.[58]
Whether all this will lead later in the decade to major policy changes,
other than any that might occur for other reasons, has yet to be seen.
High unemployment figures, for example, in practice help the pro-
nuclear case: "All we are concerned about here is jobs", as the leading
trade union convenor at Dounreay has been reported as saying.[59]
More likely is a continued, but not drastic, slackening of the pace of
thermal reactor construction and of the fast reactor programme. The
impact on public opinion of a large export contract for a nuclear power
station would be the topic for an interesting case study, but
circumstances are unlikely to conspire to allow this to be carried out.

CONCLUSIONS: BRITAIN'S NUCLEAR EXPORTS AND NON-PROLIFERATION

Official hopes of Britain eventually obtaining a major share of the world nuclear trade were kept alive in the 1960s and 1970s partly as a means of defending programmes from critics who saw in nuclear power development little but lost money and dangers to life and health. Though a flourishing export trade has developed in fuels, radio isotopes and certain kinds of equipment and related materials, the bigger prizes of turnkey contracts for nuclear power stations in developing countries eluded Britain's grasp. Part of the reason lies in the fact that the pursuit of exports was not the sole objective of the nuclear power programme, so that decisions on reactor choice which affected British fortunes in world markets could have their origins in quite different considerations. Britain, moreover, did not from the mid-1950s to the early 1980s commit itself firmly to one reactor type around which export programmes could be centred. A record of past failures is difficult for a salesman to shake off. And the particular reactor types chosen for the domestic nuclear programme, some not least with the aim of preserving older traditions of British nuclear technology, did not for various reasons fit well into export markets. This was a particular blow to the SGHWR, one of the defences of which in 1974 was its suitability for the power needs of developing countries. Other problems beset the AGR; its on-site construction requirements have been compared to those of trying to build jet engines in an airport hangar.[60] Until the early 1970s, too, important questions of industrial structure went largely unresolved. Finally, Britain came late in the day to an appreciation of the implications of the effective domination of world markets by light water systems.

Britain's participation in the non-proliferation debates of the 1970s was based, then, on her role in this international trade, but also followed on from commitments made to a nuclear future which comprised first the reprocessing of spent nuclear fuel and later the development of a commercial fast breeder reactor programme. United States thinking in the early months of the Carter Administration posed a direct, if veiled, threat to the political viability of these kinds of enterprises. The results of INFCE, however, helped both to clear the air and also to reassure the British atomic energy establishment that once the matter had been thought through Washington was prepared to accept the requirements of countries like Britain for different nuclear strategies. Questions of supply, moreover, emerged from

INFCE as a core issue; British officials accordingly viewed the IAEA's Committee on Assurance of Supply, created in 1980, as a main vehicle for serious nuclear policy debate and for the easing of Third World doubts about the trustworthiness of the nuclear supplying states. It was in this context that London was able to sound a cautious note of welcome to the Reagan Administration's seven-point policy statement of July 1981. It was regarded as being based on more realistic assessments and assumptions than had been common at least during the first half of the previous Administration, but at the same time appreciation of the vulnerability of domestic and international nuclear issues in the United States to changes in the public and Congressional climates checked a more positive response.

From the perspective of the AEA, there were at the turn of the decade some grounds for believing that as far as Britain was concerned the initiative in the broader public and parliamentary debate on the future of nuclear power had returned to the pro-nuclear forces. The reprocessing tumult, at any rate, had subsided. With it, too, had gone the chances of nuclear export and non-proliferation issues becoming a focal point of the nuclear power debate. On the other hand, there were implications for exports of the kinds of nuclear issues coming more into prominence in the early 1980s – the criticism, for example, of the PWR safety record. But these implications are not likely to be far-reaching. Britain's stake in the international nuclear trade remains comparatively small and specialised. Hopes of a nuclear export reviviscence tend to be grounded in the uncertain terrain of the middle and later 1990s, the road to which is charted through a series of thermal and fast reactor decisions of perilous aspect.

NOTES

1. Walter Patterson, *The Times*, 23 Oct. 1980.
2. "Nuclear Power in Disarray", editorial, *The Times*, 19 Feb. 1981.
3. Roger Williams, *The Nuclear Power Decisions: British Policies, 1953–78* (London: Croom-Helm, 1980) p. 13.
4. N. T. Marsham and R. S. Pease, "Nuclear Power in the Future", *Atom*, 196 (Feb. 1973) pp. 46–62.
5. Margaret Gowing, in the *New Scientist*, 19 June 1980, p. 329.
6. The major study dealing with this background is Margaret Gowing, *Britain and Atomic Energy, 1939–1945* (London: Macmillan, 1964); and *Independence and Deterrence: Britain and Atomic Energy, 1945–52* (London: Macmillan, 1974). Other works dealing with nuclear power issues in Britain include Duncan Burn, *The Political Economy of Nuclear*

Energy (London: Institute of Economic Affairs, 1967); Henry R. Nau, *National Politics and International Technology: Nuclear Reactor Development in Western Europe* (Baltimore: Johns Hopkins University Press, 1974); E. F. Wonder, "Decision-making and the Reorganisation of the British Nuclear Power Industry," *Research Policy*, 5 (1976) pp. 240–68; and Peter DeLeon, "Comparative Technology and Public Policy: The Development of the Nuclear Power Reactor in Six Nations", *Policy Sciences*, 11 (1980) pp. 285–307.

7. *House of Commons Debates*, 872 (2 May 1974) col. 1394.
8. Williams, *op. cit.*, p. 125.
9. For the view of the system's future potential in world markets see *Atom*, 138 (Apr. 1968) pp. 72–3.
10. Varley, at *House of Commons Debates*, 872 (2 May 1974) cols 1356–8. See also ibid., 876 (10 July 1974) col. 1367; and 883 (20 Dec. 1974) col. 2032.
11. R. McKeague, "The Suitability of the SGHWR for the Power Requirements of Developing Countries," *Atom*, 215 (Sept. 1974) pp. 200–14.
12. Benn, at *House of Commons Debates*, 926 (21 Feb. 1977) cols 1011–13; and ibid., 925 (8 Feb. 1977) col. 1266.
13. *Financial Times* conference, reported in *Atom*, 242 (Dec. 1976) p. 307.
14. *Atom*, 239 (Sept. 1976) pp. 232–5. Cf. Marshall's remarks to the 1977 Sunningdale conference, reported at *Atom*, 251 (Sept. 1977) p. 203.
15. "The Choice of Thermal Reactor Systems", report by the NNC, republished in *Atom*, 251 (Sept. 1977) pp. 208, 213.
16. Williams, op. cit., p. 259.
17. *Financial Times*, 6 Apr. 1981.
18. David Fishlock, "Full Steam Ahead for the 'British PWR'", *Financial Times*, 13 Dec. 1979; and CEGB, *Proposed Sizewell 'B' PWR Nuclear Power Station. Project Statement* (mimeo., n.d.)
19. D. E. H. Peirson, "Twenty Years On", *Atom*, 255 (July 1975) pp. 103–4.
20. *Board of Trade Journal*, 190, 3613 (17 June 1966) p. 1349.
21. *Atom*, 158 (Dec. 1969) p. 309.
22. See reports in the *Board of Trade Journal*, 191, 3628 (30 Sept. 1966) p. 814; and *Trade and Industry*, 9, 8 (23 Nov. 1972) p. 363.
23. *Atom*, 208 (Feb. 1974) p. 45.
24. *Trade and Industry*, 1, 7 (2 Dec. 1970) p. 378.
25. *Board of Trade Journal*, 191, 3628 (30 Sept. 1966) p. 814.
26. *Atom*, 157 (Nov. 1969) p. 305.
27. *Trade and Industry*, 21, 3 (17 Oct. 1975) p. 140.
28. E. P. McTighe, "The Development of the UK Nuclear Power Industry" *Atom*, 170 (Dec. 1970) pp. 246–7.
29. *House of Commons Debates*, 768 (17 July 1968) cols 1429–35.
30. *Atom,* 152 (June 1969) p. 150.
31. With occasional higher points, for example in 1964 and 1974. See *House of Commons Debates*, 746 (9 May 1967) col. 211 (written); and *ibid.*, 912 (9 June 1976) col. 682 (written).
32. *Atom*, 154 (Aug. 1969) p. 238.
33. *House of Commons Debates*, 912 (9 June 1976) col. 682 (written).
34. British Nuclear Fuels Ltd, *Annual Reports and Accounts* (1971/72 to 1979/80).

35. Sir John Hill, "The Scope and Limitations of International Cooperation concerning the Nuclear Fuel Cycle", *Symposium on International Cooperation in the Nuclear Field: Perspectives and Prospects. Proceedings* (Paris: OECD/NEA, 1978) p. 53.
36. William Wallace, *The Foreign Policy Process in Britain* (London: Royal Institute of International Affairs, 1975) p. 142.
37. Ennals, *House of Commons Debates*, 895 (16 July 1978) cols 481–2 (written).
38. *Financial Times* conference, reported in *Atom*, 242 (Dec. 1976) p. 307.
39. *Atom*, 239 (Sept. 1976) pp. 233–4. Cf. *The Guardian*, 16 Sept. 1980, on international collaboration.
40. "Future Prospects for Energy: Supply and Demand", *Atom*, 196 (Feb. 1973) pp. 38–40; and Marshall interview in *Atom*, 294 (Apr. 1981) p. 102.
41. *Nuclear News*, Oct. 1979, p. 38.
42. *Atom*, 150 (Apr. 1969) p. 78.
43. "The Abuse of Nuclear Power", ibid., 239 (Sept. 1976) pp. 237 ff.
44. See *Nuclear Fuel*, 28 Apr. 1980, p. 9; and *Financial Times*, 14 July 1978.
45. J. G. Collier, "The Nuclear Fuel Cycle and Proliferation", in *Environmental Impact of Nuclear Power* (London: BNES, 1981) pp. 273, 275.
46. *Financial Times*, 29 Mar. 1978.
47. *Atom*, 239 (Sept. 1976) pp. 237 ff.
48. *Draft UK Statement at INFCE Primary*, mimeo (Feb. 1980). See also reports in the *Financial Times*, 19 July 1979, and 26 Feb. 1980.
49. *Energy Daily*, 6 July 1980.
50. *Atom*, 294 (Apr. 1981) p. 102; cf. AEA, *Annual Report*, 1978/79, pp. 6–7.
51. *Nuclear Fuel*, 26 Nov. 1979, p. 7.
52. AEA, *Annual Report*, 1978/79, pp. 6–7; BNFL, *Annual Reports and Accounts*, 1977/78, p. 12.
53. *The Times*, 24 Sept. 1980.
54. The manner of nuclear decision-making became an important sub-issue in the debates of the second half of the 1970s, especially the secrecy and the excessive power of certain senior officials which critics claimed to find there. A document was leaked in 1979 which purported to reveal official thinking on the feasibility of maintaining a low profile on PWR development (*Time Out*, 7 Dec. 1979, p. 7).
55. *Daily Mirror*, 21 Oct. 1975; *New Scientist*, 9 Oct. 1980; *Home and Country*, July 1977.
56. *Royal Commission on Environmental Pollution (Chairman, Sir Brian Flowers), Sixth Report: Nuclear Power and the Environment*, Cmd 6618 (Sept. 1976) p. 76; the government response in *Nuclear Power and the Environment*, Cmd 6820 (1977) p. 11; and *The Windscale Inquiry: Report by the Hon. Mr Justice Parker*, vol. 1 (London: HMSO, 1978) pp. 14 ff.
57. *Atom*, 251 (Sept. 1977) p. 202.
58. House of Commons, *First Report from the Select Committee on Energy* (1981); the poll is reported in *The Times*, 6 Aug. 1980.
59. *The Guardian*, 11 Sept. 1980.
60. David Fishlock, in *The Financial Times*, 13 Dec. 1979.

7 Australian Uranium Exports: Nuclear Issues and the Policy Process

Russell B. Trood

Over the past decade the controversy which has surrounded nuclear power and technology since the end of the second world war has increased in intensity. The changing tempo of the international debate over the issue has been most noticeable in the nuclear consuming countries of western Europe, North America and in Japan where the expansion of commercial nuclear facilities to meet the rising demand has attracted considerable domestic opposition. However, the debate over nuclear power has not just been confined to these countries. It is perhaps one further indication of the growing interdependence of states in the international system that during the 1970s a debate over the safety and utility of nuclear power developed in Australia which was equal in intensity to any of those taking place around the world. Yet in contrast to those other debates Australia's did not emerge from the process of formulating national defence or energy policies; rather it arose in conjunction with policy decisions regarding resource development and more particularly the exploitation of Australia's uranium reserves. Put another way, Australia approached the dilemmas posed by the use of nuclear power from the standpoint of being a supplier of nuclear material rather than as a consumer of nuclear energy.

Before the advent of the uranium debate, nuclear power was an issue of little importance in Australian domestic politics. Periodically, concerns surfaced over the problem of nuclear proliferation and there was sporadic discussion of the possibility that Australia might develop nuclear weapons for defence purposes and perhaps construct nuclear power plants as sources of energy supply. But neither of these issues nor the first phase of uranium development, between 1954 and 1971,[1] attracted the controversy which accompanied the discovery of substantial new reserves of uranium in the early 1970s.[2] The need to formulate policy regarding the future of these reserves brought the issue of nuclear power on to the political agenda and led the federal government to review Australia's external policy regarding nuclear proliferation and management of the international nuclear industry.

This chapter examines the evolution of Australian uranium export policy during the 1970s and several issues associated with the development of Australia's uranium resources. Broadly, the essay is divided into two parts. The first reviews three important elements of the policy process; the public debate, the role of the Ranger Uranium Environmental Enquiry (the Ranger Enquiry) and the government's decision to proceed with mining. The second part analyses five specific issues; safeguards and non-proliferation policy, uranium enrichment, government involvement in the uranium industry, environmental protection and the impact of uranium mining on Australia's aboriginal people.

THE FORMULATION OF URANIUM POLICY

The formulation of public policy integrates issues and processes. Arguments continue as to how rational a process may be, but it has long been recognised that the process may frequently be as important as the issue itself in determining the nature of a particular policy decision.[3] In Australia this was certainly true of the uranium issue; the final decision to proceed with mining was made by the federal government, but the process included, in addition to the usual paraphernalia of bureaucratic machinery, the elements of a public enquiry (the Ranger Enquiry) and an extensive public debate. The prominence of the second and third elements in this process distinguishes the uranium issue from many other issues in Australian politics. Traditionally, public policy is decided in secret, amongst senior public servants and the members of the government. Public debate usually succeeds, rather than precedes, the announcement of policy. Departure from this tradition in the case of uranium policy can be explained, in part, by the controversy which often surrounds nuclear issues. But it is also the consequence of a government decision to open the policy process to direct public participation through the medium of a public enquiry.

(i) The Public Debate

Australia's public debate over the mining and export of uranium began to take form during 1975. In these early stages the development of Australian uranium reserves was favoured by all major political parties;[4] the Liberal and National Country parties (L–NCP), on the conservative side of Australian politics and the Australian Labor Party (ALP), on the other.[5] This bipartisanship only lasted while the full implications of uranium development remained largely un-explored. Once the issue was examined more closely the consensus began to fracture and constituencies in support of and in opposition to mining began to build within the parties. Since all shared the philosophy of promoting mineral exports as a source of economic development, the problem for each was essentially the same: how to balance the economic considerations of mining, such as export earnings and economic growth, against non-economic concerns like proliferation and environmental protection.[6] For the ALP the issue was of the most profound kind, of a nature which reached back into its history as a force for social advance, touching matters of prin-ciple and expediency and thus calling attention to its heritage as a home for both the realist and the romantic. For the Liberal and National Country parties, the issue was no less profound, but rather less complicated. Traditionally, both identified with business and development interests and the romantic had always tended to lead a rather tenuous existence within their ranks. By mid-1976 the lines dividing supporters and opponents of mining were evident, both between parties and within them. The ALP was divided for and against. The differences were noticeable, but not particularly divisive, during the party's period in government between 1972 and 1975. Afterwards they became much more obvious as the issue began to split the rank and file. Some members, mainly of the former government, were prepared to support mining under certain strictly controlled circumstances; however, with the more radical elements of the party gaining control of the uranium issue, the ALP's position moved, effectively, to one of outright opposition, the party calling for a moratorium on all mining until the hazards associated with mining had been eliminated.[7] The ALP-affiliated trade union movement was similarly divided, as several conservative trade unions, notably the Australian Workers Union, with members in the mining industry, supported the further development of uranium reserves while many others did not. The tension between the two positions led to uneasy compromises in policy and left the movement as a whole in an ambivalent position over the issue.[8] In contrast, the theme within the conservative parties was essentially one of harmony in favour of mining with one or two discordant notes of opposition. This was the L–NCP's position while in opposition in the federal parliament, and became government policy once the coalition achieved office in 1975. Once bipartisanship disappeared these positions characterized the major parties' approaches to the uranium issue throughout the debate.

That debate was all the more intense because, as Thomas Smith has pointed out, it came at an unusual time in Australian political history.[9] At a federal election in December 1972, the L–NCP coalition government was defeated after 23 uninterrupted years in office. The event marked a clear break with the past in Australian politics, and the new ALP government was resolved to make it more manifest through an innovative programme of policy reform. Many of the government's more significant proposals were opposed by conservative state governments and the federal opposition and there was considerable dissatisfaction with Labour's style of government. In November 1975, after three controversial years, Prime Minister Whitlam and his Ministers were dismissed from office by the Governor General exercising executive powers. The manner of the government's removal and the part said to have been played in that event by the new Prime Minister, Malcolm Fraser, generated a political climate which went beyond controversy to one "filled with acrimony, distrust, suspicion and a lingering feeling on the part of the ALP and their supporters that they were 'done in' by establishment interests".[10] This atmosphere infected Australian politics throughout 1976 and beyond. It reinforced, generally, the policy disagreements which existed between the parties and, in relation to uranium in particular, put an end not only to any thoughts of sustaining a bipartisan approach to policy but of any useful and constructive party debate on the issue.

While Australia's major political parties were the principal protagonists in the uranium debate, the issue drew supporters and opponents from a wide spectrum of the community. In addition to the L–NCP coalition and some trade unions, the supporters of mining included: uranium mining companies, several prominent nuclear scientists, and the Australian Atomic Energy Commission (AAEC), a statutory nuclear research body.[11] As well as sections of the ALP and the trade union movement, the opponents of mining included groups representing environmental and aboriginal interests, some nuclear scientists and doctors and the fledgling Australian Democrat party.[12] The Ranger Enquiry became a major forum for the presentation of arguments for and against mining, but for the most part the debate was unstructured. Participants used a variety of means ranging from the relatively passive, such as writing letters to the Editor, to more disruptive strikes and marches to publicise the issue and draw public attention to the arguments.[13] Since the issue tended to excite passions, some of the more demonstrative expressions of opinion led on occasions to ugly and violent incidents.[14]

The mining and export of uranium was an Australian domestic political issue, but it fitted into a mosaic of international controversy surrounding nuclear weapons and the generation of nuclear energy for commercial purposes. Misgivings over the military and civilian uses of nuclear power translated into numerous specific concerns: the danger of nuclear war, the threat of nuclear terrorism, the hazards both environmental and personal of the nuclear fuel cycle, the difficulty of waste disposal, and so on. These were widely discussed aspects of nuclear power in nuclear consuming countries such as Japan, West Germany and the United Kingdom, and they were seen as being no less relevant to a debate over nuclear power in a nuclear supplier country such as Australia. Hence, much of Australia's uranium debate was taken up with discussion of the general dangers associated with the generation of nuclear power even though Australia was not using this form of energy.[15] Nor was it that issues alone crossed over national borders. Much of the information and material presented in arguments during the course of the Australian debate drew on overseas experience with regard to nuclear technology or cited studies and statistics by internationally distinguished individuals, organisations and government agencies.[16] Moreover, some participants in the debate such as the Friends of the Earth organisation were affiliated with similar organisations overseas.

While the debate was international in scope as well as being comprehensive and protracted, few of the participants were involved in government or in positions where their influence could directly affect the making of policy. The anti-mining lobby was most disadvantaged in this regard; once Labour left office its position was largely unrepresented in government. As a consequence there was only a very slim possibility that its maximum demand – a ban on uranium development – would be met. But, as already mentioned, the public debate in the case of the uranium issue was of more significance than normal in the policy process. While the lobby's maximum demand was unattainable, its campaign against mining was not without impact. By consistently drawing attention to the hazards of uranium development, opposition groups reinforced the findings of the Ranger Enquiry and put considerable pressure on the government to incorporate extensive regulatory mechanisms into its policy.

In effect, the public debate limited the government's usually considerable area of discretion in policy making, performing functions which are normally the government's prerogative. First, it established and confirmed the agenda of issues for resolution, principally whether or not to proceed with the mining and export of uranium, but also whether to impose safeguards, proceed with enrichment facilities, require environmental precautions, acknowledge the concern of aborigines, and so on. Second, the public debate established the parameters within which each of these might be resolved. In other words, it provided a range of possible options and policy alternatives; for example, to mine and export uranium with a restrictive or a liberal safeguards policy, to mine and export uranium in conjunction with, or independent of, enrichment technology. Denis Stairs has argued that public opinion may perform similar tasks with regard to foreign policy.[17] Australia's experience with uranium suggests an application to domestic policy and further that the impact of an extensive and informed public debate on policy can be considerable.

(ii) The Ranger Enquiry

The Ranger Enquiry was announced, with little public fanfare, in April 1975 and established in July of that year.[18] Three commissioners were appointed, with Mr Justice Fox of the Supreme Court of the Australian Capital Territory presiding, to enquire into all the environmental aspects of a proposal by the AAEC and Ranger Uranium Mines Pty Ltd to develop certain uranium deposits in the Northern Territory of Australia. The Enquiry took nearly two years to complete its work and produced two reports. The first, in October 1976, was a generic report dealing with the broader issues of nuclear power and technology. The second report, of May 1977, addressed the particular questions raised by the Ranger development proposal.

The first point to make in relation to the Ranger Enquiry is that its purpose was to examine the environmental impact of a particular uranium development project. This was a relatively narrow objective. Further, in contrast to other ALP government commissions which had reviewed major areas of policy, the Ranger Enquiry was quite differently constituted, having been appointed under the specific provisions of the Environmental Protection (Impact of Proposals) Act.[19] Moreover, it came at a time when the ALP government's uranium policy was largely in place. As the Enquiry went about its business most of these matters were forgotten and it became something it was not intended to be: a vehicle for the comprehensive appraisal of Australian uranium policy. The second point to note is that L–NCP governments of the past have shown little inclination to appoint public enquiries to consider and make recommendations upon important areas of policy, preferring instead to decide issues behind closed doors. When the ALP government was dismissed from office in November 1975, with the Ranger Enquiry only part of the way through its business, the new government inherited an approach to policy making not very much to its taste. The Commissioners were asked to conclude their Enquiry quickly, but they refused on the grounds that it had been appointed under a statutory instrument and was not subject to the directions of ministers.[20] The government, having agreed to await the Enquiry's findings and recommendations before deciding upon its own policy towards uranium development, was largely forced to suspend its efforts at policy formulation. Third, the Enquiry became a focal point for the public debate over uranium. Its terms were interpreted as being wide enough to allow a comprehensive examination of nuclear power. This reinforced the community's perceptions of the broad issues which were involved in deciding whether to proceed with the mining and export of uranium. As a result, the Enquiry's activities received a great deal of media attention and attracted widespread public support. For the new government this had two consequences: first, in an already difficult political climate, it was possible to request, but almost impossible to force the Enquiry to terminate its activities; second, with such public support it would be difficult to ignore the Enquiry's findings and recommendations if they proved unacceptable. Finally, the Enquiry's two reports avoided making any final recommendation on whether or not to go ahead with uranium development, although they contained numerous recommendations regarding the Ranger project to be implemented should mining in fact proceed. The closest the Commissioners came to recommending general development was the first finding of the first report:

> The hazards of mining and milling uranium, if those activities are properly regulated and controlled, are not such as to justify a decision not to develop Australian uranium mines.[21]

To the Commissioners' regret this was interpreted by many, the government included, as approval, albeit qualified, to proceed with development. On one view this may have been so, but in their report the Commissioners had expressed the hope that the "findings of fact . . . [would] . . . prove more valuable than . . . [the] . . . final recommendations",[22] and later on urged that there "be ample time for public consideration of . . . [the] . . . report and for debate upon it".[23] In short, the Commissioners saw their role as contributing to the public debate over uranium and not ending it. With this objective in mind they produced comprehensive reports which discussed the complex dimensions of the nuclear and uranium industries in a clear, critical yet balanced fashion. As a result, most of the participants in the uranium debate found something in the reports to support their position.

(iii) The Government's Decision

Although the new L–NCP government agreed to await the final recommendations and findings of the Ranger Enquiry before announcing its own uranium policy, Ministers made little secret of their preference for mining to proceed. The Minister of Trade and Resources, Mr Anthony, was particularly outspoken in support of development. On one occasion, shortly after taking office, he was reported as warning that "Australia had to make its uranium available to other countries or face the risk of having it taken by force."[24] This proposition was roundly criticised, with one newspaper calling it "scare-mongering, silly and dangerous",[25] but few doubted it to be a clear indication of the government's wish to proceed with uranium mining. While Mr Anthony's views seemed to give the clearest insight into the government's thinking, its policy intentions were evident in other ways: in the frequent assurances given to the Japanese government to the effect that all existing contracts for uranium would be completed and in the Prime Minister's clear endorsement of President Carter's April 1977 proposals to limit proliferation.[26] Each hint of the government's plans drew criticism from the anti-mining lobby which saw them as evidence of an intention to disregard the Ranger Enquiry's findings.[27]

If the government did little to disguise its policy intentions while the Ranger Enquiry was in progress, with one exception, it also did little in the way of actual policy formulation. Announcements were made of changes in the foreign equity guidelines, and of the role of the AAEC in uranium development and some broad indications were given of the areas of policy which the government was likely to review.[28] While each announcement irritated the anti-mining lobby, it was the government's statement of nuclear safeguards policy in May 1977 that created the greatest outcry. In announcing the policy the Prime Minister said that it "in no way preempted a decision on the question whether any . . . new contracts for the export of uranium will be permitted".[29] But few were impressed. The Labour Party's spokesman for Minerals and Energy, Mr Keating, saw it as a statement "to usher in a policy of uranium exports",[30] while a spokesman for the Movement Against Uranium Mining said it was "clear the government had decided to establish a large-scale mining industry".[31]

To an extent both were correct, since the odds in favour of mining proceeding had increased substantially following publication of the first report of the Ranger Enquiry in October 1976. This long-awaited document did not contain a firm recommendation that mining should proceed, rather it discussed the broad implications of uranium development in the general context of an international nuclear industry. Nevertheless, the Minister for Environment, Housing and Community Development, Mr Newman, told parliament that the thrust of the Report's findings and recommendations "is broadly acceptable to the government and provides a basis for future decisions on the industry".[32] If the government had said nothing further this enigmatic response might have enabled it to argue successfully that further uranium mining was still an open issue. As it was, this reaction, when taken with the remainder of the Minister's remarks, left a clear impression that the government saw the report as being generally favourable towards mining and reinforcing its own stand on the issue. Several newspapers reported that the Ranger commissioners were displeased with this interpretation of their findings.[33] The Commissioners had hoped to stimulate informed public debate on the whole issue of uranium mining, thereby elevating the existing discourse to a more constructive level. Instead, their report was being used by the government as affirmation for a position already taken. Nor was the government alone in its approach. The ALP, among others, found it to contain material which also supported its position. According to the Leader of the Opposition in the federal parliament, Mr Whitlam, the government's actions with regard to the report were "misrepresentations". It was "overwhelmingly concerned with the hazards of nuclear development", and in accordance with ALP policy no Labour government would agree to uranium mining until satisfied that the hazards had been eliminated and that a satisfactory method of waste disposal had been developed. Furthermore, Labour would not honour contracts for the sale of uranium entered into by the present government.[34]

By the time the second report of the Ranger Enquiry was published on 25 May 1977, the decision to proceed with mining seemed to have been all but announced. As with the earlier report, the second made no recommendation on whether general uranium development should take place, although it did conclude that the Ranger project should be allowed to proceed within certain strict guidelines which were set out in considerable detail. The government's immediate response was to announce that a final decision would probably be months away, and that an interdepartmental committee (under the Chairmanship of the Prime Minister's Department) was to be established to examine both of the Ranger reports.[35] The committee was struck a short time later and was composed of representatives of all departments with an interest in uranium policy, principally: Trade and Resources; Foreign Affairs, Aboriginal Affairs, Environment, Housing and Community Development, and Health. In conformity with the usual practice, decisions were reached by way of consensus although in this case the Prime Minister's preference for mining to proceed was reflected in the Chairman's strong leadership. The committee's work was completed by mid-May, allowing cabinet to spend several days deliberating the details of policy before the budget session of parliament in mid-August.[36]

The Prime Minister announced that the government had decided "there should be further development of uranium under strictly controlled conditions", on 25 August 1977.[37] Since the government had done little to disguise its attitude, few were surprised by the decision. *The Australian* called it "realistic" while *The Age* approved of it on ethical and pragmatic grounds.[38] Public opinion polls reported that the decision had the support of a majority of Australians.[39] By contrast, members of the anti-mining lobby were universal in their condemnation. Mr Whitlam said the decision "is not only premature, it is precipitate. The Opposition rejects it". Mr Tom Uren, an ALP member of parliament and a committed opponent of mining, argued that a "pitiful philosophy of short term greed" underlay the decision.[40]

The government's decision was motivated by four broad considerations which were mutually reinforcing. First, it was dictated by a "high sense of moral responsibility"[41] which imposed two obligations upon Australia: one, not to "abandon the world's energy poor countries", and a second to do what could be done to arrest the problem of proliferation – "to help make a safer world". The second motivation was international influence. This was a corollary of the first. Being a significant supplier of uranium would confer influence and make "certain that Australia's voice . . . will be heard" in international forums where proliferation was being discussed. The third consideration was economic. Not to proceed with mining would "deny Australia significant economic benefits". Finally, the government believed that while the hazards accompanying uranium development could not be ignored, they could be minimised through "proper regulation and control".

For some of these arguments there was credible supporting evidence. On the matter of economic benefits, for example, the Ranger Enquiry had found that a uranium industry in Australia would bring substantial economic benefits to several sections of the Australian community.[42] Yet the benefits were hardly guaranteed. They depended on such unpredictable factors as the demand for and price of uranium, both of which would fluctuate, perhaps to Australia's advantage but not necessarily. Similarly, the Ranger Enquiry appeared to believe that government regulation might ameliorate some of the hazards of uranium mining. But once again this was not a certainty; overseas experience has shown that even with substantial regulation accidents could happen with potentially alarming consequences. On both of these matters, economic benefit and hazards, the government balanced risks against the potential advantages and decided in favour of the latter. By way of contrast the ALP had weighed the same issues and found the scales to tip in the opposite direction. On the subject of whether Australia had a "moral responsibility" to supply uranium there could be a range of judgements based on differing standards of conduct in international politics. Even if it made sense to speak of morality in the affairs of states it was not patently obvious that this was a situation which actually called for Australia to fulfill its particular moral responsibility.[43] Far from abandoning other states, the Ranger Enquiry had shown that should Australia not develop its uranium reserves other sources of supply would be available.[44] This conclusion suggested that the dire consequences implied by "abandonment" were perhaps overstated. Similarly, it was possible to counter the argument that the export of uranium would make a safer world, with the observation that one of the most effective means of containing proliferation might be to limit the availability of nuclear fuel altogether. This perspective on non-proliferation understandably made little impression on a pragmatic government. That the export of uranium would confer "influence" was little more than an optimistic expectation on the part of the government.[45] Power may be one of the more recognisable features of international politics but it is also one of the more evanescent. It was doubtful that Australia would acquire greater influence as a result of one policy decision. Furthermore, the premise upon which the proposition rested, namely that Australia was a major supplier of uranium ore, might be easily and quickly undermined should further substantial deposits of ore be found elsewhere in the world. The government's decision did bring an end to the uncertainty over whether Australia would proceed with uranium development, but it did not end the controversy which surrounded the whole issue. Since 1977 new contracts for the export of the uranium have been signed and shipments of yellowcake have taken place;[46] yet the opponents of mining, including the ALP and the trade union movement, have continued to call for a moratorium on further uranium mining.

ISSUES

The principal issue for Australians to decide was whether to proceed with mining and export of uranium. The debate revealed that there were several dimensions to this question, among them: non-proliferation and safeguards policy, uranium enrichment, government regulation of the uranium industry, environmental protection and aboriginal welfare. Not all of these subjects were especially controversial during the uranium debate, but they were all relevant to the making of Australian uranium policy and for this reason deserve consideration.

(i) Non-proliferation and Uranium Safeguards Policy

As with nuclear issues generally, concern for the problem of nuclear proliferation was only of sporadic interest in Australia's domestic politics prior to the controversy over uranium development. The early phase of uranium mining attracted very little public discussion and the implications for proliferation were barely mentioned. One or two domestic issues inspired some thoughtful consideration of the problem, but for the most part Australia's nuclear conscience was vicarious in nature, largely being aroused by periodic international crises. In contrast, an appreciation of the problem of proliferation had always been a feature of Australia's foreign policy. Australia had been a founder member of the IAEA and had always taken an active part in its work as well as participating in other multilateral efforts to strengthen the fragile international non-proliferation regime. With the emergence of the uranium issue domestic interest in non-proliferation moved into closer alignment with the country's foreign policy, and indeed much of the uranium debate focused on the problem. Supporters of mining argued that the export of Australian uranium would either strengthen the non-proliferation regime, as the government contended, or that it would have little impact one way or the other. On the other hand, opponents of mining were generally adamant that export could only substantially increase the dangers of proliferation. The key to the problem lay in preventing the unauthorised diversion of nuclear fuel and technology for military purposes. An extensive system of international safeguards had been established to this end but it was widely recognised as having numerous weaknesses and shortcomings.[47] These highlighted the unpalatable fact that virtually no system of safeguards, however comprehensive, could prevent a determined state from clandestinely diverting nuclear fuel or technology to military purposes and probably avoid both bilateral and international sanctions in doing so.

In recognition of growing public concern, the government placed considerable emphasis on the non-proliferation aspects of its uranium export policy. When responding to the first Ranger Enquiry report, the Minister for Environment, Housing and Community Development, Mr Newman, made a particular point of supporting a recommendation to the effect that any future export of Australian uranium be subject to the "fullest and most effective safeguards agreements".[48] The government would not permit export, the Minister advised parliament, "unless . . . satisfied that there are adequate and proper safeguards on the handling, transport and processing en route and in respect of the ultimate consignee".[49] The Prime Minister sought to convey the same firm resolve in May 1977 when announcing the government's safeguards and non-proliferation policy. He told parliament that the establishment of a framework for the peaceful use of nuclear energy was an issue of "major international importance" and that Australia was determined that nuclear material supplied for peaceful uses not be misused.[50] To this end the Prime Minister announced a dual approach to the problem of proliferation. Firstly, Australia intended to apply strict safeguards to the sale of its uranium. These would require that a state proposing to purchase uranium be a party to the NPT and, before making any purchases, enter into a bilateral safeguards agreement with Australia covering the use of Australian supplied nuclear material. More particularly, the agreement would require an undertaking that Australian nuclear material be used only for peaceful purposes; provide for the application of IAEA safeguards; require prior Australian consent to the enrichment of Australian uranium beyond 20 per cent; prevent reprocessing and transfer to third parties without prior Australian consent; incorporate "fallback" safeguards, and provide for the physical safety of the material. The second element of the policy was an "important complement to these measures". Australia would participate in multilateral efforts to coordinate safeguards policy, to upgrade existing standards and seek to promote consensus between supplier and consumer countries on effective controls in the nuclear industry.

Although the Prime Minister's announcement met with some criticism, the policy did attempt to confront the problem of proliferation in a comprehensive manner.[51] It proceeded on the premise that as a potentially significant supplier or uranium Australia would be favourably placed to make a direct contribution to non-proliferation through the imposition of its own safeguards, and through diplomatic initiatives could encourage other states to make a similar commitment. The government probably overestimated its capacity to move other states in the direction of non-proliferation, but it seemed to have a realistic appreciation of the commercial and political forces which would affect uranium sales. The policy attempted to strike a balance between stringent safeguards conditions and being too liberal. Even so, the policy was not without its restrictive aspects. In this regard the conditions to be included in bilateral agreements which required consent to the transfer, reprocessing and enrichment of Australian uranium were especially noticeable and likely to prove unacceptable to some of Australia's potential uranium customers. These requirements seemed to leave little room for compromise in the negotiation of export conditions and they gave the whole policy something of a high-handed air, of unilaterally imposed obligations, being offered on a take or leave basis. In fact, the conditions in agreements were to prove more flexible than the Prime Minister's statement of policy suggested. Moreover, the core of Australia's safeguards policy was to be the system of safeguards developed by the IAEA. As parties to the NPT, it could be anticipated that most consumers of Australian uranium would be familiar with the demands made by these safeguards in the areas of disclosure and inspection, so in reality Australia's conditions offered few surprises. But as the Ranger Enquiry had pointed out, the IAEA safeguards system was not without its shortcomings. In part, the bilateral agreement was designed to overcome these by imposing additional conditions such as "fallback safeguards", which would apply to nuclear material in the possession of consumer states if IAEA safeguards became for some reason inoperative. In setting the standards for safeguards, the policy built on the experience of other states, such as Canada, and the government made it clear that it would continue to monitor practices elsewhere as part of a comprehensive plan of coordinating international safeguards policy.

Australian safeguards policy has continued to evolve in the years since 1977. Some of the developments have clarified the policy, while others have raised something of a question mark over the government's long-term commitment to a strict safeguards regime. Of the former, the most significant has been the announcement of conditions for consent to reprocessing, a subject upon which the Government had been reserving its position until completion of INFCE. The Minister for Foreign Affairs, Mr Street, announced Australian policy on reprocessing in a statement to parliament in November 1980.[52] Broadly, it proposed that a state interested in reprocessing would provide information to the Australian government outlining the reasons why it had become necessary. If the need to reprocess nuclear material of Australian origin "is demonstrated to the satisfaction of the government" and controls and safeguards met all existing requirements, consideration would be given to the granting of consent in certain limited situations; on the basis of agreement in advance to reprocess for energy use or to facilitate the management of materials, and on a case-by-case basis where reprocessing was intended to produce material for peaceful, non-explosive purposes or for the storage and use of plutonium in ways that do not contribute to proliferation. The conditions of consent were to be subject to review and states were to undertake to support measures for the more effective control of reprocessing. The policy provided a narrow range of circumstances in which reprocessing might be permitted and with the possible exception of the "management of materials" category left little room for other needs. Nor would the policy permit reprocessing for all peaceful purposes. Consent would not be given, for example, to reprocessing to produce explosive grade material for use in mining or engineering projects or like purposes. Australia intended to keep an intrusive hand on reprocessing by reserving the right to decide if the need to reprocess had been demonstrated. If this provision operates as apparently intended, decisions on requests to reprocess may well create some problems for the Australian government.[53] It is not inconceivable that as part of an effort to surmount them a practice will evolve in which a state supplying the necessary information could expect to receive consent provided reprocessing is for an enumerated purpose. The option to reprocess is an important matter for some states and the absence of clear guidelines for consent has long been a noticeable shortcoming in Australian safeguards policy. Now that the matter has been settled it is arguable that the task of marketing Australian uranium will be more straightforward.

Giving consent to reprocessing is not without its risks, but from the perspective of non-proliferation two other developments in safeguards policy are arguably more disturbing. First, there has been a change in the policy requiring the signing of bilateral agreements before uranium sales contracts can be signed. This change took place, amid some criticism, in 1978 when protracted safeguards negotiations with the Japanese and West German governments seemed likely to threaten lucrative uranium contracts.[54] Australian policy now permits uranium contracts without an agreement, but prevents their completion until one is in place. Clearly this is a compromise of the original policy and, it might be argued, evidence of the government's inclination to lower its safeguards standards. Such a view is perhaps a little uncharitable, since there is no concerted movement in this direction. Moreover, this particular change will not substantially weaken safeguards conditions, provided uranium is not supplied until such time as a bilateral agreement has been concluded. There is a danger, however. It lies in the possibility that a contract for the supply of uranium which is nearing its completion date will become a source of pressure encouraging negotiations on a bilateral agreement to be brought to a hasty conclusion with a compromise in safeguards standards. The second development which gives rise to some concern is the government's departure from the policy of confining uranium exports to states being parties to the NPT. To date the only manifestation of this intention is the signing in 1981 of a bilateral safeguards agreement with France.[55] Since France already possesses nuclear weapons, this development may be of less significance than first appears; and the government had indicated earlier that non-signatories to the NPT already possessing weapons would constitute an exception to the general rule requiring all importers of Australian uranium to be parties to the treaty. Accordingly, the agreement with France is not a surprising development. The primary reason for the treaty rule and the exception, namely the diversion of weapons grade material, is obvious, but, as Martin Indyk has pointed out, there may still be hazards in dealing with non-parties, even if they possess weapons.[56] The possibility exists, for example, that Australian safeguarded uranium supplied to a state will free other non-safeguarded supplies for export to a third party who may use them for weapons production. Australia would have had no direct dealings with the third state, but would have unwittingly facilitated its acquisition of nuclear weapons. With its export-oriented nuclear industry, France is one state to which this kind of problem is apposite. There is no evidence that the government intends to liberalise its policy to the point of exporting generally to non-NPT countries, but clearly any movement in that direction would compromise substantially the principles which underpin Australia's safeguards policy.

Since 1977, then, Australia's safeguards policy has evolved in response to the international system in which it is required to operate. Yet measured against the number of bilateral agreements which have been signed, the policy has still to gain widespread international acceptance. To date only nine safeguards agreements have been concluded, most with states strongly committed to the same ideals of non-proliferation as Australia.[57] As yet there is no evidence that the lure of Australian uranium is proving so irresistible to those states not so committed that they would be willing to compromise options of further nuclear development by agreeing to Australia's conditions of purchase. Indeed, the modest nature of the achievement so far suggests international resistance to the conditions attached to the sale of Australian uranium. Moreover, the bilateral negotiations already completed or in progress have not always proceeded smoothly. Problems have delayed the completion of an agreement with Japan, a country often seen as a major customer for Australian uranium. And there were obstacles to be overcome in the negotiations with both France and the United Kingdom,[58] although in the latter case they were attributable more to constitutional issues surrounding the United Kingdom's membership of the European Economic Community than substantive disagreements over the conditions of the agreement.

Clearly, Australia's efforts to implement a safeguards policy have met with mixed results. This, together with the very short period of time which has elapsed since the policy was announced, make assessment of its long-term viability a difficult task. Even so, it may be ventured that in implementing its safeguards policy the government has attempted to maintain fidelity with the objectives of non-proliferation announced in May 1977. This has posed several problems and Australia's opinion has not always prevailed. But the former Minister for Foreign Affairs, Mr Peacock, predicted as much in 1977 when he observed that:

> If one country says another country ought not to reprocess, does anyone think the second country would greet that statement with relish? Come into the real world, for goodness sake. . . . The future will unquestionably see a process of international give and take on both sides.[59]

This remains an accurate assessment of the international environment in which Australian safeguards policy must operate and suggests three alternatives for the long-term: firstly, Australia taking more than it is required to give to gain acceptance of its safeguards conditions. To the Australian government, this is no doubt the preferred alternative, but at the same time the least likely. Secondly: balancing the principle of a strong safeguards policy against the pragmatic demands of a uranium export industry. This, in essence, is the existing policy and the government seems willing to engage in the compromises and trade-offs which will enable it to continue. Thirdly, Australia might give up more of its safeguards policy in order to ensure markets for its uranium. At present this is an unpalatable thought, but it may become less so in the event the conditions attaching to the sale of Australian uranium are perceived as being too onerous and limiting export potential.

In addition to implementing its safeguards policy, the Australian government has pursued non-proliferation objectives by means of more general diplomatic activity – the second facet of the policy announced in May 1977. Mr Justice Fox, Chief Commissioner of the Ranger Enquiry, was appointed Ambassador at Large for Non-proliferation and Safeguards in December 1977. His Honour spent a year advocating and explaining Australia's safeguards policy overseas and representing Australian interests at international conferences such as INFCE. Neither the Australian government nor Mr Justice Fox himself expected that the appointment of a special ambassador would bring any immediate breakthroughs in strengthening the international non-proliferation regime. Even so, in the long term His Honour's contributions in this direction may well turn out to be of considerable importance; in the meantime, his appointment and work served to publicise Australia's status as a major uranium producer with a strong interest in non-proliferation.[60]

Similar motivations were behind Australia's active support of President Carter's proposals of April 1977. Coming at a time when the government had not yet made its final decision on uranium mining, but was anxious to do so and looking for arguments to justify its position, President Carter's plan offered both a partial rationale for development and a context in which Australia's own safeguards policy would be reinforced by the international regime. At the same time, the Carter proposals added a further dimension to the co-operative relationship which has traditionally existed between Australia and America on matters of foreign policy.[61]

Australia's participation in INFCE followed naturally from the government's uranium development and non-proliferation policies. Australia's "sought and secured" the co-chairmanship of Working Group 3 of INFCE, which dealt with assurance of long-term supply, because it was seen as providing a useful vehicle for pressing Australian interests in the area of non-proliferation and because it dealt with other relevant interests such as future uranium supply.[62] This study was not intended to yield decisions for formal endorsement in a treaty, although an attempt was made to define areas of agreement. From Australia's perspective this process produced some useful conclusions on matters such as demand for uranium, the adequacy of existing world enrichment capacity and on progress towards non-proliferation. The findings on these and several other subjects provides Australia, and other participating nations, with some valuable guidelines for the future development of policy. Earlier, President Carter might have hoped that his proposals would be accepted in this way, but the widespread international criticism which they attracted made this extremely unlikely. The Carter proposals envisaged a significant role for Australia in the international nuclear industry and in continuing efforts to secure non-proliferation. The results of INFCE suggest that for Australia these opportunities will continue to exist even in the absence of President Carter's policy.[63] In addition to its contribution to INFCE, Australia has actively contributed in the past few years to the work of several other international agencies concerned with the regulation of the nuclear industry and the problems of proliferation.[64] Given Australia's traditional involvement in international efforts to establish an effective non-proliferation regime, none of these activities are surprising.

However, the enthusiasm with which they are now being pursued reflects the conviction, common amongst members of the government, especially the Prime Minister, that with substantial reserves of uranium Australia has acquired a new status and influence in the international community, one that requires it to speak, and commands that it be heard, on issues like proliferation.

(ii) Uranium Enrichment in Australia

Once large reserves of uranium had been discovered in Australia it became realistic to consider the possibility of establishing a local uranium enrichment industry. Although the substantial costs of such a project made it necessary to think in terms of overseas assistance with financing, the idea had a particular appeal for the ALP government because it accorded with the general policy of encouraging the processing of minerals in Australia. Besides maximising the value of resources prior to export, an enrichment facility would also contribute to the expansion of Australia's industrial base and provide a source of additional employment in the mineral industry.

In several statements during 1973 and 1974 the Minister for Minerals and Energy, Mr Connor, made it clear that the government was giving serious consideration to an enrichment proposal and was, to this end, discussing the possibility of setting up a joint enrichment feasibility study with the Japanese government.[65] The talks continued through 1973 and 1974 but seemed to be making little progress. However, late in 1974 the Japanese government agreed to participate in what became known as the Japan–Australia Study on Uranium Enrichment. The Japanese government explained its decision as a practical implementation of its own policy of diversification of enrichment supply. Even so, Australian newspapers had been reporting that Australia was applying considerable pressure to obtain Japanese agreement.[66]

While the L–NCP government also came to office espousing a policy of processing resources in Australia, the establishment of an enrichment facility was not a high priority. The possibility of a project getting under way in the near future receded into the background, as something to be considered once the threshold question of whether to proceed with mining had been resolved. The government did, however, encourage interested companies to discuss enrichment technology with the AAEC, and the AAEC itself continued to conduct research into enrichment methods. Moreover, the government supported the Japan–Australia Enrichment Study programme, and between 1976 and 1978 participated in a series of bilateral discussions covering future supply and demand for enriched material, the availability of raw material, capital requirements and the availability of technology from third countries.[67] From the outset these talks were intended to be no more than of a preliminary nature and they involved no obligations or commitments to proceed further. When they concluded in 1978, a final report, not yet made public, was made to each government.

One of the difficulties in conducting talks at this time was that they took place in an atmosphere of international uncertainty over the future of nuclear power. Just as the second round of discussions was beginning in April 1977, President Carter announced his proposals to limit proliferation. For Australia, they appeared to pose a dilemma. While encouraging uranium producing countries, like Australia, to expand their export markets, the plan proposed and placed great emphasis on limiting the expansion of uranium enrichment facilities around the world. Australia gave more or less unambiguous support to the Carter proposals, but in doing so the government seemed to favour the uranium export side of the plan and to largely ignore its implications for enrichment. Some of the uncertainties surrounding the future of nuclear power have clarified as a result of INFCE. On the specific issue of uranium enrichment, INFCE has pointed to the necessity for expansion of the world's existing capacity to meet expected demand after 1990. The Australian government has interpreted this as providing encouragement to proceed with the establishment of a local industry.[68]

Even before the final plenary session of INFCE, in February 1980, the government had been showing increased interest in the establishment of an enrichment facility. In January 1979 it announced that feasibility studies would proceed with the URENCO consortium, Japan, France and other interested governments.[69] These studies as well as the actual establishment of an enrichment industry were supported by a report of the Uranium Advisory Council in October 1979.[70] More recently, a consortium of companies known as the Uranium Enrichment Group of Australia has also recommended that an industry be established and suggested that work commence on a comprehensive engineering study.[71] If this goes ahead, as seems likely, there will be a noticeable escalation in the already obvious efforts of several state governments to attract enrichment facilities to their states.[72]

The Australian government has moved slowly over the issue of enrichment. It has been at pains to point out the complex matters which are involved in the decision: environmental impact, choice of partners, appropriate technology, problems of proliferation, and so on. Until these issues are resolved the government will remain reticent about making final decisions and giving dates for the actual commencement of enrichment operations.

(iii) Government Involvement in Uranium Development

From its inception the uranium industry in Australia has been under the close scrutiny of the federal government, which has acted as its primary regulator. This situation has been reinforced as a result of the uranium debate and as a further consequence there has been a substantial increase in the federal uranium bureaucracy.

Government participation in the regulation of the uranium industry expanded appreciably during the Labour Party's period in office. The basis for this expansion was the Party's objective of "enlarging the opportunities for Australians to share in the ownership and development of Australia's mineral resources".[73] This policy was universal, in the sense that it applied to the development of all of Australia's mineral resources, including uranium. As applied to the uranium industry it meant a substantial redefining of the role of the AAEC; its research function remained, but in future the AAEC was also to participate in uranium development projects, act as the sole, licensed explorer for uranium in the Northern Territory, and assume responsibility for the marketing of Australia's uranium reserves.[74] More generally, the uranium industry was affected by the ALP government's more active role in regulating mineral resource development. This took a number of different forms including setting strict foreign equity guidelines, requiring environmental impact statements, the monitoring of commodity sale prices and protection of aboriginal land rights. Some of these were new controls, while others merely built on existing procedures.

Few of Labour's policies were to the liking of the mining companies or to the L–NCP opposition which had an aversion to too much government involvement in the private sector. It was, therefore, hardly unexpected, that after taking office in 1975 the new government gave notice of its intention to reverse several of Labour's initiatives. In one of his earliest statements on uranium policy, the Minister for Trade and Resources, Mr Anthony, indicated that exploration for uranium in the Northern territory would be returned to private enterprise, that foreign equity guidelines would be eased (but none the less remain in existence), and that in general the government believed "companies should be relatively free to plan the development of their deposits . . . (of uranium) . . . and to negotiate their sales contracts, subject to export controls . . . safeguards . . . environmental considerations and the protection of Aboriginal interests".[75] The government has taken some steps to further these objectives but they fall well short of the goal of corporate freedom.[76] Indeed, there now exists a maze of legislative and regulatory measures which cover most aspects of the uranium industry and provide for extensive government intervention of one form or another.

Many of these new measures are a reflection of the public anxiety over uranium mining as expressed during the uranium debate. Most have their origin, more specifically, in the findings and recommendations of the Ranger Enquiry. In their carefully drafted Reports, the Ranger commissioners set forth the dangers of nuclear power as well as their reservations concerning uranium mining. At the same time, they expressed the belief that many of the hazards could be ameliorated by the government establishing standards and taking an active role in the management of the industry. Consistent with this view the Commissioners suggested regulatory controls throughout the industry, covering all stages of the mining, milling and export process.[77] In formulating its uranium policy, the government was faithful to most of these recommendations. Of course, the uranium industry is not unique in being subject to government regulation. But the special considerations of safety and health which have been applied to it have had as their consequence a regulatory regime which is probably more comprehensive and burdensome than in most other industries.

The expansion of the government's management role and of the Australian uranium industry in general has created a substantial administrative burden for several government departments and spawned a number of new administrative bodies. The department primarily responsible for the formulation and administration of uranium policy is Trade and Resources. Politically, this has been the bailiwick of the National Country party for many years and for its present leader, Mr Anthony, a coveted asset as the party sought to expand its traditional rural base of support to urban areas. The department is largely the old Minerals and Energy of the ALP government, though the Energy function was passed to a new department of National Development and Energy which was created after the 1977 federal elections. In the period since the ALP left office the uranium section of the department has expanded from a few people to the status of a separate division, indicating that uranium is a growth industry in more ways than one. Although Trade and Resources dominates, other federal departments have been, and continue to be, active in the formulation and/or administration of uranium policy. Foreign Affairs has borne the primary responsibility for negotiating Australia's safeguards agreements and for developing approaches to the problems of proliferation. In accordance with their expertise, lesser roles have been played by Aboriginal Affairs; Environment, Housing and Community Development (before being broken up in 1977); Health and Attorney Generals. The Prime Minister's interest in uranium policy has been reflected in his department's active role in coordinating much of the policy process.

Administrative burdens are frequently a source of power in government bureaucracies. In Australia there has been a degree of departmental and ministerial rivalry over the control of uranium policy. Mr Anthony argued strongly to keep uranium policy within his responsibilities when the present department of National Development and Energy was established in 1977 and placed under the control of a relatively junior Liberal party minister, Mr Newman. Mr Anthony was successful in this contest despite the fact that policy functions in relation to other resources were passed over to the new department. Nevertheless, National Development and Energy has secured some policy functions in the uranium area and presently has primary responsibility over radioactive waste disposal, and is actively engaged in formulating enrichment policy. The Department also chairs an interdepartmental committee on the latter subject and this has been the subject of some differences of opinion with Trade and Resources, sections of which believe the control of enrichment policy to be more properly the function of that department. Recent newspaper reports suggest that the present minister for National Development and Energy, Mr Carrick, will not yield easily on this issue and is in fact anxious to expand his Department's role in the uranium policy area.[78] Similarly, the area of safeguards policy has been a contentious issue between the departments of Foreign Affairs and Trade and Resources. At present a rather nebulous division of functions gives Trade and Resources responsibility for its implementation prior to export and Foreign Affairs afterwards with the negotiation functions being shared between the two.[79] As with enrichment policy, the differences which exist over safeguards seem likely to continue while the responsibility for specific aspects of uranium policy remains divided between two or more departments.

Finally, several new administrative bodies have been established as a result of Ranger Enquiry recommendations. The Uranium Advisory Council was established in 1978 as an independent body reporting to the Minister of Trade and Resources. Its functions are to investigate and report, as it sees fit, on the overall problems and impact of the uranium industry. To date it has reported on several matters, including uranium enrichment, sequential development of uranium mines, the future of the AAEC and the Harrisburg nuclear reactor accident.[80] The second body recommended by the Ranger Enquiry was that of Supervising Scientist, an office now responsible to the Minister for Home Affairs and Environment. The office is to manage the environmental aspects of uranium mining in the Alligator Rivers region of the Northern Territory. Thirdly, the enquiry recommended a marketing authority with general powers to control and supervise marketing, sales, and commercial arrangements with regard to Australian uranium. At present this authority exists only in the form of an Australian uranium exports office within the Department of Trade and Resources. The government has delayed constituting the authority until it examines implications of Foreign Anti-trust laws as they affect the marketing of uranium.[81]

(iv) Uranium Development and Environmental Protection

The uranium issue emerged at a time when sections of the Australian community, along with others in the western world, were taking an increasingly active interest in new areas of public policy. The appearance of a "social conscience" was particularly evident in the field of environmental protection. By the early 1970s conservation groups and trade unionists in most Australian states were actively engaged in efforts to preserve Australia's natural environment. Environmental concerns had been minimal during the first phase of Australia's uranium development.[82] By contrast, the existence of a vocal, domestic environmental lobby and the high visibility which the hazards of nuclear development had attained internationally, made it likely that any new decision to proceed with mining would be profoundly effected by environmental considerations.

To conservation groups, the impact of resource development projects on the natural environment was a matter of special concern, with uranium mining an obvious target of opposition. It was not so much that uranium mining was inherently more destructive of the environment than other kinds, radioactivity problems aside. Rather, uranium deposits had been found in some environmentally sensitive locations. This was certainly the case with the Ranger uranium deposit, around which much of the environmental controversy was focussed. This deposit, along with several others, was situated in the magnificent Alligator Rivers region of the Northern Territory, a wilderness area which had been proposed as the site for a national park. It was for the purpose of assessing the environmental impact of the development of this deposit that the Ranger Enquiry had been established in 1975. Evidence presented to the Enquiry pointed to the adverse impact that mining would have on the water, soil, flora and fauna resources of the region, as well as upon the local fishing, pastoral and tourist industries.[83] Much of this evidence was accepted by the Ranger commissioners and they recommended that the project, as proposed, not be allowed to proceed. However, they were satisfied that if their recommendations and stipulations were implemented the environmental impact of mining could be limited to the point that the damage would be minimal, and mining should therefore be allowed to proceed.[84] This conclusion stood in stark contrast to that of the environmentalists of the anti-mining lobby. In the Ranger Enquiry's detailed findings of the adverse effect of mining on the ecology of the region, they found ample evidence to support their contentions regarding the hazards of uranium development. At a joint press conference shortly after release of the second report, representatives of the conservation lobby saw its findings as providing sufficient evidence to justify a ban on mining for years to come.[85]

While much of the controversy over the environmental consequences of uranium mining concentrated on its impact in the immediate vicinity of mining operations, environmentalists also had misgivings of a wider nature. The accumulating evidence from overseas, which pointed to the hazards of operating nuclear reactors and the problems of waste disposal, together with rising perceptions of the dangers associated with the proliferation of nuclear technology, created a constituency concerned for the global implications of growing dependence on nuclear power. This perception of the danger to man's global habitat provided another motivation to resist uranium mining, since it was only by opposing the expansion of the nuclear industry in specific countries that an attack could be made on the overall problem.

Misgivings over the impact of uranium mining in Australia and the implications of nuclear dependence gave the environmental issue considerable salience and made it one of the more coherent themes of the uranium debate. From the government's point of view the pervasiveness of the environmental concerns made the issue a difficult one to de-fuse. In an attempt to do so the government accepted most of the Ranger Enquiry's recommendations pertaining to environmental protection.[86] While this did help to mollify environmental objections to mining, it did not quell all opposition. Environmental considerations remain amongst the most frequently articulated reasons for a ban on uranium development. In part this is because environmental concerns have usually been at the core of most opposition to mining. They were prominent at the outset of the debate and are now sustained by continued ALP and trade union opposition to mining which is based on essentially environmental considerations. Moreover, the issue remains one of high visibility because of widespread public appreciation of the adverse environmental impact of some resource development projects. Yet another reason for the continuing opposition is to be found in the public's perception of the L–NCP government as being less than completely dedicated to environmental protection in relation to uranium mining. The origins of this perception lie in part in the government's rejection of some of the Ranger recommendations which, from an environmental perspective, were amongst the most important. Most notable in this regard is the decision not to proceed with the plan for sequential mining development as proposed by the enquiry.[87] But also damaging to the government's environmental image has been the continuing controversy surrounding alterations in the boundaries of the area in which miners will be able to operate in the Kakadu National Park. In short, it is unlikely environmental objections to uranium mining in Australia will be allayed completely in the near future. They will remain a substantial part of the continuing controversy over whether development should have begun in the first place.

(v) Uranium Development and the Australian Aborigines

The need to reconcile uranium development with the competing interests of Australia's aboriginal people added a further dimension to the uranium debate. This issue was largely overshadowed by other matters during the early part of the debate and did not emerge into full public prominence until the mining companies began negotiating royalties and conditions for mining with aboriginal leaders in 1978. Even so, within the cluster of interests most directly concerned with uranium development, the mining companies, the ALP government and the aborigines themselves, it was clear from the outset of the debate that the impact of mining on aboriginal interests would be an important aspect of the whole uranium issue. In part this was because uranium mining would have a direct, adverse impact on several aboriginal communities and with its potential for large profits political considerations, if not equity, dictated that they should be shared with the inhabitants of the mining area. Beyond these considerations, however, the recognition of the aborigines' stake in uranium development was indicative of a considerable change in the public's attitude towards the aboriginal people. For nearly two hundred years the European population of Australia had studiously avoided paying anything but perfunctory attention to either aboriginal culture or welfare. By the early 1970s growing public interest in these matters contributed to making the cause of the aboriginal people an important facet of the uranium debate.

The uranium issue was little more than of potential interest to many aboriginal communities. But to others, such as those in the Alligator Rivers region of the Northern Territory, it was of direct and immediate concern since this was not only the site of several large deposits of uranium ore but an area of traditional tribal lands. Mining would involve "trespass" upon these lands and, perhaps more importantly, threaten the desecration of certain sacred sites. Having to reconcile these interests was an awkward problem for the ALP government which was committed to recognising aboriginal land rights as well as honouring all existing contracts for the supply of uranium. These two objectives were not necessarily mutually inconsistent, but the government found itself split over the issue on several occasions.[88]

The aborigines' ability to protect their interests against the onslaught of uranium development was greatly enhanced by the results of two enquiries appointed by the ALP government. The first, the Woodward Commission, was established in 1973 to examine the whole question of aboriginal land rights.[89] The commission reported in 1974 and recommended that aboriginal land claims be recognised and that they be accompanied by the right to receive royalty payments with respect to any mining development and to restrict access to recognised land. The report also proposed a procedure for establishing and securing land claims.[90] These recommendations were incorporated into the Aboriginal Land Rights (Northern Territory) Act of 1976. Although this was an important beginning, it was the work of the Ranger Enquiry which facilitated the grant of land rights in mining areas and responded directly to the aborigines' misgivings over uranium development. In their second report the Ranger commissioners reviewed the existing circumstances of the aboriginal people in the Alligator Rivers region and devoted considerable space to an assessment of the impact of mining on aboriginal society. They found that the "arrival of large numbers of white people in the region will potentially be very damaging to the welfare and interests of the aboriginal people".[91] Nevertheless, the Commissioners concluded that the Ranger project should be allowed to proceed "but only in the circumstances stipulated in this Report and subject to the recommendations we make in it".[92] As they affected the aboriginal population of the area, those stipulations included a scheme to improve the morale and welfare of the aboriginal people of the area, reduction in the area of the Ranger project site to further remove it from the vicinity of aboriginal sacred sites, employment and training of aboriginals in the area, improvements to the land rights legislation, and the restriction of mining in certain areas of aboriginal land.[93]

Aboriginal reaction to these findings was mixed. The Northern Lands Council thought the Enquiry had "taken very careful note of aboriginal concerns" and seemed to be willing to accept mining on this basis. In contrast, the Federal Council for the Advancement of Aborigines and Torres Strait Islanders observed that the report recognised that "there would be great destruction of aboriginal society in the Alligator Rivers region", and because of this seemed opposed to uranium development.[94] The L–NCP government accepted most of the Ranger Enquiry's recommendations with regard to the aboriginal population of the Alligator Rivers region.[95] As with the environmental lobby (the two were not always easily distinguished), this helped to mollify some of the objections to mining although it never fully satisfied the government's most trenchant critics.

Once the government's policy was announced, the effect of mining on the aboriginal people began to attract greater public attention. Interest centred on the consequences for aboriginal culture and the traditional association of the people with the region, but there was also public interest in negotiations regarding royalties and conditions of mining. These were to be conducted between the Northern Lands Council, on behalf of the aboriginal people, and the mining companies, and except in the case of the Ranger project were not to take place until the traditional owners of the land gave instructions to that effect. Negotiations have either been completed or are in progress with regard to four projects in the Northern Territory, Ranger,

Nabalek, Jabiluka and Koongara.[96] For some aboriginal people, however, they have proved to be a difficult undertaking. It is not so much that the mining companies have been unrealistic in the terms they have offered to secure the rights to proceed with mining. Naturally they have been determined to gain the most favourable terms possible. With professional assistance from lawyers and other outside advisers, some from overseas, the aboriginal interests have been expertly represented in the negotiations. But in some aboriginal communities it has proved to be very difficult to secure the necessary consensus on a negotiating position. Several newspapers have reported that from time to time disagreement amongst tribal interests and between different factions of the Northern Lands Council has interfered with the progress of negotiations.[97] While it is not clear that these differences of opinion have irrevocably jeopardised aboriginal interests, or that they should be regarded as unusual or excessive given the cross-cutting interests involved, they have been divisive within the aboriginal community. In this respect they provide further evidence of the capacity of the uranium issue to divide sections of the Australian community.

CONCLUSIONS

In recent Australian political history only Australia's participation in the Vietnam war and the dismissal of the Whitlam government have attracted as much controversy as uranium development. That this would be so was hardly perceived before the debate actually began, even by those who were later to take an active part in it. Australia had mined and exported uranium for nearly two decades; and, although not a consumer of nuclear energy, was an established supplier of nuclear material, a role which in the past had attracted little controversy. Moreover, nuclear issues in general had been the cause of few controversies in Australian domestic politics. But Australia's uranium debate came at a time when apprehensions over the civilian and military uses of nuclear energy were building in a crescendo of international opposition against further nuclear development. Although environmental hazards, the impact of mining on Australia's aborigines and the dangers of proliferation provided sufficient reason for opposition to uranium development in Australia, the debate took much of its inspiration from the world-wide opposition to nuclear power. The Ranger Enquiry was to serve as a focus for this debate, providing a forum for the presentation of arguments both for and against. Had the Enquiry not been appointed, uranium development would still have been an issue of intense controversy. The Enquiry was to legitimise the opposition to mining. Without this legitimacy it is arguable that the misgivings of the anti-mining lobby would have made less impact on the public and been of less interest to the government. In the event, both the public and the government became aware of the hazards associated with further uranium and nuclear development and both were required to respond to the implications.

In the past Australia had taken an active part in international discussions of the problems of nuclear proliferation, safeguards policy and the hazards of the nuclear fuel cycle because it had a modest uranium export industry and because successive governments have believed these to be matters of concern to all states in the international system. Following the discovery of considerable reserves of uranium and the decision to proceed with mining, the L–NCP government perceived a change in Australia's circumstances, one attributable to Australia's potential of becoming a major world producer of uranium. From this, a number of things follow. The government, along with other supporters of mining, believes that Australia has the opportunity to establish a new and profitable local industry which will eventually develop a reprocessing and enrichment capacity. Equally important, however, are the international implications. The government believes that Australian uranium exports will help stabilise the international market for nuclear fuel and this in turn will aid the cause of non-proliferation. Furthermore, substantial uranium exports will give Australia, for the first time, a direct significant interest in the international nuclear industry and entitle it to a more influential role in the management of the industry's affairs.

It would be unrealistic to suggest that these aspirations can be realised merely by Australia becoming a major uranium producer. Generally a matrix of factors make for influence in international relations and there is no particular reason why this should not be the case with regard to nuclear issues. Even so, being a substantial uranium producer will give Australia direct, bilateral contact, and perhaps influence with several consumer states and be to Australia's advantage in any international discussion of non-proliferation, safeguards policy and other related matters. At present, these prospects rest upon somewhat uncertain foundations. It will take several years before Australia's production of uranium reaches significant levels relative to other world producers. In the meantime,

Australia will be relying on its potential as a uranium producer to confer the influence which it courts. Potential can be a valuable asset in international politics, but it has an ephemeral quality. Clearly, Australia will not only have to produce large quantities of uranium, but be successful in marketing the commodity, if it is not to be an asset of declining utility. Mention has already been made of the constraints which Australia's own safeguards policy may impose in this regard. Allied to this problem is the fact that uranium is a reasonably abundant resource in the western world. As reserves are developed, competition for markets will become more intense. Moreover, markets can be expected to become more elusive if there is an appreciable decline in the demand for nuclear fuel as a result of continued domestic opposition to nuclear power generation in developed countries. Furthermore, when considering Australia's nuclear future, it must be remembered that the opposition Labour party has a uranium policy which if implemented would effectively ruin any prospects which Australia may have to become a major producer. In response, the L–NCP government is inclined to minimise the problems facing Australia's uranium export industry. It dismisses ALP policy as irresponsible and in all probability privately hopes that, should Labour win office at some future date, the pressures to continue exporting uranium will prove too great to resist. Being optimistic over the future of nuclear power, the government has encouraged mining companies to begin uranium production as soon as possible and occasionally gone to great lengths to assist them to do so. At the same time, the government sees Australia's economic and political stability as a definite asset in attracting uranium sales, one that gives an advantage over a potentially large producer such as South Africa. As evidence of the viability of an export industry it points to recent successes in securing uranium sales contracts in difficult market conditions. However encouraging these early results may be, Australia has yet to establish itself as a major uranium producer and yet to overcome the several challenges which may stand in the way of such prominence. Although much remains uncertain about Australia's future as a uranium exporter, it seems clear that one legacy of the government's decision to proceed with development is that Australia is becoming more closely integrated into the network of interdependent relationships between states which constitute the international nuclear regime. In the future Australia's uranium and to an extent its foreign policy options will be conditioned by this reality.

NOTES

1. For details of the first phase of Australian uranium development, see: R. K. Warner, "The Australian Uranium Industry", *Atomic Energy in Australia*, 19(2), (Apr. 1976) pp. 19–31; and William Wright, "Historical Background to Uranium Development in Australia", paper delivered to the Edlow International Inc. symposium in Washington, D.C., 5 Mar. 1981. For a review of the Australian government's present policy see James A. Brooks, "Australia: A Major Uranium Supplier: Government Policies and Attitudes to Development and Trade", paper delivered to the Edlow symposium.

2. As of 30 June 1980 Australia was estimated to possess 299 000 tonnes or about 21 per cent of the western world's 'reasonably assured reserves' of uranium recoverable at a cost of up to $US80/kgU. Australia is also thought to possess 'estimated additional reserves' of 208 000 tonnes, in the cost range of up to $US80/kgU and further smaller reserves in the $US80 – $US130/kgU range. See AAEC, 28th *Annual Report*, Parliamentary Paper 37/1981. For additional statistical information on uranium use see *Uranium, Resources, Production and Demand*, joint reports by OECD/ NEA and IAEA, Dec. 1975, 1977 and 1979.

3. For instance, see the studies on the influence of bureaucratic politics on the making of foreign policy, for example, Graham T. Allison, *Essence of Decision: Explaining the Cuban Missile Crisis* (Boston: Little, Brown & Company, 1971); Morton H. Halperin and Arnold Kanter (eds), *Readings in American Foreign Policy: A Bureaucratic Perspective* (Boston: Little, Brown, 1973).

4. For details of the ALP government's policy which, for the most part, had the support of the opposition, see "Statement of the Minister for Minerals and Energy, Mr Connor, Northern Territory Uranium Programme, 31 Oct. 1974", reprinted in *Australian Government Digest (AGD)*, vol. 2, no. 4, pp. 1225–8. For an analysis of the minerals and energy policy of the ALP government and its L–NCP successor, see Gary Smith, ch. 14 in Allan Patience and Brian Head (eds), *From Whitlam to Fraser: Reform and Reaction in Australian Politics* (Melbourne: Oxford University Press, 1979).

5. The National Country Party was formerly known as the Country Party of Australia. The present name has been used throughout this essay to avoid confusion.

6. Gary Smith, *op.cit.,* p. 249.

7. For developments in the formulation of ALP policy towards uranium development, see: *Sydney Morning Herald*, 5 Feb. 1975, 14 June, 18, 22 Nov. 1976; *Australian*, 13 June 1977; *Australian Financial Review*, 28 Nov. 1978; *Canberra Times*, 2, 7–9 July 1977; *Age*, 4 July 1977. Also see the ALP booklet published to present the arguments in the uranium debate, A. Manning (ed), *Uranium: A Fair Trial* (Canberra: ALP, 1977).

8. In an effort to de-fuse uranium mining as an issue in the trade union movement, the union's umbrella organisation, the Australian Council of Trade Unions (ACTU), adopted a policy of calling for a national referendum on the matter. The government found little merit in the idea

and refused to agree to it. See Judith Walker, "The Trade Unions and the Uranium Issue", *Current Affairs Bulletin*, July 1978, pp. 18–30; and R. M. Martin, "The ACTU Congress of 1977", *Journal of Industrial Relations*, Dec. 1977, pp. 424–34.

9. Thomas Smith, "Framing a Uranium Policy: Why the Controversy?" *Australian Quarterly*, vol. 51, no. 4, (Dec. 1979) pp. 32–50.

10. Ibid., p. 34.

11. The mining companies operated through a coordinating organisation, the Uranium Producers Forum. The most prominent scientists were Sir Ernest Titterton of the Australian National University and Sir Philip Baxter, a former head of the AAEC. Also prominent among the supporters of mining were the Premiers of Queensland, Mr John Bjelke Peterson, and Western Australia, Sir Charles Court, in whose states mining was to take place.

12. In the union movement the Australian Railways Union, the Electrical Trades Union and the Transport Workers Union, were among those most strongly opposed to uranium development. Environmental and Aboriginal groups included the Australian Conservation Foundation, Friends of the Earth, Movement Against Uranium Mining and the Federal Council for Advancement of Aborigines and Torres Strait Islanders. Scientists opposed to uranium included Sir McFarlane Burnett and Professor Charles Birch of Sydney University.

13. Reports of some of these activities are to be found in the following newspapers: strikes and stoppages, *Sydney Morning Herald*, 20, 21, 24, 26 May 1976, *Financial Review*, 6 July 1977; rallies and demonstrations, *Age*, 2 Apr., 4 Oct. 1980, *Sydney Morning Herald*, 4 Apr. 1975, *Australian*, 28 Aug., 23 Oct. 1977; symposiums, *Sydney Morning Herald*, 8 Sept. 1976; advertising campaigns, *Australian Financial Review*, 5 Apr. 1977; special publications, Manning, *op.cit.*, and E. W. Titterton, F. P. Robotham, *Uranium, Energy Source of the Future* (Melbourne: Thomas Nelson in association with the Australian Institute of International Affairs, 1979).

14. The situation became so tense at several rallies that the President of the ACTU, Mr Hawke, warned that there may be bloodshed in the streets if the government continued to refuse the union movement's demands for a national referendum. See *Sydney Morning Herald*, 8 Sept. 1977.

15. This was true of the arguments made at public rallies and in the literature of the debate. On the latter see: Manning, *op.cit.*, and Titterton and Robotham, *op.cit.*

16. Ibid.

17. Denis Stairs, "Publics and Policy Makers: The Domestic Environment of the Foreign Policy Community", *International Journal*, vol. XXVI, no. 1 (Winter 1970–1) pp. 235–48.

18. For ministerial announcements regarding the Enquiry, see: *Australian Government Weekly Digest (AGWD)*, vol. 1, no. 1, p. 5; *AGWD*, vol. 1, no. 16, p. 556.

19. During its three years in office the ALP government established numerous enquiries to examine different areas of policy. Unlike the Ranger Enquiry they were not generally established pursuant to specific legislation but rather by ministerial fiat. For a discussion of environmental impact legislation in Australia, see: J. Formby, "Environmental Policy Review

and Project Appraisal – The Australian Experience," in T. O'Riordan and D. D. Sewell (eds), *Environmental Policy Review and Project Appraisal* (London: John Wiley, 1980).

20. The new Prime Minister, Mr Fraser, pressed the Enquiry to produce its report by 30 Jan. 1976. Later, in June it was reported that the Enquiry was under strong pressure to finish its work. See *Sydney Morning Herald*, 4 Feb. and 16 June 1976.

21. *Ranger Uranium Environmental Enquiry: First Report* (Canberra: Australian Government Publishing Service [AGPS], 1976) p. 185.

22. Ibid., p. 5. See also Thomas Smith, *op.cit.*, p. 34.

23. *Ranger Enquiry, First Report*, p. 186.

24. *Sydney Morning Herald*, 30 Mar. 1976.

25. *Sydney Morning Herald*, 31 Mar. 1976.

26. As regards Australia's relations with Japan, see: *Sydney Morning Herald*, 3 Feb., 16, 18, June 1976. For reports of Australia's response to the Carter proposals, see *Sydney Morning Herald*, 9, 19, 23, Apr. 1977.

27. As early as February 1976 the president of the Australian Conservation Foundation, Dr Mosely, accused the government of breaking a 1975 election promise not to decide uranium policy until after the Ranger reports had been received. See *Sydney Morning Herald*, 3 Feb., 31 Mar. and 25 May 1976.

28. On the role of the AAEC, see *Sydney Morning Herald*, 2 Feb. 1976. As to foreign investment see statement of the Treasurer, 1 Apr. 1976, *Australian Parliamentary Debates* (APD), *Weekly Hansard* (House of Representatives), no. 6, (1976) pp. 1288–92. As regards uranium development in general, see Media Release, 1 Feb. 1976, *Department of Overseas Trade and National Resources*, Canberra.

29. "Government Policy on Nuclear Safeguards", Ministerial Statement by Mr Fraser, 24 May 1977, *APD*, Weekly Hansard (House of Representatives), no. 10 (1977) 1701. The statement is reprinted in *Uranium: Australia's Decision* (Canberra: AGPS, 1977).

30. *APD*, *Weekly Hansard* (House of Representatives), no. 10 (1977) p. 1706.

31. *Sydney Morning Herald*, 25 May 1977.

32. "Ranger Uranium Environmental Enquiry", Ministerial Statement by Mr Newman, 11 Nov. 1976, *APD*, *Weekly Hansard* (House of Representatives), no. 22, (1976) p. 2635.

33. *Sydney Morning Herald*, 9 Nov. 1976, 23 Mar. 1977; *Australian Financial Review*, 30 Nov. 1976.

34. *APD*, *Weekly Hansard* (House of Representatives), no. 24 (1976) p. 2979.

35. *Sydney Morning Herald*, 28 May 1977. Mr Anthony's reaction was less restrained. He told parliament that Australia could be in a questionable position if it refused to export to countries in desperate need of energy. Amongst other reactions the spokesman for the uranium moratorium committee said the second report was another set-back for business; the Friends of the Earth spokesman suggested that miners would not be happy with the report and noted that the report showed that mining would greatly affect the environment; the Australian Uranium Producers Forum said that the mining companies would not find it difficult to meet the very strict

environmental standards recommended.
36. Interview, officials of the Australian Public Service, June 1981. Also see *Canberra Times*, 14 July 1977.
37. "Australian Uranium Policy", Ministerial Statement by Mr Fraser, 25 Aug. 1977, *APD*, *Weekly Hansard* (House of Representatives), no. 13 (1977) pp. 645–51. The Prime Minister's statement was followed by statements by the Ministers for Overseas Trade and National Resources, Foreign Affairs, Aboriginal Affairs, Environment, Housing and Community Development and Health, ibid, pp. 651–76. All are reprinted in *Uranium: Australia's Decision*, op.cit.
38. *Australian,* 26 Aug. 1977; *Age*, 26 Aug. 1977. Most of Australia's other major daily newspapers approved of the decision.
39. See Thomas Smith, op.cit., p. 40.
40. The speeches of Mr Whitlam and Mr Uren are reported in *APD*, *Weekly Hansard* (House of Representatives), no. 13 (1977) pp. 688–93 and pp. 694–6, respectively. For reports of other responses to the decision see *Canberra Times*, 26 Aug. 1977, and *Australian Financial Review*, 30 Aug. 1977.
41. This and the other quotations in the paragraph are from the Prime Minister's statement, "Australian Uranium Policy", 25 Aug. 1977, op.cit.
42. *Ranger Uranium Environmental Enquiry, Second Report* (Canberra: AGPS, 1977), ch. 8 and appendices V and VI. Also see Stuart Harris, "Economics of Uranium Mining in Australia", *Current Affairs Bulletin*, Apr. 1978, pp. 18–30.
43. The L–NCP government was not alone in seeing the possession of extensive uranium resources as both a benefit and a burden. In 1974, the ALP Minister for Minerals and Energy, Mr Connor, explained the burden in terms of "an obligation to those members of the world community with limited access to energy resources". See statement on N. T. Uranium programme, Oct. 1974, op.cit., p. 1228.
44. *Ranger Enquiry, First Report*, ch. 8, esp. p. 68.
45. The ALP government also believed that the world-wide demand for Australian minerals would confer bargaining power on Australia. See Gary Smith, op.cit., p. 236.
46. The first contracts for the sale of Australian uranium since 1972 were signed with the Republic of Korea in November 1979. Since then, contracts have been signed with Japan, Finland, West Germany and the United States. In 1980 approvals for the supply of U_3O_8 to these countries amounted to 37 000 short tons and in the same year 1200 short tons was actually exported. See Media Releases, 9 Nov. 1979, 13, 18, Aug. 1980 and 8 Jan. 1981, *Department of Trade and Resources*, Canberra.
47. The Ranger Enquiry referred to defects in the existing safeguards regime "such as may provide only an illusion of protection". *Ranger Enquiry, First Report*, ch. 13, p. 147. For a discussion of the application of IAEA safeguards to Australian uranium and of Australia's non-proliferation policy in general see Martin Indyk, "Australian Uranium and the Non-Proliferation Regime", *Australian Quarterly*, vol. 49, no. 4 (Dec. 1977) pp. 4–35.
48. *Ranger Enquiry, First Report*, p. 185.

49. "Ranger Uranium Environmental Enquiry", Ministerial Statement by Mr Newman, 11 Nov. 1976, op.cit., p. 2635.
50. "Government Policy on Nuclear Safeguards", Ministerial Statement by Mr Fraser, 24 May 1977, op.cit., p. 1701. Also see the Background paper on Nuclear Safeguards in Uranium; Australia's Decision, *op.cit.*
51. The ALP's spokesman on minerals and energy, Mr Keating, described the policy as exhibiting "some good intentions" but absolutely naive of international realities. See *APD Weekly Hansard* (House of Representatives), no. 10 (1977) p. 1207. For a more considered evaluation see Martin Indyk, op.cit.
52. Press Release, "Conditions for Australian Consent to Reprocessing", 27 Nov. 1980, *Department of Foreign Affairs*, Canberra.
53. As examples, consider the implications in the event that Australia denies consent for what are perceived to be inadequate reasons or alternatively grants consent which attracts domestic opposition, perhaps because the state concerned has a poor record on non-proliferation.
54. The change in policy took place quite quickly. The Minister of Trade and Resources announced the possibility of a change in January 1979 and advised that there had in fact been a change in February 1979. See Media Releases, "Uranium Sales Contracts", 15 Jan. 1979 and 1 Feb. 1979, *Department of Trade and Resources*, Canberra. Another noteworthy change in policy was the removal of the requirement that Australian uranium remain under Australian ownership until converted for use. See News Release, "Nuclear Safeguards Policy, Control Arrangements", 18 July 1979, *Department of Foreign Affairs*, Canberra.
55. The agreement with France was announced on January 7, 1981. See *Commonwealth Record (CR)*, vol. 6, no. 1, p. 11.
56. See Martin Indyk, op.cit., p. 19. France is a party to the EURATOM agreement with the IAEA for the application of safeguards to European Community nuclear facilities. The agreement, however, has yet to be implemented. For an exchange of opinion between Australian political leaders on the implications of this agreement see speech of the Leader of the Opposition, Mr Whitlam, to the National Press Club, 20 July 1977, *CR*, vol. 2, no. 29, and the reply of the Prime Minister, Mr Fraser, 21 July 1977, *CR*, vol. 2, no. 30.
57. Up until the end of May 1981 agreements had been concluded with: Finland (July 1978), Philippines (August 1978), Republic of Korea (May 1979), United Kingdom (July 1979), United States (July 1979), France (January 1981), Sweden (March 1981), Canada (March 1981), EURATOM (May 1981).
58. Negotiations with France were delayed because of the reprocessing issue. See *Australian Financial Review*, 12 Sept. 1980. On the negotiations with the United Kingdom see *Sydney Morning Herald*, 3 July 1978.
59. Cited in Martin Indyk, op.cit., p. 23.
60. Reports of His Honour's activities suggest that he may well have contributed to the resolution of several difficult issues regarding matters of non-proliferation, for example the impasse over the acceptability of the international control of plutonium. His Honour's activities were not without controversy; he was largely opposed to the Carter proposals,

reluctant for Australia to move into uranium enrichment and was criticised by the Minister for Foreign Affairs for releasing the details of a confidential report to the government on the subject of safeguards. See *Sydney Morning Herald*, 2 May 1977, *Age*, 11 Nov. 1979, and *Bulletin*, 16 Jan. 1979.

61. Prior to the announcement of Australian safeguards policy there was an exchange of correspondence on the subject between the Prime Minister and the President. See *CPD*, *Weekly Hansard* (House of Representatives), no. 10, 1977. Shortly after President Carter's policy announcement a high-level Australian delegation visited Washington to discuss safeguards policy. US officials were reported as having made it clear that exports of Australian uranium were a key element in US policy. Later, after a visit in May, Mr Anthony said Australian exports were indispensible; however, US officials were more restrained. See *Sydney Morning Herald*, 19, 23, 26 Apr., 11 May 1977; *Australian Financial Review*, 4 May 1977. For further discussion of the point see Martin Indyk, op.cit.

62. Statement on INFCE by the Minister for Foreign Affairs reprinted in *Australian Foreign Affairs Record (AFAR)*, Mar. 1980, pp. 52–8.

63. Ibid., pp. 52–8.

64. In addition to INFCE, between 1976 and 1979 Australia participated in the work of the Nuclear Energy Agency of OECD, the Nuclear Suppliers Group and the IAEA, while representatives of the AAEC attended numerous symposia and conferences and arranged international exchanges of scientific personnel. For details see the *AAEC Annual Reports* for 1976–7, 1977–8 and 1978–9 (AGPS, Canberra).

65. See *Sydney Morning Herald*, 8, 31 Oct., 8 Nov 1973, 14 May 1974, 10 June 1975.

66. *Sydney Morning Herald*, 31 Oct. 1973.

67. *AAEC Annual Report, 1976–77*, Parliamentary Paper 58/1978.

68. AFAR, op.cit.

69. Media Release, "Uranium Enrichment", 23 Jan. 1979, *Department of Trade and Resources*, Canberra. At the end of 1978 it was reported that a Japanese study had recommended the establishment of a uranium enrichment facility in Northern Australia. See *CR*, vol. 4, no. 1, p. 25.

70. *Uranium Advisory Council, Second Annual Report* (AGPS, Canberra, 1980).

71. *Australian*, 22 Apr. 1981.

72. South Australia has been considering the possibility of an enrichment/ reprocessing facility for some time and the subject has been a source of considerable controversy. See *Advertiser*, 2 Aug. 1980; *Canberra Times*, 10 Aug. 1978, 1 Jan. 1979; *Sydney Morning Herald*, 3 July 1976. More recently Queensland has shown an active interest in establishing an enrichment facility. See *Australian*, 12 Dec. 1979.

73. This was one part of a comprehensive minerals policy which Labour brought to office. See Gary Smith, op.cit., p. 236. Also see the speech of the Prime Minister to the Australian Mining Industry Council reprinted in *AGD*, vol. 1, no. 1.

74. "N. T. Uranium Programme", Statement by the Minister for Minerals and Energy, 31 Oct. 1974, op.cit. Also see a statement of 6 Mar. 1975, *AGD*,

vol. 3, no. 1, pp. 138–9.

75. Media Release, 1 Feb. 1976, *Department of Trade and Resources*, Canberra.

76. After relaxing foreign equity guidelines early in 1976, the L–NCP government announced a further liberalisation in 1979. See *Age*, 19 Apr., 11 June 1979. More controversial was the government's decision to dispose of its share in the Ranger development. See Media Releases, 6, 14 Aug., 3, 26 Oct. 1979, 23 Jan., 10 Aug. 1980, *Department of Trade and Resources*, Canberra.

77. Uranium mining may not begin until foreign equity requirements, state and federal environmental procedures and developmental regulations have been satisfied. Mining and processing operations are controlled by state and federal mining and milling codes relating to health and environmental matters. Sales and exports are regulated as to purchasers, price, duration of contracts, use of ore, safeguards and all require export permits. The implementation of such a comprehensive code of regulations involved the federal government in some delicate negotiations with the states. See *Australian*, 19 Sept. 1977, *Advertiser*, 19 April 1978, *Sydney Morning Herald*, 4, 29 May 1978.

78. *Australian Financial Review*, 16 Feb. 1981.

79. Interview, officials of the Australian Public Service, June 1981.

80. These reports are reprinted in the Uranium Advisory Council, Second Annual Report, op.cit.

81. "Uranium Export Policy", Ministerial Statement by Mr Anthony, 1 June 1978, *CPD, Weekly Hansard* (House of Representatives), no. 10 (1978). Also see Media Release, "Australian Uranium Export Office", 12 Oct. 1978, *Department of Trade and Resources*, Canberra; *Sydney Morning Herald*, 2 June 1978.

82. The absence of environmental protection measures during the development of the Rum Jungle uranium deposits was commented upon by the Ranger Enquiry. See *Ranger Enquiry, Second Report*, ch. 6, p. 109.

83. *Ranger Enquiry, Second Report*, chs 9 and 11.

84. Ibid., p. 335.

85. *Sydney Morning Herald*, 26 May 1977.

86. For an outline of the government's policy see "Uranium: Environmental Protection", Ministerial Statement, Mr Newman, 25 Aug. 1977, op.cit., pp. 669–74. Also see the *Canberra Times*, 25 Jan. 1978. The enabling legislation was introduced into parliament in Apr. 1978.

87. *Ranger Enquiry, Second Report*, p. 328. The sequential development of uranium mines was also considered by the Uranium Advisory Council which advised a continuation of the present policy which it described as sequential. See Report on sequential development in uranium mining, November 1977, reprinted as *Appendix D*, Uranium Advisory Council, *Second Annual Report*, op.cit.

88. In November 1973, for example, the government split over a decision to renew exploration licences of three companies. Several ministers argued that the decision should be delayed until the report of the Woodward Commission was available. See *Sydney Morning Herald*, 30 Nov. 1973. For details of the ALP government's policy towards aborigines see

Statement of the Minister for Aboriginal Affairs, 24 Apr. 1974, *AGD*, vol. 2, no. 2, pp. 309–16.
89. For announcements relating to the Land Rights Enquiry see Press Statement, 14 Feb. 1973, *AGD*, vol. 1, no. 1, p. 70; and 3 May 1973, *AGD*, vol. 1, no. 2, p. 507.
90. *Aboriginal Land Rights Commission, Second Report* (Canberra: AGPS, 1974). The implications of the Commission's findings and of the Land Rights legislation were discussed by the Ranger Enquiry. See *Ranger Enquiry, Second Report*, ch. 14.
91. *Ranger Enquiry, Second Report*, p. 232.
92. Ibid., p. 335.
93. Ibid., pp. 329–30.
94. *Sydney Morning Herald*, 26 May 1977.
95. For an outline of the government's policy see "Australian Uranium Development: Impacts on Aboriginal Society", Ministerial Statement, 25 Aug. 1977, op.cit. The government's relations with the aboriginal community have not been particularly harmonious since the announcement of its mining policy. While a number of specific matters acted as irritants, much of the problem seems to be related to the fact that the government was anxious to move quickly to begin mining operations. See *Canberra Times*, 5, 7, 8 May, 17 Oct. 1978.
96. For details see Media Releases, 9 Jan. 1979, 24 Jan. 1981, *Department of Trade and Resources*, Canberra. Also see *Canberra Times*, 4 Nov. 1978, 10 Jan. 1979, *Northern Territory News*, 23 Jan. 1978.
97. *Bulletin*, 10 Oct. 1978, *Australian Financial Review*, 1 Aug. 1978.

Part III   The Nuclear Non-proliferation Regime: Challenges and Problems

8 Nuclear Energy, Nuclear Proliferation and National Security: Views from the South

Ashok Kapur

A study of nuclear energy and nuclear proliferation in the 1980s requires an assessment of efforts in the post-1945 world to develop international regimes to control proliferation and the nuclear trade.[1] So far efforts at regime-making have been based essentially on northern initiatives and northern interests. The approaches adopted – through the mechanisms of the NPT and IAEA safeguards – have contributed to the southern view that the United States and its northern partners (including the USSR) were, and remain, unwilling to permit change in global power relations. In that sense the issues of nuclear trade and nuclear proliferation go beyond the safe management of fissile materials. Since the mid-1940s international nuclear negotiations and the process of gradual nuclearisation of the southern international environment reveal a linkage between nuclear power development, nuclear trade and power politics.

The term "south" has been defined in a number of ways. It refers here primarily to states which are usually described as "near nuclears". The long list of these includes Spain, South Korea and Taiwan; the short list stresses imminent proliferation cases such as India, Pakistan, Israel, South Africa, and possibly Iraq, Argentina and Brazil in the 1980s. While our focus is on the short list it should be emphasised that there is no certainty that all, or any, of these countries will develop nuclear arms forces. The short list, then, deals with countries which are located south of North America, Europe, the USSR and China. Apart from this geographical aspect, the southern nuclear states are outside the normal sphere of NATO and Warsaw Pact influence; indeed

163

politically, military and culturally they are outside the mainstream of northern international relations or East–West relations. Alienated from the north, they see themselves forced to achieve temporary and tacit alliance relations with northern partners. These partners are not, however, reliable, and consequently the southern states seek self-reliance and a capacity to manipulate the northern states for their own advantage. As secondary powers with proud cultural and political heritages, the southern nuclear states sense that strategic conflict is also cultural conflict. Thus the economic status of these states is not the crucial determinant of the definition of the south. Most have viable economies, though economically and politically they are unevenly developed. Their strategic and political behaviour flows less from their economic situations, and more from their cultural and strategic perceptions. In this context, "power politics" is a useful term to describe both an attitude and the policy of engaging regional neighbours and the superpowers by all available means, including threat and violence. The intent is to develop some sort of constant relationship which satisfies southern interests. The long-term aim is to establish a relationship of exchange, then, even though the method at present may be that of confrontation politics and intervention or counter-intervention.

In the coming decade proliferation is likely to be a southern phenomenon. The relationship between nuclear trade and power politics should therefore be examined in order to explain the underlying factors behind proliferation. This paper is a preliminary attempt in that direction.

ATOMIC ENERGY AND NUCLEAR PROLIFERATION: FIVE PHASES

Since the mid-1940s the world community has been subjected to a number of attempts by the United States to set up a regime to control atomic energy. American international policies about the atom may be divided into five periods.

(i) 1946–53

The first entailed technology denials to Canada, Britain and France, the allies who had contributed to the Manhattan project. The US Atomic Energy Act (1946) cut off even the flow of information on civil nuclear power development which had been anticipated under wartime agreements. At that time only the United States had knowledge of how to make a nuclear weapon. The denials were accompanied by a proposal, the Baruch Plan of 1946, to internationalise the ownership of "dangerous" atomic activities and materials. It was based on the Acheson–Lilienthal report's conclusion that international inspection was insufficient to control peaceful atomic activities and that international ownership and management was required. The policy of denials to wartime collaborators led to their developing "go it alone" policies: Britain entered the nuclear club in 1952 and France in 1960. The Soviet Union, for its part, rejected the Baruch Plan, seeing it as a trap whereby the US could retain its monopoly and retard the nuclear development of others. Overall, American denial policy created mistrust among allies and enemies alike, and led to the first wave of horizontal nuclear proliferation in the world.

(ii) 1954–64

A period of consensus-building followed. Its hallmarks were the Eisenhower "atoms for peace" plan (1953) and the establishment of the IAEA (1957). Strictly speaking, the first was not a non-proliferation enterprise. It stemmed from the notion that nuclear weapons proliferation resulted from national political and security decisions; if a country was determined to proliferate it would do so, and efforts to deny nuclear power would stimulate "go it alone" efforts. The atoms for peace approach thus represented a bargain between nuclear suppliers and recipients. Assistance in the peaceful uses of nuclear materials and equipment was given in *exchange* for acceptance of safeguards against diversion to military use. The IAEA was given a dual mandate: to promote peaceful uses of nuclear energy, and to promote safeguards. It was intended to follow a policy of anti-diversion with regards to safeguarded supplies; it was not intended to inhibit the military nuclear programmes of its members. Thus IAEA members with military nuclear programmes were still eligible to receive peaceful uses assistance. Two major international conferences on the peaceful uses of nuclear energy took place during this period, in 1955 and 1958; and a good deal of US technical information was declassified. The first power and research reactor sales occurred, with the initial orders being taken by Canada, Britain and France. A noteworthy feature of this period was that the USSR, in 1963, dropped its opposition to international safeguards and joined Washington in advocating the IAEA safeguards regime – a major departure from its original opposition to international controls over atomic energy. This was a basis for the quest for non-proliferation by the superpowers in the mid-1960s.

(iii) 1965–74

The third period is one of active anti-proliferation advocacy and regime-formation. However, no neat periodisation is possible because developments in the second period paved the way for the third. Thus the Soviet policy change in 1963 paved the way for the subsequent concert of the superpowers with regard to Article III of the NPT. Secondly, the NPT deliberations were a consequence of the Irish initiative in the early 1960s to prevent dissemination – the aim of Article 1 of the NPT.[2] Thirdly, by the mid-1960s the IAEA had assumed the task of safeguards from bilateral safeguards agreements. The transfer was limited to the terms and conditions originally negotiated in bilateral nuclear supply agreements; but despite this role, the IAEA in the mid-1960s was clearly an Agency in search of a mission, and the NPT was instrumental in saving it from a retarded and marginal existence. Fourthly, non-proliferation advocacy by the superpowers was not simply a world order and arms control concern. It was a method of bilateral détente-building. The superpowers had started to make eyes at each other in the second half of the 1950s, and the NPT was one product of a process begun then.

Finally, non-proliferation advocacy occurred at a time when the world was on a low proliferation curve. The Soviet allies (except China) had renounced nuclear arms, and Soviet nuclear supplies to bloc members entailed return of spent fuels to the USSR. In the spirit of socialist division of labour, the East Europeans provided the uranium, and the USSR provided the reactors and the fuel. So at the time the NPT was negotiated the USSR had no fear of proliferation within the East European bloc. Article 1 (non-dissemination by existing nuclear weapon states) was not relevant to Sino-Soviet nuclear cooperation because (a) by the mid-1960s nuclear technology, equipment and materials had been transferred to China, except for the sample of the bomb; and (b) the NPT excluded China from inspection and control because it was already a nuclear weapon state by treaty definition. For the rest of the world also the picture was one of non-proliferation. Germany and Japan had both renounced nuclear arms:

the FRG as a condition for NATO entry and access to conventional armaments; and Japan by virtue of its national law prohibiting their acquisition. Much of the third world was on a low, if not a non-existent, proliferation curve – that is, if proliferation is defined in terms of the quest for nuclear arms and not of access to nuclear science or nuclear equipment and materials. In the third period it is noteworthy that anti-proliferation advocacy came from powers who were themselves the prime global proliferators, in terms of acquisition of nuclear arms, nuclear testing and an unending arms race.

The first period was based on denials and failed to establish an anti-proliferation regime; the second established international confidence in a peaceful nuclear supply safeguards regime, but in another sense it created mistrust in the thinking of states outside the European–North American–Japanese network of nuclear supply relations. Confidence now rested on the fact that the NPT regime confirmed the "atoms for peace" approach: societies were free to adopt the sensitive aspects of the full nuclear fuel cycle – including plutonium reprocessing, uranium enrichment and the fast breeder reactor cycle – provided the nuclear supplies were safeguarded. Articles III(3) and IV of the NPT accepted the concept of safeguarded supply of sensitive nuclear equipment, materials and technical information. There was no question in the NPT of denying the supply of such items. It definitely accepted the role of the plutonium economy and the enriched uranium economy. Safeguards were seen as part of a bargain – in return for assured supplies. Indeed Articles III(3) and IV called for the fullest possible peaceful nuclear trade. A balance was seen to exist between Article III and Article IV. Even peaceful nuclear explosions under an international regime were permitted (Article V). Furthermore, the nuclear weapon states, particularly the superpowers, assumed an international obligation to take steps towards nuclear disarmament.

For those states able to publicly adhere to the NPT, that is, to assume an obligation not to make nuclear weapons for the duration of the NPT (25 years), the bargain seemed to be a good one. But several states were unable to accept the treaty for domestic, regional and international reasons which impinged on political, diplomatic, security, legal and economic considerations. To them, whether as treaty law or international norm, the treaty was a cultural, mischievous, unrealistic and insincere document. Their reasoning was somewhat as follows.

First, the NPT was a cultural document because it defined a NWS as one which had exploded a nuclear device by January 1, 1967. This meant the global nuclear (and power) status quo was to be frozen permanently at five – the permanent members of the UN Security Council. Proud and potentially powerful societies like Argentina, Brazil, and India could not accept the implication of a concert of great powers directed against secondary powers which were upwardly mobile in the international system.

Secondly, the NPT was mischievous because it insinuated that states not adhering to it were likely to seek nuclear weapons. It shifted the burden of proof of nuclear intentions on to the NNWS, whereas it is an elementary rule of law and evidence that the onus is on the prosecutor to prove the other side's bad faith and guilt. The NPT parties, particularly the superpowers, tried to foster public hysteria by creating a clear public identification with this insinuation; and were able to succeed to the extent that public psychology feeds on anticipated bad news, and arm chair advocates of worst contingency scenarios are not usually punished for issuing false alarms.

Thirdly, the treaty was realistic in the sense that it recognised that countries faced with danger to national survival would likely withdraw from it. The premise was sound: legal and technical barriers could not prevent proliferation if the national political factor[3] so required. To cope with this contingency the treaty framers conceived the possibility of withdrawal with three months notice in case supreme national interests were jeopardised. In the real world, however, the withdrawal clause is an absurdity. When the norm is universally that of government secrecy in questions of national security it is hard to believe that any government would want to alert its enemies by giving three months notice. It is more likely that a government would renounce its NPT obligations quickly in a condition of war or crisis. (In November 1980 Iraq refused to allow IAEA inspection for a few months on the ground that it was in a war situation with Iran.) Furthermore, it is unrealistic to expect a country facing a crisis to abide by safeguards and the NPT. There is strength in the view that the NPT is a good treaty for good times but it could be a bad treaty in bad times.

Finally, the treaty has come to be widely regarded as insincere, because of the record of non-implementation of Articles IV and VI. Many non-adherents of the treaty felt from the outset that these articles were inserted only to induce countries to sign the treaty; that the heart of the treaty, in superpower thinking, consisted of Articles II and III; and that the superpowers were interested in disarmament talk and disarmament meetings but not in real disarmament, that is, that superpower agencies of arms control and disarmament were actually agencies for disarmament-control and stable arms racing. And it was naive to expect them to reduce their military capacities when they saw themselves as international powers because of their great military strength.

Although the NPT has not to date been officially repudiated, the third phase – the NPT phase – became problematic in the mid-1970s. Several developments undermined the NPT regime. Consider the following:

(1) The NPT rested on the premise that no state would dare challenge the nuclear prescription against horizontal proliferation laid down by the superpowers. If it did, it would face international sanctions and the prospect of pariah status. India's 1974 test, officially a peaceful one but technologically no different from a military test, called the superpowers' bluff, without visible punishment. This was the most dramatic development in the 1970s which hurt the NPT regime.

(2) President Nixon offered nuclear reactors to Egypt and Israel under safeguards although both states were located in a region of high tension and neither was a party to the NPT. The offer seemed to reveal a weakened commitment to non-proliferation, and, in the context of the US debate about proliferation in the mid-1970s was widely criticised as a step which could lead to proliferation in the Middle East.

(3) The NPT was negotiated on the premise that proliferation could be stopped if states assumed international obligations renouncing nuclear arms. According to this premise the national political factor, which might lead to a nuclear weapons decision, had to be curbed; and it could be if a state accepted the NPT regime. But after the NPT regime came into being a new fear emerged, namely, the prospect of terrorists acquiring plutonium. Consequently the basis of the NPT regime was altered when possible illegal sub-national activity became a focal point in the definition of the proliferation problem.

(4) Whereas the NPT's focus was against nuclear weapons proliferation, the early 1970s saw the growth of environmental lobby groups. These argued against the bad environmental impact of nuclear energy *per se* and drew international attention to the safety aspect of civilian nuclear power. Such groups, which functioned effectively and visibly in North America, Europe and Japan, saw the nuclear industry as a social and military danger despite the existence of an international safeguards regime. In some instances links were made between a recipient's human rights record, the danger of a regional nuclear race

and nuclear supply relations. Nuclear trade itself was viewed as either a deliberate or an unintended method of external and internal aggression by a recipient state despite its acceptance of a safeguards regime.

(5) Among safeguards experts a belief arose during the 1970s that safeguards could at best detect diversion of sensitive nuclear materials from peaceful to military use; safeguards could not prevent such diversions. One concern was that the IAEA's capability to safeguard was not fool-proof: that the figure of 1 per cent of material unaccounted for (MUF) taken as an acceptable limit in verifying safeguards was enough to make a few bombs, or that a need existed to shorten detection time. It was thought necessary to improve the national political factor to ensure full cooperation by the safeguarded state and a continued disincentive against withdrawal from the NPT and the safeguards regime. Above all, it was argued, something had to be done to prevent proliferation by controlling nuclear trade of sensitive equipment, materials and technology. This line of thinking became the basis of the London Nuclear Suppliers Group.

(6) Also during the 1970s the Soviet Union and Europe (URENCO and EURODIF) emerged as enriched uranium suppliers on a large scale. Consequently the US monopoly of enriched uranium was broken, and its capacity to enforce anti-proliferation policy through supply restraints was diminished.

(7) Finally, European industry emerged as a strong competitor of the United States for LWR sales. The FRG–Brazil full fuel cycle sale (including enrichment and reprocessing) was a major signal of the German nuclear industry's attack on American dominance of the export market.

(iv) 1974–8

By the mid-1970s these developments had cast doubts on the effectiveness of the NPT regime. Nuclear power, including reprocessing and uranium enrichment capacities, had spread world wide; and the adequacy of IAEA/NPT safeguards was being questioned because of the proliferation of sensitive nuclear equipment, materials and technology, and because North American suppliers could no longer exercise monopolistic control over this trade. The Indian test of 1974 dramatised the concerns, particularly since it did not violate any international obligations of the recipient. But even before this, the tendency in supplier thinking was to see proliferation in terms of the export and/or acquisition of sensitive nuclear equipment, materials and supplies. The result was that Canada announced a new policy in December 1974 which unilaterally required re-negotiation of old contracts. For the first time in post-war nuclear history a unilateral suspension of contractual obligations became a bargaining tool in inter-state behaviour.

These events are important for the present study in a major way. The NPT regime had been meant for two diverse groups of states, but in the circumstances of the mid-1960s the diverse needs were not apparent. For the superpowers' allies who were protected by military alliance, the NPT was a bargain between assured supply and safeguards. For the Europeans and the Japanese Article VI was a cosmetic gesture, in the short term, because their national security was protected by alliance membership. But for the second group of nations – those outside the major global alliance systems – the NPT had to satisfy two balances: one between assured supply and safeguards, and the other between renounced nuclear weapons options and general nuclear disarmament, including regional disarmament measures such as nuclear weapon-free zones. The first was meant to satisfy the long-term requirements for nuclear energy of those countries which felt entitled to its benefits – given the shortage of fossil fuels. The second was meant to satisfy national security planners who felt obliged to keep their nuclear option open (i.e., not to decide to make nuclear weapons) provided there was a likelihood of a toned down process of international and regional militarisation and nuclearisation. The NPT, however, did not address the peculiar problems involved in the security planning of states outside the major alliance systems. Indeed the security assurances offered by the superpowers through the Security Council were worse than what the UN Charter offered: whereas the Charter offered Security Council support against aggression irrespective of adherence to the NPT, the assurances offered by the superpowers to states not members of alliance systems made Security Council support conditional on adherence to the NPT.

For the northern industrial nations, then, the NPT regime was viable as long as it left intact the balance between assured supply and safeguards. It was a basis for nuclear energy security because alliance relations provided national security. The argument, for example for the FRG and Japan, was not about national sovereignty and the right to make nuclear weapons; rather it concerned national sovereignty expressed in terms of the right to enjoy the full benefits of the full fuel cycle without external dictation, provided the activities were safeguarded. The erosion of confidence in northern thinking occurred when even safeguarded activities were constrained with threats of external vetoes. For the southern states the tensions between these two balances in the NPT system came to a head in the mid-1970s. The inadequacy of the NPT system was revealed in regional security crises. Israel in 1973 is alleged to have made several bombs because it saw itself losing the war with the Arabs; and India's 1974 test was a political demonstration to friends and enemies alike that nuclearisation of the regional environment would occur if external powers did not exercise restraint in their strategic behaviour. The national security argument became important in the perception of regional powers in South Asia and the Middle East precisely because these states were outside major alliance systems. But the argument cut two ways. On the one hand, a nuclear arsenal was not necessary: national security could not be served in mid-1970s strategic scenarios in South Asia and the Middle East (and Southern Africa) with acquisition of nuclear arms. Yet on the other hand, a refusal to sign the NPT meant a decision to keep the nuclear option open, if necessary, in the future. Thus the political demonstration of nuclear weapons potential was seen as adequate for the strategic circumstances of the time.

In other words, just when tension between supplier and recipient perspectives was taking root in northern international relations in the mid-1970s, at the same time in southern international relations – particularly in regions of tension – the national sovereignty/national security argument was gaining ground. The tension between northern and southern perspectives could not be resolved because the assumptions about the strategic context varied. The northern premise was that of military security; the southern premise was that of military insecurity. The northern perspective saw nuclear energy security in the context of secure military relations, whereas the southern perspective sought both energy and military security via the bargaining tool of the nuclear option. For the northern states the concern was to restore confidence by restoring the balance between assured supply and safeguards. This balance had a limited meaning as far as southern states were concerned: it meant acceptance of partial safeguards in return for materials supplied and not full scope safeguards. Furthermore, it had to be accompanied by another balance: one permitting the use of nuclear power as an instrument of regional deterrence; recognising the utility of calculated ambiguity to achieve deterrence; and drawing a fine line between threatening to convert the nuclear option into a weapons programme and not doing so. Because northern states operated from the context of alliance security, they seemed, however, unable to appreciate the difficulty which southern states faced in coping with a nuclear strategy which partly supported the NPT regime (by not overtly crossing the threshold of nuclear arms) but which at the same time was outside it.

The NPT regime was conceived in the mid-1960s. In the strategic context of the time the treaty made sense. The network of nuclear supply and alliance relations between the United States, Europe and Japan satisfied and accommodated security and energy requirements. Tension between nuclear supply and non-proliferation concerns could be handled within the alliance framework. But in the strategic context of the mid-1970s the NPT regime appeared fragile. The focus of international tension shifted to regional politics – in South Asia, the Middle East and Southern Africa. The changed strategic context pointed to the legitimate advocacy of self-help by regional powers. Israel, India, South Africa, Brazil and Argentina emerged as prime practitioners of self-help, even though their strategic circumstances varied, as did their behaviour and rhetoric. Israel threatened the use of nuclear bombs when it saw itself threatened during the 1973 crisis. India chose in 1974 to give a political demonstration after it perceived the danger of forcible intervention and diplomatic isolation in the 1971 crisis. Thus the theoretical objections to the NPT voiced in the mid-1960s by states who chose to remain outside the constraints of alliance politics became policy relevant a decade later when these same powers found themselves executing regional crisis management policies.

The fourth period, then, was one of crisis. The crisis came about because of a tendency on the part of Canada and the United States to view proliferation in religious terms. After the Indian test of 1974 Canada became a self-appointed guardian of world nuclear order. It seemed that the less the power, the less the responsibility, the greater was the noise level of Canadian non-proliferation advocacy. This concern seemed ironic because, before 1974, Canada had done everything possible to sell its reactors to areas of regional tension – India and Pakistan, South Korea, and Argentina. Particularly during the 1950s Canadian reactor salesmen had over-stated the economic benefits of nuclear power and of the CANDU reactor both to potential recipients and to Canadian audiences. Indeed the individuals in charge of officially condemning the 1974 test – External Affairs Minister Mitchell Sharp and Under-Secretary of State E. Ritchie – were among those who had sold, or oversold, the concept of the Indian reactor market to Canadians and Indians in the 1950s and 1960s. There was a clear over-reaction to the test because Indian bomb intentions were clearly, but privately, advertised by senior Indians to senior Canadians during the 1950s, literally from the day Indo-Canadian nuclear cooperation agreement was signed.

Compared to the impact of the event on Canada, the Indian test was a less dramatic source of re-thinking about proliferation in the United States. The new thinking crystallised in the Ford–Mitre study released shortly after President Carter's election. This study provided an optimistic view of the availability of uranium and implicitly emphasised the once-through use of uranium in American LWRs; and called for delay and suspension of reprocessing and uranium enrichment in countries which were moving in that direction. There were differences between Canadian and American attitudes. For instance, Canada had an open-minded position on reprocessing. Nevertheless the demand for application of full scope safeguards, and the insistence on "prior consent" of the supplier before reprocessing and enrichment occurred, strained relations with EURATOM, Japan and various third world states. Anti-proliferation seemed like virtue rather than as a problem in inter-state relations; casting anti-proliferation advocacy in theological terms, with injunctions against plutonium reprocessing, uranium enrichment and fast breeders presented as scriptural dictates, created a crisis of confidence for the recipients of nuclear supplies. Furthermore, a question arose about the credibility of legal contracts between states when a supplier state sought to make a new bargain by breaking an old one. The fourth period thus revealed a fundamental tension between states who insisted that old contracts must be carried out, and those who insisted that contracts were open to re-negotiation to save humanity from war.

This tension was really between two general schools of thought. It has never been resolved. The first consisted of believers in safeguards, who recognised the limitations of safeguards because of the political context of international safeguards regimes. First, it was felt that if, for reasons of national security, a country felt impelled to acquire a level of nuclear armament, then no international regime could prevent it. Secondly, even if a country accepted NPT/IAEA safeguards, their implementation required the full cooperation (indeed the assistance) of the safeguarded country. National political will was expressed in the form of adherence to the NPT regime, but this was a political act which states had the right to renounce. Consequently the regime was the best under the circumstances. In discussions in the London Nuclear Suppliers Group (1975 to 1978) this school therefore advocated restrictions on nuclear exports of sensitive materials and technology if a state refused to accept safeguards. (France, however, did not accept this view, arguing that insistence on full-scope safeguards and a nuclear embargo could encourage independent nuclear programmes.)

The second school of thought started with a different premise about human nature. If the temptation of nuclear energy was placed before (unstable? ignorant? insecure?) nations, it was felt, they would foolishly adopt nuclear power and start making bombs. States developed nuclear weapons if they had access to fissionable materials: access to nuclear capability with civilian and military uses meant that nuclear bombs would be made. This temptation ought to be removed by denying the proliferation-prone states any access to nuclear power, or at least access to fissionable materials should be curbed.[4] There is in fact no evidence to support the theory that states go nuclear militarily simply because of a temptation to do so. But the temptation school was the basis of President Carter's approach. It meant that possession of plutonium was itself sin, and that the acquisition of a plutonium and enriched uranium economy and fuel cycle was itself proliferation. This school had no use for the bargain of the NPT. It cited developments in the 1970s as a reason to downgrade the commitment to supply, and to upgrade emphasis on supply restrictions to prevent proliferation, and on improved safeguards technology (such as containment, surveillance, accountancy and physical protection) to shorten detection time.

To date no international regime has settled this debate. The IAEA safeguards regime of the 1960s, and the NPT regime of the late 1960s and early 1970s, accommodated the two schools of thought, but the accommodation was overtaken by the deliberations in secret among nuclear suppliers during 1975–8. Here, in the NSG, the nod was in the direction of the temptation school. The debate was not settled, however, because failure to accept the notion of full-scope safeguards implied the validity of the first school. Thus Canada's nuclear export policy review of December 1974, President Carter's April 1977 statements, and the US nuclear export Act of 1978 leaned towards the second school; but because of international criticism of Canada's and the United States' policies, the INFCE exercise – a multilateral exercise meant to cool tempers in Washington and Ottawa – took the debate back to the first school of thought.

(v) Post-1978

The fifth period was that of crisis management. It was a response to the havoc created by Canadian and American re-negotiation demands. INFCE bought time, and the North American demand for "prior consent" for reprocessing was diluted. The INFCE dialogue recognised the utility, indeed the necessity, of a plutonium and enriched uranium economy in the future. This new focus has restored confidence among EURATOM states and Japan. Although INFCE was meant to be a technical exercise it had a hidden purpose. First, it was designed to legitimise the notion internationally that there was no alternative to reprocessing and enrichment, and that the question of entitlement to these activities flowed from the concept of national sovereignty. The political and economic wisdom of a particular activity, however, was open to discussion at the discretion of the states concerned. Secondly, the exercise was to give enough time for North American anti-proliferation bureaucracies to work out their reactions, and to seek harmony between supplier and recipient views and interests. These purposes have been achieved only in northern international relations, where the most important suppliers and recipients are located. In this sense, a regime – with the prospect of stabilising expectations, perceptions and relations – does exist in the field of nuclear energy at present in the north.

THE NATIONAL POLITICAL FACTOR IN THE SOUTH

This periodisation of efforts to develop a viable international nuclear supply and nuclear non-proliferation regime reveals a quest for a balance between assured supply and safeguards. After 1974 a consensus emerged that there was a need to slow the supply of sensitive materials to regions presumed to be tense, such as South Korea and Pakistan. Denial of sensitive nuclear materials, equipment and technology was thought likely to slow proliferation. In the north, as we have argued, the national political factor and alliance relations do not presently favour military nuclearisation. Given a stable strategic context, the aim, for example on the part of the FRG and Japan, is to develop a supply regime which responds to market mechanisms, and which curbs restrictive political interventions.

In the south, on the other hand, the international system is still growing. International military conflict is today located essentially in the south. One third of the global arms race (measured in terms of the arms trade) is in the developing world, a third among Middle East OPEC states, and a third in the north. Intervention in the south by northern states continues as a legitimate activity. Regional security mechanisms do not yet exist in any stable institutional sense. Attempts at regional dialogue and regional conflict limitation began to take root in the 1970s, but there is much to be done before regional identities become institutionalised. The strategic and political setting in the south, then, is one of mixed signals at present. We see the proliferation of conflicts in the south and the proliferation of conventional arms; there is a steady militarisation of regional environments. The argument about the implications, however, can go in two different directions. On the one hand, militarisation can be seen as the first step to regional arms races given the history of regional rivalries (Argentina/Brazil, India/Pakistan, Israel/Arabs). The introduction of nuclear energy could lead, therefore, to regional nuclear wars which could drag in the superpowers. But on the other hand, regional militarisation can be viewed as a consequence of the national political factor: the primary motive, in other words, is to find third party checks to superpower intervention in regional crises (for example, India in 1971; Israel in 1967 and 1973; Vietnam throughout the Vietnam war; and South Africa in the 1970s).

Regional tensions are manageable, according to this second line of thinking, if the superpowers can be kept out. And the way to keep a superpower out is to increase its margin of uncertainty, and to raise the stakes of conflict and superpower involvement: after regional balances (or imbalances) have come into being, then the superpowers can be persuaded to mind their own business. Thus the central motivation in the process of regional militarisation is not really to create military machines to fight local neighbours. In part the existence of visible and viable military forces acts to deter the use of force between regional adversaries. But, more importantly, it is part of a larger strategy to re-orient the relations between superpowers and regional states. The premise is not that the middle power will ever be able to match the military and economic capability of the superpower. Catching up is not possible. But it is possible, it is felt, to manipulate the margin of safety of the superpower, and hence to inject uncertainty into its style of thinking.

In this perspective we need to study the hidden agenda of the NPT regime. For the superpowers, the NPT, with its two classes of states, was an instrument of power politics. The ban against further proliferation was a self-serving exercise designed to preserve the privileged position of the superpowers. The victory of the NPT framers was that they managed to deceive the innocents in Asia, Africa and

Latin America who naively thought that the NPT bargain could, and would, be kept. But the superpowers failed to deceive the secondary states, who also saw the NPT as an exercise in power politics. The mistake which the superpowers made is that in the process of advertising their belief in non-proliferation, their discriminatory approach released the very national political factors which have stimulated proliferation in the past. The list of near-nuclears is noteworthy – India, Pakistan, Argentina, Brazil, South Africa, Israel and Iraq – because it includes all major countries in the world which seek to alter the existing world order. The NPT framers understood these tendencies. Indeed it could be argued that they side-stepped the real issues precisely because of the implications these had for their future position in international life. Admittedly a multilateral forum like the NPT was not the place to discuss sensitive strategic and political factors – perhaps that is why the superpowers chose a multilateral vehicle. So superpower posturing resulted in counter-posturing: the hidden agenda could not be discussed, and could be mentioned only obliquely. Given the United States' experiences with its allies, and the Soviet Union's with China, the timing of the NPT deliberations also suggests an awareness of the challenge proliferation posed to superpower authority. These began when the rest of the world was on a low or non-existent proliferation curve. To date this has not changed (see Table 8.1).

TABLE 8.1 *Known and presumed nuclear explosions up to 31 December 1979*

Nation	16 July 1945–4 August 1963			5 August 1963–31 December 1979			Total		
	A	U	T	A	U	T	A	U	T
USA	193	110*	303	—	362	362	193	472	665
USSR	161	3	163	—	262	262	161	265	426
United Kingdom	21	2	23	—	7	7	21	9	30
France	4	4	8	41	37	78	45	41	86
China	—	—	—	21	4	25	21	4	25
India	—	—	—	0	1	1	0	1	1
Total	379	119	498	62	673	735	441	792	1233

NOTES
* Some of these may have taken place after 5 Aug. 1963.
A = Atmospheric; U = Underground; T = Total.
SOURCE *SIPRI Yearbook*, 1980; UN General Assembly, 35th Session, *Report of the Secretary-General: Comprehensive Study on Nuclear Weapons*, (12 Sept. 1980, Doc. A/35/392).

For the major states in the south the national security issue – the role of the national political factor – was not unimportant in the mid-1960s, but it was not central. No real external or internal pressure existed to make nuclear weapons decisions. This trend continued into the 1970s. However, the national political factor required a challenge to a process of international regime formation which could cut off the nuclear option in the future. It is important to note that all the major near-nuclear states in the world today reached similar conclusions about the importance of developing all aspects of nuclear science. From their perspective, the cold war ritual covered a reality of superpower concert in selected international security matters. Third parties had therefore to negotiate from a position of weakness. India found the right diplomatic strategy when it used Soviet arguments against the Baruch Plan as the basis of its objections to Soviet and American support of the NPT. Even Moscow could not reject out of hand a re-cycled version of its own earlier speeches on the implications for national sovereignty of international atomic energy controls. Thus access to all aspects of nuclear science was seen as a worthwhile scientific, industrial and political activity. Efforts were also made, at various times, to gain full control over the full fuel cycle. Yet once access to nuclear science was assured, and the infra-structure for civil and military applications acquired, the states in the south decided both not to accept the constraints of a restrictive regime *and* not to make nuclear weapons – because these were costly in every sense and were not really required.

There is a discontinuity between the weapons acquisition processes of the five NWSs, then, and the refusal of the near-nuclears in the south to cross the threshold of nuclear weapons production and deployment. As suggested earlier, the term "near-nuclear" is, however, misleading. It implies a tendency to move towards nuclear weapons when a capacity to do so exists. This is the logic of what we have called the temptation school. Such imagery in the north is basically anti-intellectual, anti-empirical, anti-historical and self-serving. Adherence or non-adherence to the NPT is not the dividing line in predicting proliferation. The point is rather that access to nuclear science had occurred among the near-nuclears before the NPT was conceived; and the efforts to slow the flow of sensitive nuclear equipment, materials and technology served to strengthen the quest for acquisition of nuclear science and industry under national control. Whether or not the near-nuclear states move towards nuclear weapons in the future depends on developments in their environment.

THE PROCESS OF NUCLEARISATION IN THE SOUTH

We now turn to the attitudes and nuclear capabilities of selected regional powers in south Asia, the Middle East, southern Africa and South America. These regions are the principal centres of international conflict. Three of them constitute the Indian Ocean arc (from southern Africa to south-east Asia, including the Indian Ocean). South America is worthy of study because of its projection of political and economic influence *vis-à-vis* North America and Europe and in south–south relations. These regions contain unsafeguarded nuclear facilities and the states in them project revisionist views about nuclear regime-making. The post-1945 nuclear development of states in the south can be understood both as a historical and a cultural process. It occurred as an aftermath of colonialism – a factor more important for some states than for others – and has taken place in the context of unequal relations between the north and the south. But the "real" motives for seeking nuclear power can only be conjectured. Information in the public domain does not fully explain why any particular country chose to soil its hands with nuclear technology. And speeches by government leaders and others give little help. Anti-proliferation debates are essentially exercises in posturing and counter-posturing; speeches represent "noise" and do not necessarily express national intentions and capabilities.

First, some general observations can be made about the process of nuclearisation in the south.[5] This is not simply a repeat of the story of nuclearisation in the north. The decisions of southern states to move along various nuclear paths – in terms of their development of nuclear science and industry as well as of nuclear weapons potential – paralleled American efforts to formulate an international nuclear control regime in the period from 1946 to the present. Indeed to the extent that interest in nuclear science goes back to the late 1930s, initial nuclear decisions in the south can be regarded as preceding US plans to control atomic energy. The Baruch Plan's demand for international ownership, widely regarded as a front for a desired US monopoly, then stimulated national atomic energy development, for example in India. Subsequent policies to deny the transfer of sensitive nuclear technology had the same effect, for example in the case of Pakistan. Further, regime formation efforts also created anti-regime and pro-nuclear constituencies in the south as opportunities emerged for in-house government debates about nuclear policy to be transformed into public and nationalistic debates. As a result, the trend towards nuclearisation of the south seems irreversible. The role of nuclear energy for civilian purposes has been slower than expected, but the demand for nuclear energy is likely to grow in the future. In the period 1990–2020 the oil economy is likely to be replaced mainly by a coal and nuclear energy economy (see Figure 8.1) as the slow curve of southern nuclear energy development accelerates. The states in the south being studied here managed, moreover, to escape international controls over their nuclear programmes. Present international controls can at most slow down the acquisition of full fuel cycles in these countries; so the parallel development of a nuclear supply/nuclear safeguards regime in the north, and the unsafeguarded development of sensitive nuclear technology and nuclear industry in the south, is likely to continue as a pattern during the 1980s. Intrusiveness of the northern regime in the south seems to be a finite phenomenon.

During the 1970s a number of southern states developed ambiguous nuclear weapons potential or nuclear options (for example Israel, India, South Africa and Argentina). National nuclear weapons decisions involve a mix of capability, incentives and disincentives. So far the incentives have been towards development of nuclear weapon potential, while disincentives exist against overt crossing of the weapon threshold. If Soviet–American and Sino-Soviet rivalries persist, and if regime-making continues to have loopholes which allow the flow of sensitive nuclear materials to the south, then the 1980s is likely to remain a period of ambiguous nuclear options in the south. Restraint on the part of states in the south flows from the perceived disutility of nuclear arms at present, and the perceived manageability of their strategic environment. International regimes like the NPT are not real barriers against further proliferation. Change in the international strategic environment, therefore, will likely – if it occurs – be the major variable causing nuclear weapons decisions to be made in the south. This is because multilateral anti-proliferation regimes cannot usually address the specific policy concerns of the southern near-nuclears. The nuclear policy process, we suggest, should instead be treated as part of a mix of energy, military, diplomatic and domestic political issues, and as one that requires the management of constituencies at the domestic, regional and international levels. National and sub-national levels of analysis are crucial: and public multilateral diplomacy is not sensitive to these. By encouraging public posturing, moreover, it is likely to fail. The 1980s, by contrast with the 1970s, should be a decade of real negotiations. However, so long as the superpowers and other nuclear weapon states do not tone down the arms race, the southern states in regions of conflict are unlikely to abandon their nuclear weapon options – irrespective of any foreseeable international regime.

Calculated ambiguity seems likely to continue, therefore, as the name of the nuclear game of the south. Ambiguity helps manage the international bargaining process, and generates uncertainty in superpower planning. This in turn reduces the margin of safety in superpower interventionist behaviour in regional politics by increasing the risks. Nuclear option diplomacy is thus an innovative method for a weaker state. It helps buy influence and attention without incurring the cost of nuclear arms. But if southern states do decide to produce and to deploy nuclear arms, these decisions will probably be a consequence of a perceived deterioration in the regional or international environment. In order for proliferation to be prevented, the onus is on the strategic and geographical neighbours of near-nuclear states to foster in them a sense of security. In particular, since the superpowers plead a belief in non-proliferation, the onus is on them to ensure that near-nuclear states are not forced into a back-to-the-wall situation. As long as the situation remains stable, and is perceived as such, ambiguous nuclear options can be stretched indefinitely.

The data in Table 8.2 and Figure 8.1 reveal a number of linkages between nuclear energy, nuclear proliferation and nuclear trade in the south in the period up to 2010. First, the role of nuclear energy for developmental purposes is likely to increase. The estimates of the 1950s about the likely growth of nuclear energy in the world were optimistic, and were toned down during the 1960s and 1970s. Forecasts for the future, however, are based on an assumption of the declining utility of the oil economy and an increasing world dependence on coal and nuclear economies. This shift in the reliance on nuclear power is likely to affect both the north and the south.

Secondly, INFCE took place largely as a European and Japanese reaction to President Carter's anti-plutonium policy. Although its results are not legally binding on states, it nevertheless settled the international debate in the north and the south by restoring confidence in the concept of the plutonium and enriched uranium economies. Access to reprocessing and enrichment cycles under safeguards, according to INFCE, is valid. Entitlement to these cycles is an attribute of national sovereignty; but the wisdom of possessing these capabilities can best be addressed on a case-by-case basis. With the question of entitlement thus separated from its wisdom, the debate is likely to be carried on now in the context of inter-state negotiations.

TABLE 8.2 *Nuclear capabilities of selected states, 1979–2020*

Country	Fossil resource category	Nuclear capacities (GW$_e$)						
		1979	1985	1990	1995	2000	2010	2020
1. OPEC								
Indonesia	High	0	0	0	0	0	0.5	2.5
Iran	High	0	1.5	2.5	3.5	5	8	13
Iraq	High	0	0	0	0	0	0.5	2.5
Kuwait	High	0	0	0	0	0	1.5	4
Venezuela	High	0	0	0	1.5	4	9	19
2. LATIN AMERICA								
Argentina	Intermed.	0.3	1	1.5	3.5	6	13	25
Brazil	Intermed.	0	3	6	9.5	16	34	59
Chile	Intermed.	0	0	0	0	0.5	3	7
Colombia	Intermed.	0	0	0	0	1	4.5	10
Cuba	Low	0	0	0	0	0	1	4.5
Mexico	High	0	1.5	1.5	3.5	6	13	24
Peru	Intermed.	0	0	0	0	0	2	5.5
Puerto Rico	Low	0	0	0	0	2	8	17
3. MIDDLE EAST AND NORTH AFRICA								
Egypt	Intermed.	0	0	0	0.5	1	3.5	8
Israel	Low	0	0	0	0	1	4.5	10
Turkey	Intermed.	0	0	0	0.5	2	5.5	11
4. AFRICA SOUTH OF SAHARA								
Rhodesia	High	0	0	0	0	0	2	5
South Africa	High	0	2	2	2.5	5.5	12	20
Zambia	Low	0	0	0	0	0	0	3
5. SOUTH EAST ASIA								
Hong Kong	Low	0	0	0	0	0	2	6
South Korea	Intermed.	0.6	2	4	6	8	12	18
Malaysia	Intermed.	0	0	0	0	0	1	3
Philippines	Low	0	0	0	0.5	2	7	14
Taiwan	Intermed.	1.2	3	5	7.5	10	18	28
Thailand	Low	0	0	0	0	0	2.5	7
6. SOUTH ASIA								
India	High	0.6	1.5	4	6	11	26	50
Pakistan	Intermed.	0.1	0.5	0.5	1	2	5	10

SOURCE Connolly *et al.*, *World Nuclear Energy Paths* (ICGNE 1979) pp. 39 a–c.

FIGURE 8.1   *Future world energy demand*

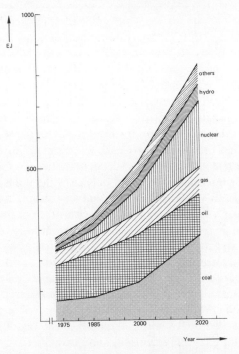

SOURCE   Connolly *et al., World Nuclear Energy Paths* (ICGNE, 1979) p. 25.

These inevitably entail a discussion of linkages between political, nuclear and other issues. In the aftermath of INFCE, then, nuclear supply negotiations have been made vulnerable to the constraints of inter-state politics for both suppliers and consumers. From theology to politics: this at least is an improvement in approach.

Thirdly, developments in 1979–80 revealed a quest for balance between nuclear supply and nuclear safeguards, the argument being that confidence is based on this balance. It is between two elements. On the one hand international nuclear trade is a function of the market, and on the other hand the nuclear trade is meant to slow proliferation. The implicit premise in this approach concerns the national political factor. According to this, a state will likely go nuclear if national security requires such a move; and excessive nuclear controls could well stimulate independent nuclear development and proliferation. So, to avoid stimulating national proliferation tendencies, it is not advisable to seek restrictive international controls.

The implication is that the real barrier against proliferation lies in the mix of incentives for, and disincentives against, proliferation – and not in international regimes. Present nuclear supply and safeguards regimes (the IAEA, NPT, the NSG trigger list and the US nuclear export Act) are likely to remain major elements which regulate the international nuclear trade; and they are also likely to be perceived – quite mistakenly – as the barriers against further nuclear proliferation. If, as we have been arguing, proliferation is a consequence of the national political factor, and if excessive controls stimulate rather than prevent proliferation, then the absence of further proliferation is not in itself a sign that the controls are working: it simply means that the near-nuclears do not presently see an incentive to cross the nuclear threshold. The regime can at present only slow the nuclear trade in the south. As Pakistan's case shows, the nuclear supply and safeguards regime has enough loopholes to permit acquisition of nuclear weapon potential by a near-nuclear state. Unless the profit motive is eliminated from national and international politics – an unlikely prospect – the nuclear supply regime will likely remain porous, and tolerant of the nuclear salesman cutting corners legally. Indeed restrictive supply relations encourage extra-legal and/or *sub rosa* international nuclear commerce. Such commerce is in any case unavoidable since some of the equipment used in the nuclear industry also has legitimate non-nuclear uses – for example generators and invertors.

Fourthly, it is impossible to separate the civilian from the military uses in the nuclear development of our selected cases in the south. There is a strong overlap between the two uses, particularly if the military motive is defined simply as the capability to make a nuclear bomb. By that definition, all the country case-studies to be summarised shortly either have, or are likely to have during the 1980s, the capability to go nuclear. That is not at issue. Rather the subject should be addressed differently. Given that there are, it will be argued, five steps to be crossed before a state acquires a nuclear force or a significant level of nuclear armament, what is the likely pattern of nuclear weapon development of southern states?

These steps are:

(1) mastery of nuclear science and technology;
(2) acquisition of nuclear infrastructure to make a bomb;
(3) open advocacy of the bomb by the government;
(4) nuclear testing; and
(5) establishment of a nuclear force which is viable and visible.

All five nuclear weapon states have crossed each of these steps. In the south, by contrast, only a few steps have been crossed by the leading near-nuclear states. Let us review briefly the cases of India, Pakistan, Israel, Iraq, South Africa, Argentina and Brazil.

India has crossed steps 1, 2 and 4. It advocates the nuclear option, but rejects nuclear weapons (step 5). It rejects regional nuclear disarmament without global nuclear disarmament; and advocates nuclear testing for the purpose of a political demonstration and as a means of staying abreast of modern science and technology. Finally, it accepts the goal of non-proliferation.

Pakistan has crossed steps 1 and 2, and may cross step 4 in the future. It advocates regional and global disarmament. At present it does not advocate nuclear testing (step 4), but its stance is ambiguous on this point. It rejects nuclear weapons, and seeks non-proliferation.

Israel has already crossed steps 1 and 2, and may have jumped to step 5. (Assuming some means to reprocess plutonium and assuming the availability of heavy water for the 26 MW reactor at Dimona, Dimona's production since 1964 could have given Israel fissile material for about 10–15 bombs during the period 1964–80. There is, however, no authoritative evidence to verify this estimate.) Its nuclear policy is ambiguous. Its declaratory policy is not to be the first to introduce nuclear weapons into the Middle East. It seeks reciprocal restraint in the region, and subscribes to the concept of regional nuclear disarmament through a Nuclear Weapon Free Zone. It does not advocate nuclear testing but it possesses the nuclear option like other states in the south. It too subscribes to the goal of non-proliferation.

Iraq had crossed steps 1 and 2 before the reactor near Baghdad was bombed by Israeli planes in June 1981. After the bombing Iraq vowed to rebuild its nuclear infrastructure, but it is reported that for the foreseeable future Iraq is not likely to have a nuclear industry because of the damage inflicted by Israel to its main nuclear facilities. The case of Iraq is highly political because it claims to be in a state of war with Israel, and has vowed repeatedly to eliminate the "Zionist entity"; and Israel has indicated by its words and actions that it has no wish to see such a proposal succeed. Because Iraq was an NPT party and its known facilities were subject to international safeguards, its cause was taken up by the IAEA after the Israeli attack. The Agency recommended to its members that the international community should help re-build Iraq's destroyed facilities. It is unlikely, however, that the French administration under Mitterrand will be as forthcoming with nuclear sales and technology transfer to Iraq as were Chirac and Giscard. A side effect of the Israeli attack is that the western nuclear suppliers will likely consider curbing their sales of sensitive nuclear equipment and materials. In view of these considerations Iraq's nuclear future appears at present to be in limbo.

South Africa has crossed steps 1 and 2, and has threatened to cross step 4. Indeed there is speculation that it may already have crossed step 4 when, according to press reports, it carried out a test in the South Atlantic/Indian Ocean area in September 1979. However, there is no conclusive evidence in this regard. There have been four theories about that event: (i) that it was a South African test; (ii) that it was a South African-Israeli test; (iii) that it was an Indian test; and (iv) that it was a French test. In any case South Africa has the nuclear option because of its capability to enrich uranium and its high technological skills. It subscribes to the goal of non-proliferation.

Argentina has also crossed steps 1 and 2. Crossing step 4 is possible under the terms of the Treaty of Tlatelolco, which Argentina accepts with some reservations. Step 5 is barred by the treaty, but peaceful nuclear explosions are permitted. This barrier is technical and legal rather than practical since there is no difference between a peaceful and a military bomb. Argentina favours nuclear disarmament based on voluntary agreement among regional states, and it subscribes to the goal of non-proliferation.

Brazil is a late-comer to the nuclear scene. In 1975 it signed a multi-billion dollar deal with West Germany which entailed transfer to Brazil of full fuel cycle technology and capability in the 1980s. Because of domestic considerations – mainly financial difficulties due to un-expected increases in the costs of oil imports – there have been delays in the implementation of the Brazil-FRG nuclear agreement. During

TABLE 8.3 *Nuclear threshold steps: nuclear-weapon and near-nuclear states compared*

Steps to cross nuclear threshold	Behaviour of five nuclear weapon states	Behaviour of near-nuclear states
(1)	yes	yes
(2)	yes	yes
(3)	yes	Advocacy of nuclear option; against nuclear weapons.
(4)	yes	Only India tested once.
(5)	yes	None crossed this line.

the 1980s, then, Brazil may be able to cross steps 1 and 2 of the nuclear threshold. It advocates non-proliferation, and indeed was a prime mover behind the Tlatelolco treaty; and in addition favours voluntary regional nuclear disarmament.

With the exception of Iraq, all these states have rejected the NPT. They reason that the NPT creates two classes of states, is directed against industrialising states, and does not move towards the goal of vertical proliferation control. But as this summary shows, rejection of the NPT should not be seen as a sign of movement towards nuclear arms. Table 8.3 offers an overview.

TWO MODES OF DECISION-MAKING BY NEAR-NUCLEAR STATES

This overview suggests two modes of nuclear decision-making on the part of southern near-nuclears. The first of these is directed against nuclear *weapons* proliferation, but for nuclear *options* proliferation. The second is of further proliferation following the approach of the five NWSs. Our prediction is that the first is the more likely development in the 1980s in the south, assuming that regional and international strategic environments do not deteriorate during this period.

The First Mode

Superpower strategic theory sees nuclear weapons possession as necessary for national security. Influence is achieved by possession of visible and viable nuclear capability and by its communication to the enemy. This is diplomacy from a position of strength. This approach, however, is not relevant for the security requirements of a near-nuclear state. The latter seeks influence not by demonstrating its nuclear capability, but rather by acquiring it and keeping it in a posture of deliberate ambiguity. The premise is that the desired effect on enemy perceptions can be achieved by nuclear ambiguity, and that nuclear ambiguity is better since it is cheaper in financial and diplomatic terms. The utility of nuclear ambiguity, though, should be studied in the context of viable and visible possession of conventional armaments. This first mode of strategic behaviour thus sees utility in a package of demonstrable conventional military power, and an undemonstrated and ambiguous nuclear capability which is deliberately kept below steps 3–5 of the nuclear threshold.

The diplomacy of near-nuclear states is the product of a different strategic context. They must negotiate from a position of weakness. In the past nuclear arms have been useful in military crises, but only in a particular way. There is only one case of use of the bomb – by the United States against Japan, at a time when America was already winning the war. There is no known case of a nuclear bomb being used by a state which perceived itself losing a war. Of course, nuclear weapons threats have been used periodically, for example in the case of President Nixon's 1973 nuclear alert and Eisenhower's threat to use nuclear arms in the Korean war. Nevertheless it is arguable that historically there has been a declining utility in the perceived value of nuclear arms in crisis. The case for nuclear arms rests rather on their utility for war-avoidance.

As long as the strategic environment is stable and manageable, according to the perceptions of the near-nuclears, the requirements of military security are best served by conventional arms. But a distinction should be made between the use of such arms in a crisis, and the use of nuclear option diplomacy in other situations. Nuclear threats by India, for example in the 1974 test, occurred as a consequence of that country's experience with the great powers during the 1971 crisis. South Africa's nuclear threat – the September 1979 event – took place in the context of pressures from Washington. Pakistan's 1972 decision to make the bomb occurred before India's 1974 test, and was possibly also a reaction to the outcome of the 1971 crisis. To be viable and visible, nuclear option diplomacy requires the crossing of steps 1 and 2; but there is then a modified version of step 3. This is open advocacy of restraint in the strategic environment so that a near-nuclear state is not forced to have its back to the wall and to move towards step 5. Reciprocal restraint is the basis of the policy of non-exercise of the nuclear weapons option. Consequently, if the strategic environments of India, Pakistan, South Africa, Brazil and Argentina remain stable in the 1980s, their nuclear behaviour is likely to remain consistent with our first mode.

The Second Mode

However, if the strategic environment deteriorates significantly, then bureaucratic politics in each country would likely have the effect of moving the country concerned towards steps 4 and 5. Up to now, advocacy in these southern states has been to strengthen the first two steps, and to draw a line against crossing the last two (although exceptions for demonstration purposes may be made with respect to the fourth). Open advocacy (the third step) can only be understood in this context. It does not involve a contradiction, and should be viewed as an innovative development of peacetime nuclear diplomacy of the weak in the south against the strong in the north – in other words, of those located outside stable alliance relations against those who benefit from them.

Generally speaking, east-west lines of international security communications are manageable and predictable. This is not the case with north–south relations. The norm of confidence-building is not yet globally accepted and practised. For their part, southern states see little utility in alliances; they are still in the process of working out policies and strategies to enhance their security and to successfully engage their northern partners and adversaries. The process of nuclearisation of the southern states is one part of an emerging southern strategy of altering the unequal structure of global power relationships.

A CONCLUDING NOTE

In early June 1981 Israel used conventional bombs to destroy Iraq's nuclear reactor near Baghdad. According to Israeli premier M. Begin the reactor was about to go critical, and because of the state of war between Israel and Iraq it posed a "mortal danger" to Israel's survival.

Several observers saw a relationship between the timing of the attack and the Israeli elections. The attack was hailed by William Safire in the *New York Times* as a "Nuclear Entebbe", and the use of force to rid the world of an irresponsible nuclear power (Iraq) was described as "moral." The Director-General of the IAEA viewed the Israeli action as an attack also on the credibility of the IAEA safeguards regime. The Agency's Board of Governors, and the UN Security Council, strongly condemned the attack. Private comment by western and Arab observers, however, stressed that Iraq was not a model world citizen. This judgment was based on the nature of the Iraqi regime, its attack on Iran, and its unwillingness to permit inspection by the IAEA of safeguarded facilities, citing "war conditions" as the reason for delay. But observers also pondered the implications of the pre-emptive use of force against a state perceived to be irresponsible in nuclear matters. The Israeli attack seemed to create a new element in Middle Eastern and international politics. During the

Cuban missile crisis in 1962, American decision-makers explored the possibility of a pre-emptive strike against nuclear installations in Cuba, citing these as a threat to US national security. In the 1960s, the USSR, through the journalist Victor Louis, also alerted international audiences to the possibility of a Soviet surgical strike against Chinese nuclear facilities. The idea itself was not new: but the action was a new element in the sense that Israel did what the United States and the USSR had in other settings only considered.

It is unlikely that Israeli decision-makers saw their action as anything more than a quest for national security and as an attempt to preclude the possibility of a nuclear arms race in the region. However, the attack had important side-effects. It postponed the peace process in the Middle East; revealed Iraq's political isolation in the Arab world; exposed the fragility of the IAEA safeguards regime; and, finally, it exposed the lukewarm commitment – if indeed there is any commitment – of the Reagan administration to non-proliferation. Because Israel is seen by many as the American cat's-paw in the Middle East, because the Reagan administration is not seen as a fierce opponent of nuclear proliferation, because UN condemnations are ritualistic acts devoid of significance, and because Iraq's regional ambition is seen by many as upsetting the Saudis, the Egyptians and the Syrians – many observers viewed the Israeli move as one codifying a consensus to isolate Iraq and to treat the question of IAEA safeguards as subordinate to larger foreign policy and security issues. Dr Eklund, of the IAEA, was right in moaning about the attack as one on the credibility of the IAEA safeguards regime, but he seemed to speak as the head of an agency with a vested interest. After all, what is the future of the IAEA without a safeguards regime?

In the longer term, the Israeli attack could serve a useful purpose if it opens up debate about the political context of this regime. The IAEA does not usually stress this point. As a technical agency, it is only competent to report that *at best* all safeguarded materials have been accounted for. Even this claim cannot be convincingly made at all times, as can be seen from reported losses from safeguarded facilities in the United Sates, and reports of possible diversions from the high seas. When confronted with a reported loss, the IAEA has in the past covered up, or diverted attention by pointing to Israel as the culprit. Israel may or may not be guilty of theft, but that is not the point. The point is that the IAEA safeguards system depends heavily on trust between the Agency and the safeguarded state, and between the Agency and the world community. The Agency certifies annually to the UN that no significant diversions, at least of safeguarded materials, have taken place. Its data, though, are not open to public scrutiny. It thus creates a false sense of security with regard to suspicious nuclear behaviour. It is a mistake to assume that if safeguarded materials are accounted for, then a state's nuclear intentions are peaceful. The IAEA's performance suggests that it certifies the obvious and may cover up the suspicious. Not once in its history has the IAEA succeeded in catching a diversion while it is taking place. The case of Pakistan is interesting in this regard. It is reported that Pakistan has been reprocessing plutonium since mid-1980. This is a suspicious development because the only known source of spent fuel is KANUPP (the Canadian-supplied reactor at Karachi) which is still under IAEA safeguards. The dilemma for the IAEA is that it must project a confident posture to the world about the reliability of safeguards, even when Agency officials are concerned about suspicious happenings in safeguarded facilities.

Although the use of force is deplorable in any situation, Israel's attack on the Iraqi reactor may thus have a sobering effect on those who wax euphoric about IAEA safeguards, and those who remain confident about technical and institutional solutions to issues which are essentially political, strategic and cultural. Safeguards are useful, but not a barrier against nuclear weapons proliferation. Indeed the NPT provides a good way to proliferate, as the concern about Iraq's nuclear intentions demonstrates. The system of IAEA safeguards can always be improved technically, as is continually being done. This, and extension of the scope of safeguards to currently unsafeguarded facilities may be helpful in building confidence; but political trust and stable political relations are an essential element too. Does the IAEA have the organisational jurisdiction and the detached perspective to relate nuclear developments to world politics? And were the non-NPT states right in saying that the NPT and IAEA regimes do not really address the basic political and cultural issues of proliferation?

During the late 1970s the suppliers' initiative passed to the Europeans, and the political initiative to the third world. Will the gang of three (the United States, the Soviet Union and Canada) survive the challenges of the 1980s?

NOTES

1. This paper relies heavily on the following works: B. Goldschmidt and M. B. Kratzer, *Peaceful Nuclear Relations: A Study of the Creation and the*

Erosion of Confidence (International Consultative Group on Nuclear Energy [ICGNE], Rockefeller Foundation/Royal Institute of International Affairs, Nov. 1978); R. Imai and Robert Press, *Nuclear Non-proliferation: Failures and Prospects* (ICGNE, n.d.); David Fischer, *International Safeguards 1979* (ICGNE, Sept. 1979); M. A. Khan, *Nuclear Energy and International Cooperation: A Third World Perception of the Erosion of Confidence* (ICGNE, Sept. 1979); T. J. Connolly *et al.*, *World Nuclear Energy Paths* (ICGNE, 1979); *Report of the International Consultative Group on Nuclear Energy* (Jan. 1980); IAEA, *International Nuclear Fuel Cycle Evaluation*, *Summary Volume*, INFCE/PC/2/9 (Jan. 1980).

2. It may be argued, however that the focus of the NPT, particularly Articles II and III, is quite different from the concept of non-dissemination originally proposed by Ireland.

3. The term "national political factor" refers to the utility for national security of either adhering to an international regime or rejecting it. Because it addresses the fundamentals of foreign and defence policy, it expresses interests and attitudes which are wider than the norm of anti-proliferation or the safe management of the nuclear industry.

4. To date, though, the identity of the irresponsible, unstable and conflict-prone leaders has not been made public.

5. For a good overview of nuclear development in various countries, see the papers in J. A. Yager, *ed.*, *Non-proliferation and United States Foreign Policy* (Washington, D.C.: The Brookings Institution, 1980).

9 Containing the Blast: Some Problems of the Non-proliferation Regime

James F. Keeley

The 1970s saw the effort to check the spread of nuclear weapons thrown into disarray. The oil crisis of 1973 contributed to an increase in interest in nuclear power as an alternative energy source. More and more states, some of them of questionable internal stability and others in areas of political instability, began to acquire or plan for the acquisition of nuclear power facilities. The spread of these facilities and growing interest in plutonium breeding promised to complicate safeguarding problems by increasing substantially the volume of material to be controlled. The Indian test of 1974, it was feared, could stimulate other powers to develop nuclear weapons potentials, either through emulation or as a result of regional rivalries. Attempts to respond to these perceived challenges were hindered by different interests and preferences regarding means. Thus, despite attempts to co-ordinate action and to strengthen the obstacles to the spread of nuclear weapons, it cannot be said that we have recovered from the shocks of the last decade.

In approximately the same period that these possible threats to the non-proliferation effort became salient, the concept of "international regimes" began to attract the attention of international relations scholars. The two developments may not have been unconnected, for although nuclear power was by no means a dominant concern of early works on this theme, a concern about the implications of technological change for international relations was.[1] Since that time, the concept has escaped from an exclusively technological focus and has been put to broader use. The intention of this chapter is to use the perspective provided by the concept of an international regime in an examination of some of the difficulties that have faced and are facing the non-proliferation effort. The first section will develop a dynamic, contextual concept of an international regime, while the second will review the evolution of the non-proliferation regime in the terms so provided. The third part will deal with some of the problems of non-proliferation so revealed.

THE CONCEPT OF AN INTERNATIONAL REGIME

As one might expect, in making use of the concept of an international regime, various authors have put forward their own definitions and approaches.[2] As a result, it cannot be said that there is one agreed definition or approach. None the less, with due regard for individual variation, there seems to be a degree of coalescence on some aspects of the concept.

This chapter will use, as a rough "pooled" definition, the following: an international regime refers to the set of purposes, norms, rules and procedures by which international actors attempt to provide a structure of behaviour governing activities in a particular area of international relations of interest to them. Without attempting to define the terms "international actors" and "international relations", this section will first develop some of the possible implications of this crude and loose notion, and then will briefly sketch a dynamic and context-based approach to the study of international regimes.

There are three broad aspects of this pooled definition that are of particular importance to this chapter: a regime consists of purposes, norms, rules and procedures; these purposes, norms, rules and procedures are intended to affect – to channel, contrain and shape – patterns of behaviour; and, such a regime is either a conscious creation of actors or at least is recognized and consciously used by them regardless of its manner of creation.

A Regime Consists of Purposes, Norms, Rules and Procedures

These are all objects of contention among the actors manipulating the regime, for the regime is an instrument of policy for the actors, not simply an end in itself. For this same reason, the purposes of the regime, even for an actor capable of influencing them, are not necessarily identical to the purposes of that actor. Indeed, if one uses regime purposes as a guide to the purposes of a particular actor, one should use not the ostensible purposes of the regime, but the purposes proposed by that actor – together with the norms, rules and procedures proposed by that actor. Because a regime may pursue more than one purpose, its purposes may come into conflict with one another. Both the multiplicity and the conflict of purposes may reflect the political contentions of actors, although the conflict in particular may also reflect inadequate knowledge about or inappropriate conceptutilizations of the issue area.

The regime's rules specify, for particular circumstances, what actions should or should not be performed, and the relevant set of actors.[3] A subset of these rules are the procedures, which specify decision-making processes and also how certain actions are to be performed.[4] "Norms" we will take as general principles meant to govern or guide the creation and application of rules and procedures.[5] They may thus serve as checks on how a regime's purposes are to be achieved. To that extent, we may find in the norms of a regime evidence of resistance, whether effective or ineffective, to its purposes. The combination of purposes, norms, rules and procedures, taken together, will define various tasks for the regime to fulfil, and the locus and nature of various capabilities for the fulfilling of these tasks.

There is no requirement that a regime take on a particular form, or that it consist of only one component or one type of form. Although international regimes might generally tend to be identified with international organizations, they may also take on other, simpler or more complex, forms. Bilateral treaties may be the most common form in which international regimes appear; on the other hand, customary international law may be the most pervasive, though organizationally intangible, international regime in existence. Ruggie goes so far as to suggest that international organizations, although the most concrete form of a regime, must themselves be interpreted in the context of a regime[6] – that is, they are themselves contained in broader regimes of which they are mere components. A given regime might thus consist of a multitude of components of different types: the non-proliferation regime, then, might consist not only of the Non-proliferation Treaty, but also of the International Atomic Energy Agency, the Treaty of Tlatelolco, various bilateral and trilateral agreements, certain informal groups, etc.

Given this possible complexity of a regime, it may also be the case that components will not have identical purposes, or purposes given the same weight. With respect to a given set of purposes, some components may be "core" and others "peripheral" in intention as well as in performance. One regime may thus shade into another, creating jurisdictional problems. The specific nature of each component of such a complex regime, its relationship to the purpose or purposes of interest to an observer, and its relationship to other components, will thus all be legitimate objects of study.

A Regime Attempts to Pattern Behaviour

It may, through the denial or provision of certain capabilities to certain actors, make some behaviours impossible and others possible. A system of regional reactor fuel reprocessing centres, for example, is intended to provide reprocessing services to states while discouraging them from acquiring their own national reprocessing capabilities. Within the rules of such a regime, a country may thus be physically prevented from carrying on a certain activity, at least in the short run. In order to acquire the relevant capability, it must first break the rules. More generally, however, a regime will not attempt physically to prevent an action from being taken. Within the context of its rules, however – that is, in so far as its rules are observed – the action will not occur. Thus, the safeguards systems of the non-proliferation regime are not intended to prevent directly and physically the diversion of materials from peaceful to military uses. The objective, rather, is to monitor compliance with the non-diversion rule and to be able to detect diversions with reasonable accuracy and in reasonable time; it is then up to the world community to take the timely and effective action needed to prevent the acquisition of a nuclear weapons capability. (Doubts about the effectiveness of safeguards have recently contributed, however, to interest in some countries in means of increasing physical barriers to proliferation – such as regional reprocessing centres.)

The attempt to pattern behaviour arises from the recognition of interdependence and its costs, and of the potential joint and individual benefits and costs of a behaviour pattern. Unless interdependence is structured by the actors, it may create uncertainties and costs to individual actors in the pursuit of their policy goals. Removing this uncertainty may thus prove beneficial, providing a form of joint advantage to the actors in the interdependent relationship.

Thus, merely by subdividing jurisdictional claims and by allowing for the extension of certain of these over waters formerly considered high seas, the proposed Law of the Sea treaty may reduce conflicts and disputes that could arise from the unregulated and idiosyncratic extension of jurisdictional claims by particular states. More positive benefits may also be available: better international management of fish stocks could not only prevent the depletion of fisheries but also might produce larger, yet sustainable yields.

Finally, of course, any pattern of relations – including that created by or embodied in a regime – may provide individual advantages to certain actors. Regimes will not be neutral in their effects, but rather will tend to favour some parties over others.[7] This is why they are objects of contention. A particular regime may thus be a device by which one or a few actors seek to enhance, confirm or obtain control over others, or by which other, weaker states seek to restrict and regularize the dominance of stronger states. Such manipulative possibilities do not rule out the attainment of joint benefits, but they will affect what benefits and costs are selected, and how they are produced and distributed.

We may in particular wish to distinguish between the *coverage* of a regime – the set of actors to which its rules are applied – and the *membership* of the regime – the set of actors who participate (with varying effectiveness) in the creation of the regime or at least in its decision-making. The possibilities of discrepancies between membership and coverage underline the non-neutral nature of regimes and the manipulative potential that makes them objects of contention. Some regimes are meant to apply only to their members: the European Community, for example, does not purport to regulate trade between South America and Australia. Others, however, are explicitly intended to apply to non-members as well as to members: the Charter of the United Nations authorizes that organization to ensure, as far as is necessary for the maintenance of international peace, that non-members as well as members act in accordance with its principles. Thus, Keohane distinguishes along these lines between "internal" and "environmental" regimes (noting that "pure" internal regimes – regimes having no effect on outsiders – are rare).[8] Challenges to a regime may thus arise from dissatisfied members, but they may also arise from dissatisfied non-members – actors to whom rules are applied and who object to the principle of application, if not also to the content, of those rules to which they have not consented.

The combintion of the membership and the coverage of a regime must be consistent with its purposes and the capabilities needed for the successful attainment of those purposes. Any regime, whether "internal" or "environmental", must include as members (or at least secure the toleration, as non-members, of) actors capable of defying the proposed rules or of providing effective support for others who defy the rules. It must also secure the support of actors with sufficient capabilities to create and support the regime, to make the rules meaningful. An "environmental" regime, to the extent that it is willing to impose its rules on others, must thus include in its membership, or secure the toleration of, all significant actors capable of breaking it, but need not secure the membership of insignificant actors. By definition, its coverage is larger than, or substantially different from, its membership. Thus, the Nuclear Suppliers' Group does not and need not, save incidentally, include major purchasers so long as it includes all major suppliers. An "internal" regime, on the other hand, would have membership and coverage identical – but still have to ensure membership by states of sufficient significance to allow the attainment of its purposes.

The Treaty of Tlatelolco, which creates a nuclear weapon free zone in Latin America, provides an additional pattern, one that approximates an "internal" regime to some degree. The Treaty requires the membership of the Latin American states, but also requires the co-operation of states – particularly the nuclear weapons states – outside of that area. In a sense, then, its membership is larger than its coverage. The broad, general non-proliferation regime, by the nature of its purpose, must either be "global internal" – i.e., virtually all states must belong, and so membership is identical to coverage – or it must be "environmental" but have all significant nuclear-capable states as members.

A Regime is Consciously Created or at least Consciously Used by its Members

That is, in order to be considered a regime by this definition, a given set of norms, rules and procedures should be perceived and used as a set by actors. In the absence of such a "recognition" criterion, any set of objective constraints, or of norms, rules and procedures which are seen by an observer to result in a patterning of behaviour could be taken as a regime.[9] This sort of approach poses some dangers and difficulties. The set of issue area characteristics of interest for a given regime – whether defined by the actors or by an observer – is not in-dependent of the purposes of those actors or that observer. Rather, the definition of the relevant relationships will depend precisely on those purposes.[10] Unless actor purposes are taken into account in the definition of a regime, it will be far too easy for an observer merely to attribute to the regime some goal that has little or no connection with how the actors see their situation or with what they themselves are attempting to accomplish. The observer is then faced with the problem of explaining why a regime does not develop as predicted – and may turn to the blindness or contrariness of the actors as explanations. Questions that require purposes in actors, as opposed to those that deal only with "objective" systems of forces and constraints, cannot be asked unless the issue of the actual purposes of the actors is addressed. There is nothing, however, to prevent an observer from asking how some goal of interest to him is attained as a result of "objective" forces and unintended consequences, or how it fails to be attained because of different actor purposes.

A related danger is that an observer may go beyond merely positing a set of consequences to which the dynamics of a system are leading. He may, instead, attribute purposes to the system *as such* – purposes that are his own values and preferences in disguise. Advocacy thus becomes disguised as objective analysis.[11] Such an approach may be profoundly anti-political: it may deny the legitimacy of clashes of opinion and interest by asserting the existence of a common interest that ought to override particular interests. Politics, for such an approach, may be "the means by which we fail to attain our objectives". An observer with such a perspective must fail to understand political phenomena; a participant with such a perspective may be dangerously intolerant of dissenting ideas and disdainful of constraints on action. If, however, one adopts a recognition criterion, then regardless of one's preferences for or interests in a given system or regime a political understanding of that system or regime becomes possible. Politics becomes fully incorporated into one's study, not as something to be overcome but as part of the process examined. Actors contend over the definition of a problem, the nature of possible solutions, and the selection and implementation of one of these solutions. They struggle with configurations of power and interest, and with changes in these.[12]

These three aspects all point to the need for a political concept of a regime – for an interpretation of regimes based on a recognition of the element of political struggle embodied in them. A formal-descriptive approach, while informative, is of necessity both partial and static; a more political approach not only adds dynamics but also increases our understainding of a regime. A political approach, however, is also incomplete. A regime arises out of a desire to structure behaviour in an area of activity. Both the characteristics of the regime as an outcome of political struggle and the performance of the regime will be affected by the nature of the activity area – its "objective" or "technical" characteristics – and how these are related to the regime. This is perhaps most obvious in the matter of regime performance. The mere absence of contention over a regime's tasks and capabilities is no guarantee of success. Inadequate knowledge of the activity area, or poorly or inappropriately defined purposes, may lead to inappropriate and inadequate tasks and capabilities, and thus to failure. Differences between performance and intention may lead to strains in the regime and to changes in it. In combination with political factors, the technical characteristics of an issue area may also produce cruel problems: the very conditions which lead to a demand for a regime may also have political or technical effects that block effective response by a regime.

We are thus led to a dynamic, contextual concept of a regime, a concept in which the regime per se – the collection of purposes, norms, rules and procedures in one or more components – is both acting and acted upon (see Figure 9.1).

FIGURE 9.1   A contextual concept of a regime

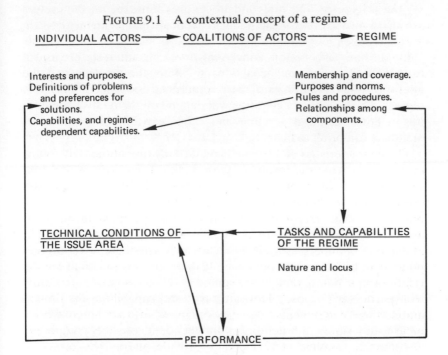

A convenient starting-point for analysis using this contextual approach is the individual actors who might take an interest in a proposed or existing regime (regardless of whether they are members or non-members). On the basis of the impact of the issue area (and of regime proposals) on them, these will take a greater or lesser degree of interest in the regime and will be more or less supportive of particular definitions of the problems to be dealt with and the means of dealing with them. Individual actor capabilities may influence attitudes to the capabilities and tasks of the regime; for example, states unable to act effectively by themselves may be more willing to accept significant regime capabilities (particularly if they can control regime rules and procedures) than states with significant capabilities. Those better able to act effectively for themselves may accept a regime only if they are granted a central role in setting its character and in its rules and procedures. The capabilities of some actors, in the issue area or generally, may be such that their toleration, if not active support, is necessary for a functional regime. Any actor that can break a regime must be persuaded at a minimum to put up with it; inevitably, such an actor will demand a greater say in the nature and the activities of the regime as its price. The rules and procedures of the regime themselves are also a source of actor capabilities – what are termed in the diagram "regime-dependent capabilities".[13]

On the basis of common, converging or parallel interests, actors will form formal or informal coalitions to affect the creation and the operation of a regime. Again, these actors need not be members of the regime. The weight of a coalition will depend on the relative capabilities – both regime-dependent and other capabilities – which its members can bring to bear.

The characteristics of a regime, and its daily operations, will follow in large part from the results of these political interactions and considerations. What problems is the regime to deal with? What purposes does it have, and within the bounds of what norms is it to pursue those purposes? What sorts of solutions is it intended to implement and what are its capabilities? What are its rules and procedures? Does it, must it, affect non-members as well as members? Are there several components in the regime or only one? If there are several, what are the relationships among them? Are some "core" and some "peripheral" to a particular purpose? How are tasks and capabilities distributed among these components? Are they organized into a coherent whole, or are they simply a hotch-pot of independent, possibly competing, institutions, treaties, etc.? Do they provide alternative forums in which actors may raise issues or act in the regime?

The assessment of performance leads naturally to a consideration of how regime tasks and capabilities are related to casual and other patterns of connection in the issue area to be regulated. If a problem is misunderstood, perhaps ignoring vital causal connections, the consequences of regime actions may be disastrous, not merely unsuccessful. For example, efforts to redistribute wealth that harm production of that wealth may end up distributing less and less, although more equally, and ultimately may work to the detriment of all. Even if a problem is well understood, inadequate capabilities may mean only partial solutions can be implemented. Improvements in oil tanker design and in navigation rules and facilities will help to reduce oil pollution in the oceans, but they do not deal with the problem of ships flushing their bilges.

As it stands, this contextual concept is merely a check-list of items to be considered and a few broad interconnections. We may also suggest broad hierarchies of relations among these groups of factors, however. "Technical" conditions in the issue area will indicate in general terms what actions are obligatory, what actions are possible, and some broad problems that will be confronted by a given regime. We cannot disobey the law of gravity, but under certain conditions we are able to fly. In that sense, then, the "technical" conditions of the issue area set possibilities. Beyond that, the distribution of capabilities among actors is often treated as a fundamental determinant of what possibilities (sometimes what impossibilities) will be taken up by a regime.[14] In combination with the knowledge at the command of influential actors, and their purposes and interests, the distribution of capabilities will help us to understand which tasks and capabilities will be granted to a regime, and what its internal characteristics are. Finally, we come full circle: if the regime is assigned inappropriate tasks or inadequate capabilities, it will be in an imperfect relationship with the technical conditions of the issue area – with the limits of the possible.

THE EVOLUTION OF THE NUCLEAR NON-PROLIFERATION REGIME

The attempt to check the spread of nuclear weapons has passed through a number of phases. The abortive initial American proposal, the Baruch Plan, was succeeded by a policy of passive denial, through, such devices as the Atomic Energy Act of 1946 (the McMahon Act);

this was followed by "Atoms for Peace" and the creation of the International Atomic Energy Agency; this, in turn, was followed by the Non-Proliferation Treaty; finally, there is the present disorder, with groupings such as the Nuclear Suppliers' Group and exercises such as the International Nuclear Fuel Cycle Evaluation. The nature of each of these phases and the transition from each phase to the next may be approached in terms provided by the concept of an international regime developed above. In particular, the characteristics and the evolution of each phase of the regime may be related to the "technical" conditions of the nuclear issue area and to its political conditions. What follows is a brief sketch of each of the five phases in these terms.

What are some relevant "technical" conditions? At least three suggest themselves. First, how far apart are the military and the civilian uses of nuclear energy? That is, how distinct are efforts in these two fields? By what means is this distinction created, maintained or even increased? Second, how difficult is it for a state to acquire nuclear energy capabilities? What "barriers to entry" exist and how formidable are they? Third, what is the state of the international nuclear market? Is the demand for nuclear goods and services high or low relative to supply? Are there several suppliers or few? What volume of flows is involved? These set broad conditions within which actors develop and pursue their goals, and with which the regime must cope.[15]

The political conditions include not only convergences and differences among actors in terms of their purposes, but also in terms of the way they define the problems to be solved and the preferred solutions. What is nuclear proliferation? It is the possession of a weapons system (nuclear weapons and a delivery system)? The mere possession of nuclear explosives, or the testing of one nuclear device? It is the possession of a capability – and thus of an option, regardless of one's present intentions – to build a nuclear explosive device at some time in the future?[16] What are the major routes to nuclear proliferation – the routes that must be blocked by a non-proliferation policy or regime? There is straightforward military production. There are a variety of broad routes from civilian programmes: clandestine diversion, spin-offs that reduce the marginal cost of military production, and "smash and grab" adaptations of civilian programmes, facilities and materials to military use. There is also the threat of the acquisition of nuclear weapons by terrorists and other non-governmental actors.[17] What are some possible solutions to the problems of nuclear proliferation? Is there to be international control over nuclear explosives, facilities, goods and services? Should one follow a policy of passive denial, refusing to assist other countries in acquiring nuclear energy and/or nuclear weapons capabilities? Should one adopt a policy of active denial, seeking to prevent more forcefully such acquisitions even through indigenous efforts? An extreme version of such a policy, apparently in combination with fears of diversion or the development of an option from what may or may not have been a civilian programme, is found in the June 1981 destruction of an Iraqi reactor by Israel. Should one depend on safeguards, on technological fixes and barriers, on political sanctions? Different problems will be associated with different routes, and may call for different solutions. States will differ on the definition of the problem, the most dangerous routes, and the preferred solutions.

(i) The Baruch Plan [18]

The Baruch Plan was presented to the United Nations Atomic Energy Commission in June 1946. Although it was never implemented, its features are nonetheless of considerable interest for any examination of the nuclear non-proliferation regime.

The plan was developed in the Acheson–Lilienthal Report of March 1946. Recognizing that nuclear energy could not be wished out of existence, the question posed by the Report was whether the military use of nuclear energy could be avoided and prevented and its beneficial civilian use encouraged. It was also recognized that, despite the great difficulties involved in the production of nuclear weapons, and the significant American advantage in this area, the American monopoly would not last. The plan's proposals were thus intended to secure effective controls over access to nuclear technology and to prevent the acquisition of nuclear weapons by other states by appropriate action while the US monopoly existed.

To accomplish these objectives, the US proposed the creation of an International Atomic Development Authority. This would not simply be a safeguards agency, nor would it be intended simply to forbid the use of nuclear weapons. Attempts to forbid the resort to force were suspect, and safeguards alone were seen as defective. Given political realities, allowing states to carry out "intrinsically dangerous activities", even under safeguard, would be inappropriate. Safeguard systems would thus be only a supplementary area of activity for the Authority.

Instead, the Authority would itself be granted broad powers to control nuclear activities, including a monopoly over "dangerous activities" and over the production of the key raw materials, uranium and thorium. It would not, however, enjoy a total monopoly in the field of atomic energy. This would be a needless irritant to states. It would, rather, have the power to control, inspect and license national activities in less dangerous areas. As a result of the erroneous assumption that plutonium-240 could be an effective denaturant, some power-producing reactors would be allowed in national hands.[19] The Authority was also expected to take a leading role in the beneficial development of atomic energy, not only so that it should not be purely negative but also so that it could keep abreast of potentially dangerous developments in nuclear technology.

A number of activities would be subject to sanction under the plan: illegal possession of nuclear weapons; illegal possession of weapons-suitable materials; seizure of Authority plant or property, or of plant or property licensed by the Authority; wilful interference with the Authority's activities; and improper or unauthorized creation or management of dangerous projects. There would be no Security Council veto to protect those guilty of such actions.

The Baruch Plan foundered on Soviet–American politics. The effect of the plan would have been to prevent Soviet development of atomic weapons, but it would have left the United States with at least the theoretical knowledge necessary to produce them should the need arise. Moreover, the Acheson–Lilienthal Report noted that there was no requirement that the US divest itself of its existing weapons, or stop production of new ones, either as soon as it presented the plan, or as soon as the Authority had been created.

> That decision, whenever made, will involve considerations of the highest policy affecting our security, and must be made by our government under its constitutional processes and in the light of all the facts of the world situation.[20]

In the absence of support from a major power, capable of producing nuclear weapons on its own, the Baruch Plan collapsed.

(ii) Passive Denial

With the failure of the Baruch Plan, the non-proliferation regime fell back on wartime and early post-war agreements among the United

States, Britain and Canada, the partners in the effort to develop the bomb. Each of the three countries had already bound itself not to give information to other countries without the consent of the other two; this was followed by an undertaking not to give detailed information on atomic energy before effective international safeguards were created, and to try to monopolize the uranium resources of the West through preemptive purchasing and other policies. In addition to this, the United States refused to share its atomic weaponry secrets with its wartime partners, and in the McMahon Act of 1946 cut off the flow of any atomic information unless and until Congress decided that effective safeguards existed. This American policy stayed in effect until the development of the "Atoms for Peace" proposal in 1953.

This policy of passive denial could impede the spread of nuclear weapons and hinder the development of nuclear power, but it could not change the basic characteristics of the issue area. Countries with significant scientific and industrial capabilities, and with access to supplies of uranium, could still press ahead. Thus, the American policy prevented neither the Soviets nor the British from developing nuclear weapons on their own, nor the French from beginning the atomic programme that would lead to a French bomb. In addition, Nieburg reports that, by the time the Atoms for Peace policy was announced, some twenty states had significant research programmes, and that both Belgium and South Africa, suppliers of uranium, were demanding changes in American policy.[21] He goes on to argue that

> The efforts of many nations to harness the peaceful atom were well advanced in 1953. The United States did not invent "Atoms-for-Peace". It attempted to climb on the bandwagon after it was already rolling, after Russia, Britain, Canada, France, and Japan had already pushed ahead without U.S. aid. In addition, other countries were moving ahead at the laboratory stage: Sweden, Switzerland, West Germany, and Communist China.[22]

Passive denial, whether practiced by the United States or by the wartime Western allies, had failed.

(iii) "Atoms for Peace" and the IAEA[23]

On 8 December, 1953 President Eisenhower presented to the United Nations new proposals for a regime to govern nuclear matters. He called for the creation of an International Atomic Energy Agency, to which states with fissionable materials would transfer a portion of their stockpiles. The Agency, in turn, would allocate this material, under safeguard, to various states for peaceful purposes, especially power generation. Unlike the Baruch Plan, these proposals depended on safeguarded access – the principle which the Acheson–Lilienthal Report had rejected as insufficient. As it was eventually designed, the IAEA was also granted the power to take over safeguard duties from bilateral nuclear co-operation agreements, and to safeguard facilities unilaterally placed under its safeguard system. The regime thus depended not merely, perhaps not even primarily, on IAEA assistance, but also or rather on the ability and the willingness of nuclear suppliers to require safeguards as a condition of supply, and the willingness of states to turn safeguards tasks over to the Agency. It thus depended on the existence of conditions in the international nuclear market which would favour suppliers, and on the willingness of suppliers to exploit those conditions for non-proliferation purposes. Ultimately, it depended on the existence of barriers to entry into the nuclear field which would encourage a resort to international, safeguarded, assistance rather than dependence on purely indigenous efforts.

The Baruch Plan seems to have defined the proliferation problem basically in terms of the possession of a weapons option, and proposed severe controls to prevent the acquisition of such an option. "Atoms for Peace" took a less ambitious, more complex and less direct approach. By using a method of safeguarded access, it dealt with two problems: acquisition of nuclear weapons, and diversion from ostensibly civilian programmes. It did not deal with straightforward military production, nor did it deal directly with the problem of uncontrolled indigenous development of nuclear energy capabilities. The latter was dealt with through the provision of the international, controlled alternative. Possession of a theoretical option would thus apparently be acceptable, so long as the largely political safeguard barrier maintained a distance between civilian and military use. The scheme thus allowed a means by which the interest of states in nuclear power could be met, yet by which the development of uncontrolled nuclear capabilities could be discouraged.

Aside from offering a solution to the problem of spreading, uncontrolled indigenous nuclear capabilities, the plan had other features that undoubtedly made it attractive to major (nuclear) states. The stress on the peaceful uses of the atom could help both to moderate fears of and to respond to enthusiasm for, atomic power. In so far as it reduced the strategic stockpiles of nuclear weapons states, it could be presented as a disarmament measure. It did not, however, put the nuclear assistance plans of these states, or of other suppliers, totally under international control. This was apparently an important factor in getting Soviet acceptance; it also foreshadowed the eventual fragmentation of the regime into IAEA, EURATOM and bilateral components. As less developed states were later quick to point out, the proposed regime would also impinge least on those states which, being most developed in nuclear energy and least dependent on the international market, had the least need for international assistance.

It took three years and complex negotiations before the proposed Agency could be created. The United States now recognized the need for Soviet agreement if the Agency was to be created, and assumed some degree of converging interests with the Soviet Union on the issue of controlling nuclear power. However, it took some time before the plan could be disentangled from broader disarmament proposals concurrently under discussion and before some aspects – such as the status of bilateral assistance – were clarified to Soviet satisfaction. In the face of such initial difficulties, the US went ahead with unilateral changes in legislation (the passage of the Atomic Energy Act of 1954, permitting co-operation), the negotiation of a number of bilateral nuclear co-operation agreements, and the holding of talks with a variety of its friends.[24] In so doing, it signalled its determination to proceed with nuclear cooperation plans with or without Soviet support and with or without the IAEA, created a possible market for the proposed Agency among the states with whom it reached these agreements, and was able to pursue and develop its proposals in a relatively amenable forum. By the time the Soviets had substantially rejoined the discussions – together with their ally Czechoslovakia, and with India and Brazil as representatives of the less developed countries – a draft Statute for the Agency had been prepared on the basis of the more limited talks and some discussions in the General Assembly. This initial draft was then adapted in response to the concerns, and the political weight, of the new members of the expanded discussion group prior to submission to a General Conference in the autumn of 1956. Thus, although the initial proposal was American, and although the Americans played a dominant role in the creation of the Agency, the desire for Soviet and indeed general membership allowed other states to have some influence over the process.[25]

Enough agreement was reached to allow a unanimous adoption of the Statute on 23 October, 1956. The key safeguards issue was only partially resolved, however, and plagued the Agency for a number of years after its creation. India in particular, with Soviet support, led the struggle against safeguards both before and after the acceptance of the Statute. They would be, it was feared, an undue interference in the sovereignty of states and a danger to economic growth. It was also quite clear that these safeguards would affect only states that drew on the Agency for assistance; states with sufficient capabilities of their own, and activities conducted without Agency assistance or without benefit of a bilateral agreement, would not necessarily have the burden of safeguards. As was the case with the Non-proliferation Treaty, therefore, one might note here a basic element of discrimination in the regime. Until 1965, when the Soviets became firm supporters of the principle of safeguards, what progress was made on this issue came through the ability of the West, led by the US, Britain and Canada, to outvote the Soviets and Indians in the Agency's Board of Governors, and the ability of the Board of Governors to dominate the Agency's General Conference.[26] It was thus not until negotiations for the Non-proliferation Treaty were well along, and probably for the same reasons, that the Agency's pre-NPT safeguards systems became more than rudimentary.

This regime did not prevent, nor was it intended to prevent, the spread of nuclear capabilities.[27] Instead, the Agency and the bilateral co-operation agreements stimulated an increase in the number of trained personnel and in the number of reactors (particularly research reactors) in the world. To that extent, it contributed to a reduction in the "barriers to entry" to the nuclear field. The most significant barrier remaining was that of enrichment technology, which remained classified. Even so, the basis for more modern and perhaps more dangerous enrichment technologies – the gas centrifuge and aerodynamic separation – was laid in this period. The dominance of the American light water reactor contributed to the important place of enrichment technology in non-proliferation. Unlike earlier power reactors, which basically combined plutonium production with power generation, the LWR, adapted from marine propulsion systems, was intended simply as an electricity producer. Being batch-loaded rather than continuously loaded, and using low-enriched uranium rather than natural or highly-enriched uranium, it offered some apparent safe-guard advantages. Above all, the choice of this type of reactor by a purchasing country meant a dependence on a supplier of enriched uranium – in essence, dependence on the United States. Selecting an American LWR could not, of itself, force a country to forgo plans more amenable to the acquisition of a weapons option, but it could create a powerful inclination against such a policy.

For its time, this regime probably seemed quite successful. The only new states to produce nuclear weapons in the period covered by it were France and China; the French programme, however, had begun well before the creation of the Agency, while the Chinese were beyond the reach of any but extreme measures. After a period of sound and fury, the principle of international safeguards was accepted – a development crucial for the NPT regime.[28] The combination of safeguards and particular technologies may have seemed to offer a means of distinguishing between peaceful and military nuclear programmes. That this regime was not seen as totally satisfactory is indicated by the creation of the Non-Proliferation Treaty; that it was nonetheless seen as providing a sound foundation is indicated by the carry-over of its principles into the NPT regime.

(iv) The Non-proliferation Treaty

The Non-proliferation Treaty's origins may be traced to a draft Irish resolution in the United Nations General Assembly.[29] Initial pressures for the treaty came from the less-developed and the non-aligned, but by the mid-1960s the two superpowers were on sufficiently good terms and had sufficient commonalities of interest to address the issue. They each presented draft treaties to the Eighteen Nation Disarmament Committee (ENDC) in 1965, and thereafter took command of the drafting process. The Soviets, with the example of China before them and a fear of a West Germany with access to nuclear weapons, became more willing to accept and support international safeguards as a central part of the non-proliferation effort. On the American side, an interest in non-proliferation had to be reconciled with NATO nuclear arrangements – arrangements that disturbed the Soviets. A balance was eventually struck that allowed the two to maintain their essential security interests in Europe while promoting non-proliferation. The United States abandoned its proposed multilateral nuclear force for NATO, but retained NATO consultation on nuclear weapons and the right to station American-controlled nuclear weapons in the territories of its European allies. The Soviets agreed, with some reluctance, to accept "self-policing" by EURATOM as an acceptable alternative to IAEA safeguards.

The United States and the Soviet Union[30] presented the ENDC with an agreed draft treaty early in 1968. This contained the key elements and articles of the treaty. Nuclear weapons states party to the treaty would bind themselves not to transfer nuclear explosives to any state, nor to encourage, assist or induce non-nuclear weapons states to acquire or develop nuclear explosives. Non-nuclear weapons states would bind themselves not to develop or acquire nuclear explosives, and to accept the application of safeguards on their peaceful nuclear activities in order to verify that this obligation was being fulfilled. All parties would have an "inalienable right" to develop and produce nuclear energy for peaceful purposes, and to exchange information on these peaceful uses (in the final draft, this was expanded to include an obligation to facilitate and a right to participate in "the fullest possible exchange of equipment, materials and scientific and technological information for the peaceful uses of nuclear energy"). The benefits from peaceful nuclear explosives were to be made available to non-nuclear states through international arrangements on a non-discriminatory basis.

The NPT represented an advance over the old regime, but also borrowed heavily from it. The definition of the proliferation problem was expanded to include all nuclear explosives, not just nuclear weapons. This would help to maintain the distinction between civil and military uses that peaceful nuclear explosives were threatening to blur. If peaceful nuclear explosives were to be made available to non-nuclear states at all, it would be under a form of international control. Whereas the old regime had allowed a distinction in the application of safeguards between fully indigenous projects and those using international or bilateral assistance, the NPT regime encouraged the application of safeguards to the entire set of peaceful activities pursued by a nuclear state, even though it did not forbid all military uses of nuclear energy. It also provided states with a means of solemnly, publicly and voluntarily renouncing the development or acquisition of nuclear weapons, thus creating an additional political barrier to proliferation. They key to the regime, however, was still safeguarded access.

The superpowers defended themselves and their draft from pressures from other states in the ENDC and in the General Assembly. Although some changes were made in the draft, the core provisions were kept essentially as drafted, and the superpowers avoided taking on additional firm obligtions on their own. The explicit discrimination in the treaty between the nuclear and the non-nuclear weapons states was the most general point of attack on the superpower draft. In return for accepting this, non-nuclear states demanded reassurances and concessions in other areas, but with little real effect. They received a commitment that the treaty would not block access to peaceful nuclear technology nor hinder economic or technological development. This was important to advanced as well as to less-developed states. They also received a commitment for a review of the treaty five years after it came into force. However, in the area of disarmament talks between the two superpowers only a general and imprecise commitment could be obtained, while states desiring security guarantees against nuclear threats had to be satisfied with vague generalities pronounced in the Security Council.

The treaty became open for signature in 1968, and came into force in 1970. It took somewhat longer to put into place the safeguards system called for under the treaty. The US, Canada and the USSR wanted tighter safeguards than did other advanced states such as Japan and West Germany; by 1972, using a German-developed technique of systems analysis, an acceptable compromise was produced.[31]

It was only in 1973 that the IAEA and EURATOM reached an agreement governing their relationship under the treaty, and only by the mid- and late 1970s did individual members of EURATOM start reaching safeguards agreements with the IAEA. A "trigger list" of exports to which safeguards would be applied was worked out by 1972, but only made in public in 1974. The list was created by a group of supplier states, the Zangger Committee. The initial members were Austria, Belgium, Canada, Denmark, West Germany, Italy, Japan, the Netherlands, Norway, Sweden, Switzerland, the United Kingdom and the United States. The Soviets became directly involved only once the Western states had reached a basic agreement on principles.[32] Thus, the NPT machinery was not fully in place before that regime was challenged.

The developments which were to strain the NPT were both political and technical. The most obvious political challenge was the refusal of a number of states to sign the treaty. France and China did not sign, but the former has generally acted in accordance with the treaty while the latter has not been a source of nuclear assistance for other states. More significantly, a number of important Third World states, such as India, Brazil, and Argentina, refused to sign. These were dissatisfied with the balance of obligations under the treaty, among other things, and did not see it serving their security and political interests. Other states, now commonly classed as pariah states, also refused to sign or else delayed ratification. Israel and South Africa had not signed at the end of 1978; South Korea ratified its signature in 1975. The state coverage of the NPT thus presents some major gaps relative to the coverage of the older IAEA safeguards system.

The delay in working out the NPT safeguards system, the need to accommodate the concerns of various advanced states, and the very composition of the Zangger Committee underline another significant development: the increase in the number of important supplier states. The number of states whose policies would have to be co-ordinated for a non-proliferation regime to be successful was increasing. For some of these states the viability of their domestic nuclear programmes could be closely linked to the health of the export market. The converse of this increase in the number of supplier states was, of course, a relative decline in the American position in the international nuclear market.

The American decline was felt not only in reactor contracts, as Canada, France, and West Germany, for example, began selling abroad, but also in enrichment, that stronghold of American technology and a key element of its nuclear export policy. While American supplies of enriched uranium were sufficiently trusted to give its light water reactor a dominant position in the world market, American restrictions, together with the development of new technology, stimulated other states to develop or expand their own enrichment capacity. There may now, or shortly, even be an over-capacity, since the Soviet Union has become an international supplier of enrichment services, and two European consortia – URENCO and EURODIF – have developed plant. Various individual countries have pilot enrichment projects. In 1974, when the United States closed its order books for its enrichment service, surprising some states in so doing, a further stimulus was given to the development of alternative sources.[33] In the areas of plutonium breeding and reprocessing, the United States has apparently fallen behind.

The growth of the nuclear market in the early 1970s, combined with this diffusion of technology and the greater problems of co-ordinating among a larger number of suppliers, helped to set the stage for the reaction to the Indian test. That test did not so much change conditions itself, perhaps, as point out that conditions were changing, and by doing so it gave greater force to concerns that were already developing.

(v) From India to INFC

India's test of a nuclear explosive device in May of 1974 signalled the start of a period of disorder in the non-proliferation regime. Together with the sale of a fuel cycle to Brazil and of reprocessors to South

Korea and Pakistan (the latter two contracts eventually being cancelled), it helped to trigger an attempt by some nuclear suppliers to redefine the nature of the problems facing the regime, and to implement new solutions. These efforts were resisted by other suppliers (many of them also purchasers), and by other purchasers who had additional sources of dissatisfaction with the regime. These challenges to the regime may be traced through three forums: the NPT Review Conference of 1975 (another was held in 1980), the Nuclear Suppliers' Group, and the International Nuclear Fuel Cycle Evaluation.

The NPT Review Conference was essentially a device by which the non-nuclear weapons states could put pressure upon the nuclear weapons states signatory to the NPT, to encourage the latter to live up to their treaty commitments. The basic issues that had existed when the NPT was created were thus re-fought, and with much the same effect. The superpowers were pressed to take more significant action in the area of disarmament; they pointed to SALT. They were pressed to provide security assurances to non-nuclear weapons states, and refused. Attempts by the less-developed countries to expand nuclear assistance and obtain preferential treatment were turned back by the developed states. Proposals by the supplier states for tighter safeguards, and for such things as regional fuel cycle centres, were seen by the others "not merely as perpetuating the discriminatory features of the NPT but as constituting a form of nuclear neocolonialism".[34] The conference thus simply underlined the fact that the political differences at the start of the NPT phase had not been resolved. This being the case, the failure of the 1975 conference and the similar difficulty of the 1980 conference point to the inherent political frailties of the regime – frailties that could become dangerous if other strains on it begin to tell.

The attempt to redefine the proliferation problem focussed on the possibility that a state might acquire capabilities that could, at some point in the future, be used to support a weapons programme. The concern was not, then, primarily with military production or even clandestine diversion, but rather with the weapons option provided by the simple possession of civilian nuclear capabilities. A state with a full nuclear fuel cycle – or at least with enrichment or reprocessing facilities – would have such an option; so would a state that had produced and accumulated large amounts of reactor grade (but weapons-usable) plutonium. The states attempting the redefinition thus sought to discourage, delay, or control the development of plutonium breeding and recycling, and to prevent the spread of "sensitive" technologies. Aside from unilateral actions – changes in their nuclear export legislation, moral suasion, political pressure, and actual or threatened embargoes – they proposed additional regime capabilities that would help to meet these newly salient problems.

Two key proposals for the new regime were for regional fuel cycle centres and for plutonium storage facilities under international control.[35] The basic idea of each was to allow states access to facilities and stockpiles under international control, removing any need to develop national capabilities and stockpiles, reducing the diversion risk and putting under international control the movement of materials through these sensitive stages of the fuel cycle. A state might thus be able to produce plutonium and have it extracted from spent fuel without itself having either a reprocessing capability or a significant plutonium stockpile under its national control. Dependence on the international nuclear market, a real but relatively informal basis for previous regimes, would thus be institutionalized. Other proposals, for an international fuel bank and for delays in adopting plutonium breeding and recycling programmes, were intended to reduce the pressure for the development of a "plutonium economy". There were also explorations of technical measures that could either avoid or at least reduce the risks seen in the large-scale production and use of plutonium.

The "redefiners" pursued their goals within two major forums: the Nuclear Suppliers' Group and the International Nuclear Fuel Cycle Evaluation. The objective in the NSG was to co-ordinate supplier safeguard policies, particularly as regards the supply of "sensitive" technologies such as reprocessing; INFCE, at least in its origins, was an attempt to find alternatives to plutonium. Both efforts ran into opposition from other suppliers and from purchasers (some states, of course, being both).

The Nuclear Suppliers' Group was formed shortly after the Indian test. It initially consisted of only seven states: Canada, France, West Germany, Japan, Britain, the Soviet Union and the United States. By 1976, these had reached broad agreement on principles, and were able to expand the group, on that basis, to include Belgium, Czechoslovakia, East Germany, Italy, the Netherlands, Poland, Sweden and Switzerland. The NSG guidelines were made public, in the form of a series of unilateral declarations, in early 1978.[36] This mode of presentation was adopted so as to avoid the too-open appearance of a suppliers' cartel; nonetheless, many purchasers saw it as precisely this, and viewed the proposed restrictions and safeguards on technology transfer as reneging on the Non-proliferation Treaty.[37] Among the ranks of the suppliers themselves, there were serious differences of opinion, so that some suggested conditions of export, such as the acceptance of full-scope safeguards, were rejected. Europe and Japan, importers as well as exporters, and with energy concerns that North Americans do not face, resisted attempts to redefine the proliferation problem and to rewrite the rules of the regime accordingly. Such attempts had affected their imports already and could have affected their exports. They tended, instead, to emphasize the political nature of a decision to produce nuclear weapons, and thus the ultimate reliance of the regime on political restraint. The United States, it was charged, was relying too much on a purely technological definition of the problem and on technological solutions.[38]

Similar differences underlay INFCE. Indeed, there is a curious refrain in the summary volume of INFCE reflecting these differences: non-proliferation is a political problem, but INFCE is purely a technical study; civilian nuclear fuel cycle capabilities could be misused, but there are other, perhaps more preferable routes to nuclear weapons.[39] The emphasis on the technical nature of the evaluation was a response to concerns that the study would be a platform for American policy. With well over sixty countries taking part, the "redefiners" would have been substantially outnumbered whether the forum was political or technical. Given that most participants were purchasers, purchaser-suppliers, or suppliers that did not share the "redefiner" perspective, it is not politically surprising, regardless of the technical merits or integrity of the exercise, that ideas of a "technological fix", including in the area of alternatives to plutonium, did not emerge with strong support, or that considerable emphasis was put on the need for stable, predictable and mutually acceptable supplier-purchaser relations as a necessary foundation for non-proliferation.

INFCE studiously avoided direct confrontation with political issues, although its "technical" issues had direct political implications. To some extent, it was used by at least one "redefiner" – Canada – to put "on hold" unilateral policy initiatives that had been meeting increased resistance.

While the outcome of the study may clear away some technical difficulties, the political problems remain to be solved. Similarly, despite the developments in the NSG, the non-proliferation regime is not yet back on firm footing. In fact, should the NSG and its guidelines be seen as too narrow and restrictive, and should states outside that group develop some significant supply capabilities of their own, the regime might come under an even more serious threat: pressures for policies unacceptable to some NSG members might split the group; NSG policies unacceptable to other states may stimulate the eventual creation of an alternative supplier network.

While proposals for new regime capabilities – for regional fuel cycle centres, plutonium storage factilities and controls, international fuel banks and the like – have come under serious consideration, these can only be regarded as possibilities, not yet fully worked out in the abstract, much less ready for implementation in the very near future.

SQUARING THE CIRCLE

A regime may be compared to a proposed solution to a system of simultaneous equations. If it is not to be defective or even infeasible, the "values," the content proposed for the regime, must be capable of satisfying the "equations", the conditions under which the regime has to exist. One set of values might be able to do this, or a solution might be impossible. It might be possible to "decompose" the system of equations into subsets or subproblems, which might then be solved independently. In that way difficulties or failure in one area need not hinder progress in another.[40] Whether or not the system can be decomposed in this fashion, each proposed solution for each problem will have to deal with two distinct but related sets of conditions. The first complex consists of the definition of the problem, possible approaches to a solution given a particular definition, and details of the regime needed to give effect to this solution. The second complex consists of the technical and political conditions out of which a given problem/solution set arises in the first complex, and to which any such problem/solution set must be applied. An answer which satisfied one of these complexes need not satisfy the other. Technical and political difficulties may block the development or successful application of an otherwise viable solution. Solutions that are politically viable might be less than adequate, or at least have very significant voluntaristic components. Changes in the technical or political conditions of a regime may make it obsolete, and may simultaneously complicate any attempt to devise a more desirable regime.

From the brief review of the evolution of the nuclear non-proliferation regime given in the previous section, a number of characteristics of the first, "problem/solution", set of conditions may be noted. First, there are multiple, co-existing problems, and similarly a number of particular instruments intended to deal with these. The result of this has been a complex regime. Second, successive problem/ solution sets have tended to be layered one upon the other. As with cities in the ancient Near East, each phase of the non-proliferation regime has been built upon, and to some degree incorporates, the remains of its predecessor. This also gives complexity to the regime. Taken together, these two conditions have been a source of a fragmentation both beneficial and harmful. Third, the definition of the problem to be dealt with has tended to broaden over time. Fourth, there have been definite limits to the effectiveness of the instruments of the regime, individually and as a whole.

As noted at the start of the previous section, one might define "nuclear proliferation" a number of ways. Broadly speaking, three definitions seem to have been employed at one time or another: possession of nuclear weapons, possession of nuclear explosive devices, and possession of an option to produce nuclear weapons or other explosives. The routes to proliferation have also been multiple: simple military production, clandestine diversion, and the acquisition of capabilities providing a weapons option.[41]

Each definition of proliferation and each route has called forth its particular form or sets of forms of response. Straightforward military production has generally been met with policies of passive denial and political commitments (such as those accepted by non-nuclear weapons states party to the Non-proliferation Treaty). The most obvious example of active denial is the Israeli attack on the Iraqi reactor; as noted, this seems to have been combined with an "option" definition of proliferation (though others might differ on this, depending on their assessments of Israeli policy and Iraqi intentions). The threat of clandestine diversion has been dealt with through safeguards and technological limitations. Safeguards maintain the distinction between civilian and military use; technological conditions, such as the use of light water reactors and a dependence on external sources of enriched uranium also help to maintain "distance" between civilian and military use. The proposed response to the "option" definition and route has included international controls and technological fixes, as well as passive denial, safeguards, and political commitments.

The broadening of the definition of proliferation has thus led to the creation of an expanded set of instruments to check the spread of nuclear weapons, and the application of more than one instrument to at least some problems. Safeguards have been applied not only to projects involving international assistance, but also, under the Non-proliferation Treaty, to indigenous projects. This increased array of instruments might be taken as a sign of increasing regime strength. This could be mistaken, however; one may argue that the broadening of the definition of proliferation (and thus the expansion of the set of instruments) was a product of weakness rather than success. Some facets of the problem proved essentially unmanageable by any means that states were willing to consider; in other areas, instruments have been devised to meet perceived new threats, rather than simply to improve the handling of old ones. In at least one basic case, an instrument used to meet one difficulty has furthered (probably unavoidably, to be sure, and probably in a way preferable to any other realistic alternative) the development of another problem. Safeguarded access, whether or not under the Non-proliferation Treaty, has helped to contribute to recent fears regarding nuclear weapons options. The increase in the volume of materials moving through nuclear facilities, and the very nature of certain phases of the fuel cycle, puts strains on the capability of existing safeguards systems to function adequately. Where a weak or a weakening instrument is applied to more than one problem, the availability and the use of that instrument does not strengthen the regime.

The "layering" of one regime phase on the other is shown in the manner in which older or simpler definitions of the problem of controlling proliferation were not abandoned, but rather were incorporated into broader definitions, together with their sets of solutions. Atoms for Peace and bilateral and trilateral safeguards arrangements have not been fully superseded by the Non-proliferation Treaty; similarly, the NPT system has not fully overcome the separate creations of the IAEA and EURATOM. Because a phase may itself contain a fragmented regime, and because each phase may not be fully incorporated into the next, each succeeding phase has also tended to be more complex, and perhaps rather less co-ordinated, than the preceding. This fragmentation has been useful to some degree, for it means that states that would not be included in the newest components of the latest phase of the regime might well be covered still by older components inherited from previous phases. This has been the case with bilateral and IAEA safeguard systems applied to many states not yet signatories of the Non-proliferation Treaty. On the other hand, insofar as the newer components are meant to remedy defects and gaps in the older ones, this fragmentation also means that these states are, in theory if not in practice, able to exploit these gaps and defects. Thus India, a non-signatory to the NPT, could develop and test a nuclear explosive device without, strictly speaking, violating obligations to which it had consented, obligations less confining than those of the NPT.

As noted, in the process of "layering" phases, the definition of the problem has broadened rather than narrowed. Initially, concern seems to have focussed on nuclear weapons, and on military production. Atoms for Peace added clandestine diversion. The NPT broadened both "proliferation" and "clandestine diversion", to include, for the first, nuclear explosives, and for the second, diversion from purely indigenous civilian capabilities. The attempt to redefine proliferation has aimed at broadening the definition still further, to cover possible weapons options implicit in civilan programmes. This broadening of the definition of the problem must inevitably affect how one assesses the proliferation threat and thus how effective one sees the regime as being. In terms of the possession of nuclear weapons and even of nuclear explosives, the regime seems to have been extremely success-ful; the number of nuclear states by these definitions is remarkably small relative to the number theoretically capable of producing nuclear explosives. Whether this success is illusory – that is, whether many of these theoretically capable states ever had any serious intention of producing nuclear weapons – is another issue. If one defines proli-feration merely in terms of the possession of an option, however, the picture is, by definition, much more alarming. Not only is the degree of proliferation much greater, but the regime has in effect contributed to it, rather than checked it, through nuclear co-operation agreements.

It must also be remarked that the broadening of the definition of the proliferation problem has not been a process by which the successful resolution of a problem has been followed by an expansion of the regime's tasks and capabilities. The proliferation problem of nuclear weapons and military production was not solved before it was redefined as a problem of nuclear explosives, military production and diversion. Rather, the expansion followed from an awareness of a broadening scope of the problem and of defects in previous ap-proaches. It was expansion because of weakness, not strength. It has also tended to be a shift from relatively unresolvable problems, such as open weapons production from indigenous capabilities, to politically more manageable problems such as diversion. Whether or not this pattern has degenerated, with the latest attempt at redefinition, into a scurrying after newly-discovered avenues of failure and a loss of attention to older, possible more important threats, is precisely one of the issues of the debate over the future of the regime.

There are two technical conditions that have a fundamental impact on the non-proliferation regime; the "distance" between civilian and military use, and the barriers to entry. Lesser effects arise from other technical factors, such as the state of the international nuclear market and the volume of material moving through the fuel cycle.

If it was possible to separate completely the military use of nuclear power from its civilian use, the task facing the non-proliferation regime would be much simpler, although not necessarily much easier. Problems of clandestine diversion, possession of options, and peaceful nuclear explosives would simply not exist. There is some distance between a power-generation nuclear programme and a weapons acquisition programme, the latter being less demanding and less costly than the former. A modest weapons programme may be within the reach of a small, or a developing, state when a civilian power programme is not.[42] This separation is not total, however, and so much of the regime's effort has been directed precisely to preventing leakage or diversion from a civilian to a military programme. The overlap between the two sorts of programmes, or at least the spin-off implications of a civilian programme for a military programme, are at the root of the concern over the acquisition of weapons options. The spread of reprocessing and the weapons-usability of reactor-grade plutonium have been major concerns behind the attempt to redefine the proliferation problem. The development of enrichment techniques both less demanding and possibly more readily adaptable from civilian to military use than the gaseous diffusion process is a longer range concern of the same sort.

The erosion of barriers to entry into the nuclear field and the diffusion of nuclear technology and capabilities exercise an equally pervasive effect on the regime. The redefinition of proliferation as the possession of a weapons option merely emphasizes, and to some degree reformulates, a major underpinning of the non-proliferation regime: the concentration of nuclear capabilities in a few hands. This concentration has allowed suppliers to demand safeguards and other requirements as a condition of supply, and has eased problems of co-ordination among suppliers. The diffusion of capabilities – the growing number of states able to meet at least some of their own needs and possibly to supply others – thus attacks the foundation of the regime. As alternative, including indigenous, sources of supply become available to states with nuclear programmes, their vulnerability to sanctions decreases and the need for their voluntary acceptance of and co-operation with the regime increases. Changing supply conditions thus alter the politics of non-proliferation.

Alternative suppliers can break a regime; thus, they must be brought into association with it. (A probably much less likely or workable alternative would be to try to block access to these alternative suppliers.) This means, however, that the policy concerns of new suppliers must be accommodated by the regime and by old suppliers. This may well lead to some dilution of the regime's capabilities, if not to a basic change in its character. Such an accommodation, whatever its form and result, merely makes more visible that which has been implicit in the regime from the start: the most powerful states in the regime are precisely those which possess the capabilities that the regime seeks to control. This provides a basic political incentive for states to acquire or to increase capabilities; the political realities of the regime may themselves provide an incentive for proliferation.

The ability of suppliers to demand safeguards as a condition of export, efforts on the part of suppliers to co-ordinate their safeguards demands, and the problems posed by the appearance of new suppliers all point to a general problem of legitimacy in the regime. The Nuclear Suppliers' Group made changes in the regime without consulting purchasers. There were fears that it would be a suppliers' cartel, and charges that it was attempting to alter the trade-off implicit in the NPT between support by the non-nuclear weapons signatories and access to nuclear technology.

The difference between NSG membership and the coverage of the guidelines generated legitimacy problems. Similarly, embargoes and threatened embargoes by individual suppliers were resented by purchaser states. If purchaser states are, or become, suppliers themselves, the legitimacy problem becomes one not simply of supplier-purchaser relations but also of supplier-supplier relations. The maintenance of the regime's legitimacy, through consultation among suppliers and between suppliers and purchasers, and through a reasonable regard for the interests of other states, is thus a basic requirement for the regime; ignoring it will provide still other incentives for the diffusion of nuclear capabilities.

The state of the international nuclear market will also affect supplier power, but with long-term effects possibly contrary to the short-term effects. Particularly if some suppliers depend on exports to preserve their domestic nuclear programme, a weak market may lead to tendencies to relax export requirements in order to secure sales.[43] Increased efforts at supplier co-ordination will be needed to counter this. Over the long run, however, weaker suppliers might well be eliminated and thus concentration in the market might be preserved or increased. A combination of recession, inflation and environmentalist politics could thus be beneficial to the regime over the long term, but dangerous in the short term. Conversely, if demand is high the position of existing suppliers is strengthened in the short term, but over time new suppliers will probably enter the market and so reduce concentration.

The interaction of technical and political conditions, as well as technical conditions and the adequacy of regime capabilities, is apparent. There is no necessity that nuclear suppliers will act wisely and thus that any particular regime will be viable or legitimate in the long run. Making the somewhat dangerous assumption that knowledge is adequate, the combination of legitimacy and capability proves to be crucial for the political conditions of a regime and thus for the regime itself. In order for a regime to be legitimate, the reasonable interests and purposes of the member states and the covered states must receive recognition. In this regard, both the interaction of nuclear policies with other policy goals and the treatment of the motivations for proliferation create potential difficulties for the regime.

As the use of nuclear power in a state increases, as the number of states using nuclear power increases, the range of interests which will be affected by the non-proliferation regime will also increase and grow more complicated. In addition, the broader definition of nuclear proliferation the broader and more complex the affected interests and purposes will be. Thus, a definition of proliferation in terms of the acquisition of a potential weapons option has led to serious clashes with the energy policies of some states. The more interests and the more complex the set of interests affected by the regime, the greater will be difficulties of accommodating all legitimate concerns in an effective regime. "Decomposing" the regime, creating several regimes of more limited scope, may be a possible solution to this problem, but whether the solution is one regime or many, the legitimate interests of the affected states will have to be taken into account at least to the degree that they have the capability to injure or destroy any regime they find unsatisfactory.

The issue of legitimacy also arises in regard to the motives for nuclear proliferation. Motivation will, to some degree, vary with definition: if one treats "proliferation" as the acquisition of an option, then under present technical and political conditions and under the current regime, energy independence is a very powerful motive for proliferation, and one which many states will find legitimate. If there are "legitimate" reasons for proliferation, however it is defined, a regime will be damaged by a failure to deal with these, or to treat them as legitimate even while trying to prevent proliferation.

This is clearest in the case of an "option" definition of proliferation, but it is also true for less expansive definitions. In the case of these narrower definitions, the non-proliferation regime displays a curious feature: even though the issue of motivation is central to the problem of nuclear proliferation, and occasionally is addressed rhetorically in debates over the regime, the regime itself does not address these issues. It does not deal with motives for proliferation, but with technical (permissive) factors, symptoms (and not all of these) and results. Treatment of the motives for nuclear proliferation is reserved for broader, high-political forums and interactions. We might note three non-competing possible reasons for this. Firstly, nuclear proliferation raises fundamental questions about world order. It cannot be treated adequately merely by the non-proliferation regime, but requires basic and far-reaching political decisions. The non-proliferation regime is not able to address these issues effectively, and would not be allowed to address them. Secondly, even if states deal with the incentives to proliferation, they still treat non-proliferation as but one goal among many, and not necessarily the goal with the highest priority. In particular, the costs and difficulties of addressing motivations for proliferation may be considerably more obvious, immediate and certain than the benefits. Are the super powers to reduce or disband their nuclear arsenals in the hopes that "horizontal" proliferation will be controlled along with "vertical" proliferation? Are they to provide meaningful guarantees of security to non-nuclear weapons states at the cost of complications, clashes, and confrontations in their international relations? States are thus restrained by their own interests from dealing with some motivations for nuclear proliferation. Thirdly, if the regime itself addresses the issue of motivation, it may be led to discriminate formally among states. Such discrimination as already exists in the regime has created legitimacy problems; attempts by the regime to distinguish between trustworthy and untrustworthy states would compound these. An alternative approach, treating each state as equally dangerous, at least formally, would either penalize some states unfairly (creating other legitimacy problems), or would treat dangerous states inadequately, as may be the present case, but avoid the legitimacy problem.

The nuclear non-proliferation regime is thus subject to a number of real and potential challenges, tied to the technical and the political conditions with which the regime must cope as well as to possible "internal" problems of matching definitions of the problem with approaches to a solution.

The challenges based on the technical and political conditions are more pressing and possibly more likely to be fatal than difficulties "internal" to the regime as such: a politically acceptable regime may be able to tolerate some minor internal defects, but an otherwise perfect regime is infeasible if it is not politically acceptable.

In order to be politically acceptable under conditions of spreading technological capabilities, the regime must have the support of as many significant supplier and near suppliers, and states capable of meeting their own needs, as possible. The support of non-nuclear-capable purchasers is not as important, but is also highly desirable. Ideally, then, as the regime develops over time, and as more states become independent and nuclear-capable, its membership should expand. The desirable pattern is that of an inverted cone or pyramid, the narrow base marking the origin of the regime. Such a pattern of membership over time requires either a strong core or an expanded appeal to the membership.

This has not been the pattern of the regime over the last 12–15 years. The core has weakened as nuclear capabilities have spread. The breadth of appeal of the regime has not widened, but rather the set of activities it has sought to control has broadened somewhat, and thus the difficulties of its relationship with state interests have increased. This is perhaps only mildly apparent in the NPT definition of proliferation as including all nuclear explosives, and its concern with diversion from all peaceful nuclear activities of non-nuclear signatories. It is more apparent in the implications of the "option" definition of proliferation. From the broad base of the Atoms for Peace and IAEA phase, regime membership has tended, allowing for the existence of new states, to narrow somewhat. Thus, a number of potentially very significant states are outside of the NPT component of the latest phase. To use our earlier analogy of an ancient city, built on the remains of its past, many states have indeed moved up and into the new city, but a number of important ones still remain behind in the old.

This pattern has fragmented the non-proliferation regime, and may fragment it further, perhaps fatally, unless these "outside" states can be brought into some relationship with the evolving regime. This may require some dilution of present regime principles; alternatively, if we are fortunate, these states will redefine their interests once they reach the status of significant suppliers, and look more kindly on the principles of the regime. Unless these are brought into some association with the current regime, they may form the core of a rival supplier network and a rival regime. We will then face a cruel choice: which is more dangerous–a diluted but unified regime, or a situation of competitive regimes? A similar problem could arise if significant suppliers within the regime prove unwilling to accept the attempts of others to strengthen and broaden the regime. A split in the present regime is as dangerous as the development of a supplier network outside the regime.

The basic political problem facing the present nuclear non-proliferation regime is that of combining a situation of spreading capabilities and more complex interests with a regime both effective and internally consistent, in such a way as to produce a legitimate whole. The problem is one of finding the highest *common* denominator. The regime per se, the sets of rules, procedures, purposes and norms, the tasks and capabilities, is not itself the true target of policy under these circumstances, but is rather the result, the outcome, of policy. The political and technical conditions affecting the regime must be the target of policy.

NOTES

1. See, e.g., J. G. Ruggie and E. B. Haas (eds) *International Organization* 29 (Summer 1975), special issue: International Responses to Technology; and E. B. Skolnikoff, *The International Imperatives of Technology*, (Berkeley: Institute of International Studies, 1972).
2. E.g., the following: H. R. Alker, Jr, "A Methodology for Research Designs on Interdependence Alternatives", *International Organization* 31 (Winter 1977) pp. 29–63; R. N. Cooper, "Prolegomena to the Choice of an International Monetary System", in C. F. Bergsten and L. B. Krause, (eds) *World Politics and International Economics* (Washington: The Brookings Institution, 1975) pp. 63–97; E. B. Haas, "On Systems and International Regimes", *World Politics* 27 (Jan. 1975) pp. 147–74 and "Is There a Hole in the Whole?: Knowledge, Technology, Interdependence, and the Construction of International Regimes", *International Organization*, 29 (Summer 1975) pp. 827–76 and "Why Collaborate?: Issue-Linkage and International Regimes", *World Politics*, 32 (Apr. 1980) pp. 357–405; R. F. Hopkins and D. J. Puchala, "Perspectives on the Inter-

national Relations of Food", *International Organization*, 32 (Summer 1978) pp. 581–616; R. O. Keohane and J. S. Nye, Jr, *Power and Interdependence: World Politics in Transition* (Boston: Little, Brown, 1977); R. O. Keohane, "The Theory of Hegemonic Stability and Changes in International Economic Regimes, 1967–1977", MS, 1979; "Market Failure and Co-ordination Failure: Microeconomic Theory and International Regimes", paper presented at the Annual Conference of the International Studies Association, 1980; D. J. Puchala and R. F. Hopkins, "Regimes and Political Theory: Lessons from Inductive Analysis", paper presented at the Annual Meeting of the American Political Science Association, Washington, 1980; J. G. Ruggie, "International Responses to Technology: Concepts and Trends", *International Organization*, 29 (Summer 1975) pp. 557–83; A. A. Stein, "Global Anarchy, State Interest, and International Regimes", paper presented at the Annual Meeting of the American Political Science Association, Washington, 1980; O. R. Young, "Anarchy and Social Choice: Reflections on the Global Polity", *World Politics*, 30 (Jan. 1978) pp. 241–63 and "International Regimes: Problems of Concept Formation", *World Politics*, 32 (Apr. 1980) pp. 331–56. While I have drawn on these and other sources in this section, they are not, of course, responsible for what follows.

3. O. R. Young, "International Regimes", p.334.
4. Ibid., pp. 336–7; see also Haas, "Why Collaborate?", pp. 398–9.
5. This use of "norm" is *not* found in the works cited in note 2 above.
6. Ruggie, "International Responses to Technology", p.573.
7. The concept of a regime is thus intimately connected to the concept of "meta-power" – the ability to structure social relations, to affect not merely how a game is played but also the rules of the game and, indeed, the very choice of the game. See T. Baumgartner, W. Buckley, T. R. Burns and P. Schuster, "Meta-Power and the Structuring of Social Hierarchies", in T. R. Burns and W. Buckley (eds), *Power and Control: Social Structures and their Transformation*, (Beverly Hills: Sage, 1979) pp. 224–5.
8. Keohane, "Market Failure", pp. 19–20.
9. Puchala and Hopkins seem to adopt such an approach, pp. 3–5.
10. Haas demonstrates this convincingly, using "ocean space" as an example; "Is There a Hole in the Whole?" pp. 834–8, 847–9.
11. On some implications of "hidden teleologies," see Young, "International Regimes", *passim*, and Haas, "International Systems", *passim*.
12. They also struggle with the state of their knowledge and with changes in their knowledge: Haas, "Why Collaborate?" *passim*; Cooper argues, regarding the international monetary system, that

> sources of disagreement do not generally arise from divergent interests, but rather from diverse perspectives and hence different conjectures about the consequences of one regime as compared with another. In short, disagreement arises mainly from ignorance about the true effects, so that we must use reasoned conjectures rather than solid fact to guide our choices, and reasonable people may and do differ with respect to their conjectures.

("Prolegomena", p. 64.)

13. Keohane and Nye, pp. 54–8; Robert W. Cox and Harold K. Jacobson, "The Framework for Inquiry", in Robert W. Cox and Harold K. Jacobson, *et al.*, *The Anatomy of Influence: Decision Making in International Organization* (New Haven: Yale University Press, 1973) pp. 12–14; John G. Ruggie, "Collective Goods and Future International Collaboration", *American Political Science Review*, 66 (Sept. 1972) pp. 874–93.

14. See, e.g., Stephen D. Krasner, "State Power and the Structure of Foreign Trade", *World Politics*, 28 (Apr. 1976) pp. 317–43; Keohane, "Hegemonic Stability", p. 8. The Keohane paper goes on to examine the limits of structural explanations of regime changes. See also Keohane and Nye, pp. 42–54.

15. As these suggestions make clear, the "technical" conditions are not restricted to engineering and physics aspects of nuclear energy. In this paper, the focus will not be on the "hard science" aspect of nuclear power.

16. For a recent treatment of nuclear proliferation in which the ambiguities of the definition of the problem are central, see Ashok Kapur, *International Nuclear Proliferation: Multilateral Diplomacy and Regional Aspects* (New York: Praeger, 1979).

17. See Victor Gilinsky, "Diversion by National Governments", in Mason Willrich (ed.), *International Safeguards and Nuclear Industry*, (Baltimore: The Johns Hopkins University Press, 1973) pp. 159–75, for a discussion of some of these routes. In the same volume, see Theodore B. Taylor, "Diversion by Non-Governmental Organizations", pp. 176–98, for a treatment relevant to the problem of terrorism.

18. This discussion is based on the Acheson–Lilienthal Report ("A Report on the International Control of Atomic Energy", 16 Mar. 1946), and Statement by Bernard M. Baruch, United States Representative to the United Nations Atomic Energy Commission, 14 June 1946, as found in United States Senate, Committee on Government Operations, *Peaceful Nuclear Exports and Weapons Proliferation: A Compendium*, (94th Congress, 1st Session, 1975, pp. 127–98 and pp. 203–13 respectively.

19. Arnold Kramish, *The Peaceful Atom in Foreign Policy* (New York: Harper and Row, for the Council on Foreign Relations, 1963) p. 25. This assumption was known to be overstated, if not false, by 1952, but it seems that only the prospects of plutonium breeding and recycling led to concern about reactor-grade plutonium. For an exhaustive study of the issue of denaturing plutonium, see Alexander De Volpi, *Proliferation, Plutonium and Policy: Institutional and Technological Impediments to Nuclear Weapons Propagation* (New York: Pergamon Press, 1979).

20. Quoted from the letter of transmittal, US Senate, 1975, pp. 133–4.

21. Harold L. Nieburg, *Nuclear Secrecy and Foreign Policy* (Washington: Public Affairs Press, 1964) p. 75.

22. Ibid., p. 86. Nieburg also notes (pp. 75–6) that there were pressures from American industry, which was anxious lest other countries get a head-start in the world nuclear market. Other states, such as Britain, did in fact enjoy an initial and very temporary advantage.

23. This section draws heavily on the following: Bernhard G. Bechhoefer, "Negotiating the Statute of the International Atomic Energy Agency",

International Organization, 13 (Winter 1959) pp. 38–59; Robert Pendley and Lawrence Scheinman, with the collaboration of Richard W. Butler, "International Safeguards as Institutionalized Collective Behavior", *International Organization*, 29 (Summer 1975) pp. 585–616.

24. These "eight-power talks" included Britain, France and Canada, all with an association with the disarmament talks (and with an historical link to nuclear weapons), and Belgium, South Africa, Portugal and Australia (all being, together with Canada, suppliers or potential suppliers of uranium): Bechhoefer, pp. 45–6. The importance of uranium suppliers and of states advanced in nuclear technology was thus emphasized from the start. It was to be institutionalized in both the composition of the Board of Governors of the IAEA and in the powers of the Board *vis-à-vis* the organization's General Conference.

25. Writes Bechhoefer of the "twelve-state talks" (p. 54),

> The commitment of the negotiating states themselves to submit a final text of the Statute to an international conference must have had a profound effect on this stage of the negotiations. If violent disagreements should take place among the twelve negotiating states, it was practically a certainty that the later Conference of all states would not agree upon a Statute. If the Soviet Union and Czechoslovakia were the sole dissenters among the twelve it was possible that after much travail an international Conference would have adopted a Statute by a two-thirds majority in the larger conference would have been out of the question. Therefore, the key task in the Working Level Meeting was to secure agreement.

He goes on to note of the pattern of negotiations (p. 58),

> In its essentials, a small but representative and interested group of states prepared the initial drafts. As the number of controversial substantive issues became narrower, the negotiating group became broader. By the time the final stage of an international conference had been reached, almost all of the issues had already been resolved along lines likely to assure conference acceptance of the main conclusions of the earlier drafts.

The dangers of unrepresentative early groups and of "premature agreement" for later stages of talks conducted along these lines are obvious.

26. See. e.g., Pendley and Scheinman, pp. 598–602.

27. Bernhard G. Bechhoefer, "Historical Evolution of International Safeguards", in Willrich (ed.), *International Safeguards and Nuclear Industry*, pp.32–35.

28. Ibid.

29. General accounts of the negotiation of the Non-proliferation Treaty and analysis of its provisions may be found in: William Epstein, *The Last Chance: Nuclear Proliferation and Arms Control* (New York: The Free Press, 1976); Georges Fischer (translated by David Willey) *The Non-Proliferation of Nuclear Weapons* (London: Europa Publications, 1971);

George Quester, *The Politics of Nuclear Proliferation* (Baltimore: The Johns Hopkins University Press, 1973).

30. Britain played a minor role in the deliberation of the superpowers on the draft NPT; the French did not participate.

31. Pendley and Scheinman, p. 612. The IAEA system under the NPT is generally described in IAEA, INFCIRC/153, *The Structure and Content of Agreements between the Agency and States Required in Connection with the Treaty on the Non-proliferation of Nuclear Weapons*, June 1972.

32. See Kapur, pp. 73–9. For the "trigger list" produced by the Zangger Committee, see IAEA, INFCIRC/209, *Communications Received from Members Regarding the Export of Nuclear Material and of Certain Categories of Equipment and Other Material*, Sept. 1974.

33. See Bertrand Goldschmidt and Myron B. Kratzer, *Peaceful Nuclear Relations: A Study of the Creation and the Erosion of Confidence* (New York: The Rockefeller Foundation, for the International Consultative Group on Nuclear Energy, 1978) pp. 16–18, 36, 43–4.

34. Epstein, p. 248. Epstein (pp. 248–56) presents an account of the 1975 review that is generally symphathetic to the non-nuclear weapons states and the Third World.

35. For a brief examination of these two proposals, from the perspective of international regimes, see Gene I. Rochlin, *Plutonium, Power, and Politics: International Arrangement for the Disposition of Spent Nuclear Fuel* (Berkeley: University of California Press, 1979) pp. 200–12, 220–35.

36. For the NSG guidelines, see IAEA, INFCIRC/254, *Communications Received from Certain Member States Regarding Guidelines for the Export of Nuclear Material, Equipment or Technology*, Feb. 1978.

37. See, e.g., Munir Ahmad Khan, *Nuclear Energy and International Cooperation: A Third World Perception of the Erosion of Confidence*, (New York: The Rockefeller Foundation, for the International Consultative Group on Nuclear Energy, 1979) pp. 13–18 for the Third World view of the NSG.

38. A particularly instructive illustration of the differences in perspective is found in Ryukichi Imai and Henry S. Rowen, *Nuclear Energy and Nuclear Proliferation: Japanese and American Views* (Boulder, Colorado: Westview Press, 1980). The two authors essentially talk past each other on a number of issues.

39. *IAEA, International Nuclear Fuel Cycle Evaluation*, Vol. 9, *INFCE Summary Volume* (Vienna: IAEA, 1980) e.g., pp. 1–2.

40. Rochlin (pp. 309–40) thus proposes dealing with the disposition of spent fuel as a number of more specific, at least semi-independent problems, which might then be solved more or less individually, although the specific solutions found will then have to be broadly compatible with each other.

41. The discussion which follows omits nuclear terrorism, for the sake of simplicity.

42. See, e.g., John R. LaMarsh, "On the Construction of Plutonium-Producing Reactors by Small and/or Developing Nations", and "On the Extraction of Plutonium from Reactor fuel by Small and/or Developing Nations", in United States, House of Representatives, Committee on International Relations, Subcommittee on International Economic Policy

and Trade, and Senate Committee on Governmental Affairs, Sub-committee on Energy, Nuclear Proliferation, and Federal Services, *Nuclear Proliferation Factbook*, 95th Congress, 1st Session, 1977, pp. 533–62 and 563–85 respectively.

43. The United States had some fears in this regard in the early 1960s. A report on the IAEA, written in 1962, stated:

> It appears to the Committee that heavy pressures are now being exerted against the Agency safeguards system and that these pressures will probably increase in the future. The world production capacity for uranium is now in excess of foreseeable needs for both military and commerical uses. There is apparently a feeling (unjustified in our opinion) among some producers that safeguards constitute a hindrance to sales. The desire to sell is strong, and growing stronger, and there is a real possibility that a number of governments of producer countries would not be willing to insist upon safeguards if a customer should refuse to buy on this condition. Such arrangements if made with increasing frequency could lead in a few years to a breakdown of the safeguards system.

Department of State, "Report of the Advisory Committee on U.S. Policy Toward the International Atomic Energy Agency," 19 May 1982, in US Senate, 1975, p. 237.

Part IV Conclusions

10 Regime-making and the Limits of Consensus

Robert Boardman and James F. Keeley

Few words so innocently incorporate into their basic meaning as much simplifying illusion as does the word policy. It means a settled, definite course of action, and yet by its very nature, policy needs to be formulated when there are complex, uncertain alternatives so difficult to analyse and resolve that it is almost impossible to settle on a single, definite course. The illusory qualities of the word have merit, however, for once the compromising, hedging judgements have been made, choosing, chances are, not one but several conflicting courses, it is comforting to be able to describe them by a word implying such wisdom, certainty, and singleness of purpose.

J. Cordell Moore, Under-Secretary of
the Interior, "Observations on US
Energy Policy", Nov. 1966

Nuclear export policy does not spring untainted from theoretical analyses of the nature of the problem of nuclear weapons proliferation. Such evaluations are certainly a part of the multiplicity of factors lying behind the formulation of policy, but, in this field perhaps more than in others, analyses can also be self-serving and the criteria of political acceptability of technical arguments may shift according to circumstance, interest, opportunity and the real or anticipated actions of others. Yet on the other hand, this is also a policy area in which states have periodically been tempted to launch crusading endeavours in the name of peace and to accept, indeed, substantial costs in terms of lost commercial deals and the erosion of diplomatic capital in order to do so. Given competition between national nuclear industries, the prospects of growing overseas sales laced occasionally with multi-billion dollar contracts, uncertainties and declines in the domestic nuclear power programmes of western countries generally, the high political character of many of the issues involved and the consequent minimal authority of international agencies, the identification of national programmes with national prestige and of certain parts of the nuclear fuel cycle with national survival – given these and other factors, supplier consensus becomes not so much an elusive ideal as an analytical conundrum: puzzling when it happens and, for some on the receiving end of nuclear supply decisions, perturbing. As with the circus dog playing the violin, it is the trick itself rather than the quality of the performance which is worthy of comment.

In the six studies of nuclear exporting countries examined in this volume, the variety of influences at work in the policy process is readily apparent. Each of these nations has responded to international nuclear issues on the basis of its own particular set of concerns and circumstances. Those that appear to be most significant and lasting will be discussed in this final chapter as a prelude to some concluding observations on the implications of these findings for the non-proliferation regime itself.

Nuclear export policy is firmly connected with other areas of foreign policy. French non-proliferation policies, for example, have been intertwined with perennial issues of European security, and more particularly with the "German problem". The suggestion that France may have joined NSG deliberations chiefly in order to secure Bonn's adherence to the NPT is an illuminating one. For other countries too nuclear policy has been inseparable from more intangible notions of national pride. Retention of distinctive and indigenous nuclear technologies as a matter of national interest has been a significant factor shaping policies in at least France, Britain and West Germany in the past; in each of these cases acceptance of the benefits as well as the costs of turning to American-style light water reactor systems of various types came slowly, and only after sometimes protracted political and bureaucratic battles in which powerful constituencies existed for the protection of nationally-based designs. Other broadly-defined foreign policy goals have left their mark on nuclear export and non-proliferation policies. Maintenance of a nuclear strategic force has been a core objective for both Britain and France for reasons outside the scope of this volume; the character of their respective nuclear programmes and policies cannot be considered in isolation from these military goals. Canberra also seems to have seized on the potential of expanded uranium exports not only because this fitted older and more specific goals of developing overseas mineral resources sales, but also out of a hunch that here might lie the sources of a bigger future "voice" in world affairs.

Since we are dealing with exports – the promotion of which generally was elevated in Britain during the 1960s and 1970s almost to the status of an overriding national interest – these kinds of links with other issues in the bilateral and multilateral relations of states form an intrinsic part of the subject. Canada's pursuit of more stringent controls on nuclear supplies clashed directly with another important foreign policy objective of the mid-1970s: that of cultivating stronger trade and investment ties with the European Community. The underlying clash of nuclear trade philosophies was muted later during the course of INFCE and bilateral Canada–EC negotiations, but not before damage had been done in this second policy area. French policies have often been evaluated domestically against criteria arising from general questions of Franco–American relations and, as Lellouche has demonstrated, steering towards and away from evolving United States non-proliferation positions while averting domestic charges of *atlantisme* or of selling out French security interests in relation to Germany posed issues of considerable delicacy for the Giscard Presidency. Western countries also tended to respond differently to the immediate problem of the Indian test of 1974 and its longer-term implications. In the United States the proposition that a low-key response might better serve American interests in Southern Asia was swamped by a mounting tide of Congressional criticism of the Administration's policies. For Britain, India's Commonwealth membership as well as traditional ties ruled out a North American reaction, as in practice did *mondialiste* ambitions for France. We will have to return later to the dilemmas posed for western countries by the setting of nuclear trade issues in north–south rather than in predominantly arms control contexts.

Nuclear export and non-proliferation policies can also be viewed as direct or indirect responses to currents in domestic politics. The formulation of Canadian and United States initiatives in the mid-1970s is perhaps the leading example. Domestic political pressures on Washington in 1976 led not only to shifts in the orientation of the Ford Administration, but also to the inclusion of a tough anti-proliferation plank in Carter's platform, the policy consequences of which began to emerge from the spring of 1977. In both the Australian and West German cases, nuclear issues of the middle and later 1970s cracked or significantly eroded earlier bipartisan approaches of the major political parties. The success of the anti-nuclear movement in the latter instance has had important repercussions, as Häckel has shown, for the nuclear policies of the SPD and the FDP, especially at local and Land levels. It should be noted, however, that in general nuclear export and non-proliferation questions have not occupied the prominent position in domestic nuclear debates in West European countries that they have in the United States and Canada (with the exception of discussion of specific deals, such as France's with Iraq and Pakistan, or Germany's with Brazil). There is a certain paradox here. Those countries relatively well-cushioned with indigenous energy sources (the United States, Canada, and Britain for the time being) have suffered far less acutely from domestic assaults on their nuclear power programmes than has, say, West Germany, a country in which a thriving anti-nuclear movement can be seen from one perspective as a highly-priced luxury good. As Trood has argued, too, much of the Australian public debate on nuclear issues has been vicarious in nature, centring – with the exception of the mining-related questions – on general problems of nuclear power affecting the consuming countries of Western Europe and North America. One constraint which has occasionally surfaced in Britain has been the contradiction inherent in the adoption both of anti-nuclear *and* of pro-Third World development positions; but in practice the lack of attention paid to the world picture has tended to muffle this conflict.

In the cases of Canada and the United States, then, the character of domestic nuclear politics has been such as to influence directly government decisions on non-proliferation issues. This has also been true of Australia; indeed there the treatment of nuclear issues from the mid-1970s can be seen as exceptional simply because of the degree to which public debate preceded and then constrained official policy. On the other hand, the impact on external policies has been for the most part indirect as far as the three West European countries examined in this volume are concerned. Cut-backs or slow-downs in domestic nuclear power programmes increase the attractiveness of export strategies or of the provision of nuclear fuel cycle services at home for foreign customers; or heightened public attention to problems of specific reactor types – safety factors in the PWR in the case of Britain in the early 1980s – can then restrict the momentum of exports of plant and equipment.

Nuclear industries themselves form the key domestic factor in the making of nuclear policy. The picture that seems to emerge clearly from Britain, France and West Germany is of nuclear policy generally, and export and non-proliferation policy more particularly, being shaped by government and industry; parliamentary and public influence tends to be rarer (though we will qualify this observation later). In the debates in these countries on reactor choice in the 1960s and 1970s, industry could be found putting the case for economic – including export – rationality: the bullet of entering into licensing arrangements with a United States company once having been bit, the argument ran, an expansion of overseas sales, as well as greater efficiency in domestic power programmes, would follow. With a successful indigenous nuclear power technology, and its own resource and mining industry, the argument in Canada tended to be more straightforward: exports were necessary for the continued well-being of the Canadian nuclear industry generally. Uranium production has accordingly been geared to global demand figures rather than to levels required by the domestic power programme.

However, the conclusion should not be drawn that governments in these countries have served in effect as little more than export pro-motion agencies for industry. More important politically, and more intriguing, have been the policy clashes that have arisen between industry and government. Succeeding governments in Britain retained as an article of faith a commitment to reactor designs in the nationally-developed gas-cooled tradition; it took the resignation of General de Gaulle in 1969 to break finally French Government resistance to the LWR; and a perennial concern underlying German nuclear policies has been the erosion of the nation's reserves of technical skills that could follow over-hasty switches to foreign technologies or a failure to develop export potential to the full. Yet on the other hand, there is some unrealism in treating government and industry as separate entities. A significant role for the state appears to be an unavoidable feature of nuclear development in western countries because of the political salience of this as of other basic energy sources, the regulatory requirements specific to the nuclear industry, the sheer size of capital and research and development investments involved, or the link (for some countries) of the industry with defence strategies incorporating nuclear weapons. The degree of public ownership or of privatisation appropriate to the industry has thus been an issue intimately connected with wider nuclear policy debates, as has the question of the optimal level of fragmentation or competitiveness. These kinds of issues have affected the ways in which non-proliferation policies have been framed. For French industry, more stringent non-proliferation controls meshed well in the 1970s with definitions of self-interest. A thriving domestic power programme could in the final analysis elimi-nate dependence on exports; while a ban on the export of reprocessing facilities boosted France's quasi-monopoly in this area. For German industry, though, exports were crucial; international regulatory measures in "sensitive" areas – suspect in any case on general free-market principles – were accepted with reluctance because of pressures from other western governments and not because of agreement with the rationales for such policies.

Of the countries examined here, it is only in the rather different cases of Australia and France that pressures arising from trade unions have left a mark on government policy. Concern for jobs in a recessionary western economy has led for the most part to pro-nuclear labour stands. An active stand against uranium mining and for more restrictive controls over exports was taken by leading unions in Australia, however, during the course of the Ranger debates. Similarly, the increasingly vocal anti-nuclear positions being voiced by CFDT, the socialist union grouping in France, combined with Socialist Party criticism of at least the Iraqi component of earlier French nuclear export policies, created for the French Government in the early 1980s a much more vocally hostile atmosphere than was present at any time in the previous decade. Competition facing the nuclear industry from utilities representing other energy sources – coal, hydro-electric, oil – has been a factor important more in the contexts of national economies than of the particular questions studied here; but it is worth noting that sniping from such quarters, in the cases at least of West Germany and Britain, has been at times a significant factor in whittling down the grandiose evaluations of export potential that have occasionally been produced by nuclear actors.

Pressures from industry have had international repercussions in one crucial area: that of nuclear futures based on fast breeder reactors and reprocessing. Given Washington's aims in the second half of the 1970s in relation to the proliferation of nuclear weapons, and its partiality to anti-plutonium arguments, the United States position here has been somewhat ambivalent; though a qualified acceptance of the role of breeders seemed to emerge during INFCE. Canadian industry over the same period was pressing firmly for government commitments to the half-way house of the thorium-cycle CANDU system. But it is in the European context that these issues have been decisive. Whereas Paris could accommodate United States calls for stricter export controls on the nuclear trade, it could not so easily cope with the related American pressure aimed against the more controversial and exotic parts of the nuclear fuel cycle. Isolation of Washington by securing a solid European front (and trying to obtain Soviet participation in INFCE) emerged as an important aim of French diplomacy, as Lellouche has argued. The British role in INFCE tended where possible to be one of mediating between the United States and the French and German (and Japanese) positions, but this did not obscure the clear British interest in helping to bring about broader international legitimacy for commercial fast breeder development and for continuation of international reprocessing business. The United States position, though, as Kramish has observed, has to be viewed in the context of the dramatic reversal that the American nuclear industry was facing in world markets in the 1970s; on the European side, growing appreciation of the loss of technological leadership by United States policy-makers indicated a hard core of self-interest behind Washington's stand that diminished in practice the seriousness with which American arguments were taken.

This brings us to consideration of the manner in which nuclear export and non-proliferation policies have been shaped by governments. Of the countries studied, only one – the United States – has a constitutional setting that allows, or encourages, clashes of opinion between the legislative and executive parts of the government machinery; while four – Australia, West Germany, Canada and the United States – have jurisdictional divisions between the federal and the state levels of government built into the nuclear policy-making process. The first point means that, here as in other areas of foreign policy, the policy process in the United States has been more vulnerable than tends to be the case with other countries to domestic political pressures being exerted through the legislature. Presidential non-proliferation initiatives – the NNPA of Carter, and Reagan's somewhat more cautious strategy in 1981/82 – have been subject to alteration and modification by Congress. Amendments to legislation initiated in the Senate have constrained Presidential freedom of manoeuvre in the nuclear export area; Congress has the option of taking up for consideration any nuclear export deal involving financing through the provisions of the Export–Import Act; and Congressional committees in the 1974/75 period both reflected public clamour for tougher non-proliferation policies and also acted to bring about policy changes in this direction in the Ford and Carter Administrations. Executives in other western countries have been more able to deflect parliamentary criticisms. But there are exceptions. As Johannson has pointed out, the House of Commons in Ottawa was a central actor in the post-India demands for application of the contamination principle to Canadian nuclear exports; and, as Häckel has shown, the Bundestag of the later 1970s had departed a considerable way from its earlier role as essentially a rubber-stamp for the government's nuclear policies.

The second division of powers, in the workings of the federal principle in some western nuclear supplying states, has a number of consequences. In Britain, a unitary state, nuclear issues have had occasionally significant regional dimensions, as in complaints by Scottish groups and party organisations at uranium exploration or nuclear waste disposal activity north of the border with England; it is interesting to speculate on what might have been the treatment of the Plogoff reactor siting issue had Brittany been a state, or part of a state, in a federal French Republic. The cases of uranium mining and export in Canada and Australia are more clear-cut, especially given the powers of the Canadian federal government in this resource area which in general constitutional terms falls under the jurisdiction of the provinces. Even so, relations between Canada and France on uranium supply and enrichment issues have been complicated by the existence of a third government, that of Quebec, with distinct interests of its own to promote. Concentration of Canada's nuclear power industry primarily in one province, Ontario, lends an additional voice to the domestic case for a more facilitating approach to export questions by the federal government. Similarly, venting of anti-nuclear arguments generally at state levels in West Germany has proved to be a strategy more likely to bring about change in party and government thinking than on balance is true at the federal level.

The national security implications for some countries, the sensitive internal security needs of nuclear installations, the potential explosiveness of many of the political and economic issues, and the size of the budgetary outlays involved, are factors that have lent nuclear policy processes a somewhat exclusive and secretive air in many western countries. The manner of government decision-making, and the alleged reluctance of ministers and senior civil servants to provide information and to be tolerant of public debate, has itself become an issue of nuclear politics in each of the nuclear exporting countries studied in this book. Some accommodation has been found, for example through the British public enquiry system or the hesitant beginnings in France of a more effective public information network. But in general such concerns are secondary. Change has been evident, however, in policy-making structures. Johannson has suggested that change in the Canadian approach under Prime Minister Trudeau has been a significant factor affecting nuclear export and non-proliferation policy. Replacing the final authority of nuclear experts with that of the

Cabinet committee, that is, opened up questions for wider high-level examination – including reactor sales to overseas customers – and in turn made bureaucratic politics a feature of nuclear policy-making.

Supplier governments have responded in various ways to the problems of policy coordination. The centralising impulse dominating the French approach to questions of nuclear industrial organisation in the late 1960s and early 1970s was paralleled at the official level, for example in the incorporation of final responsibility for nuclear policy into the President's office from 1976. The novelties and complexities, as well as the inter-departmental disputes, that set apart the uranium mining and export issues of the second half of the 1970s in Australia led to the Prime Minister's staff taking on initiating and coordinating responsibilities. Similarly, the ways in which nuclear issues of a broadly international character came to be couched in the 1970s produced in Britain a substantial revision of procedures relating to inter-departmental consultation. The earlier aims of trying to ensure some form of jurisdictional separation between technical and commercial matters on the one hand, and political and diplomatic questions on the other, could not survive the greater importance – in terms both of domestic and foreign policy concerns – of nuclear power issues from the mid-1970s. And there as in the United States patterns of regularised consultation with representatives of the nuclear industry has emerged as a norm for multilateral forums (such as INFCE) and for the routine treatment of specific export and non-proliferation regulatory questions.

Nuclear policy-making in western countries is also characterised, however, by interdependence. This general observation holds true both for more formal attempts to reach consensus on non-proliferation guidelines, and for the competitive bilateral relationships that abound in this area. As Kramish has indicated, United States fear of commercial rivalry from Britain and France in particular has been a feature of Washington's approaches to international atomic energy control issues from the Second World War to the 1980s. Britain, for its part, regarded its reactor designs of the 1960s – the AGR tradition – as a major breakthrough which would act to reverse the growing trend of American success in world markets. Lellouche has pointed out that French criticism on technical grounds of the CANDU reactor cannot be isolated from the fact of French-Canadian competition in Third World countries. There were some signs in the later 1970s that the European Community might be moving towards a situation in which a buyer's market advantage could be taken of Canadian and Australian uranium export goals. The vulnerability of Canada to shifts in purchaser country policies had earlier been demonstrated by the cancellation by Britain and the United States of uranium supply orders. Nuclear cooperation, though, has been evident at several levels: in links between national nuclear industries; transnational connections of various kinds between anti-nuclear groups in various countries; inter-state collaboration in reactor research and development, breeders, or the provision of enrichment and repro-cessing services; the implementation of bilateral nuclear cooperation agreements between governments; the scientific and technical net-work of exchange and communication; and activities in multilateral settings such as international agencies. Taken together, these kinds of factors mean that nuclear politics and policies cannot be considered simply as isloated national phenomena. Foreign nuclear policy, as we have seen, is also susceptible to pressures arising from other foreign policy areas. Just as Johannson has identified a "North American variable" as a determinant of Canadian policies – which is not the same thing as arguing that the latter can be seen as a product of successful influence attempts by Washington – so it may be useful to view French, German and British policies in the light of a "European variable", which constrains government actions and establishes certain common policy concerns in a setting otherwise characterised by competitive-ness.

We have so far been looking at the exporting nations. If supplier consensus is difficult to achieve – because of the dispersal of capa-bilities, complexity of the non-proliferation issue-area, overlapping of other foreign policy goals, and the absence of a single dominant supplier – then at first glance a global consensus embracing suppliers and consumers, and rich and poor states, seems well-nigh impossible. Commitment to the principles of the NPT represents a base level of accommodation between countries. But as Kapur has shown, a declaratory commitment to these principles can be combined with Third World denunciation of the nuclear states for failing to keep what is arguably their part of the bargain. The spread of nuclear energy facilities, that is, is not merely an arms control and weapons prolifera-tion issue – complex though that is in itself. It is also a problem that is central to North-South politics. As in the deliberations at the 1981 energy conference in Nairobi, LDCs can with some justification complain that western countries will readily enough approach Third World energy problems with discussion of "appropriate" forms like wood or biomass, but will then in practice restrict access to high technology, notably nuclear technology. Even if, by some quirk of atomic physics, the latter had no military significance whatsoever, it is likely that the transfer of nuclear technology would be an especially intractable area of high politics.

Assured access to nuclear power was a vital political feature of the NPT, in exchange for which the non-nuclear weapon states – both developed and developing – were willing to accept some measure of discrimination between themselves and the five nuclear weapon states. A related compromise existed in the security realm and centred on nuclear disarmament. Here the efforts of the super-powers to control "vertical" proliferation have been viewed by LDCs as grossly in- adequate. Many of these countries are not necessarily interested in developing nuclear weapons, Kapur has argued, but are rather interested in developing – and exploiting politically – the capabilities that *could* be devoted to the production of a nuclear weapon force. The politics of calculated ambiguity, in other words, is intrinsic to the problem. It follows too that the nuclear export philosophies espoused by the supplying nations cannot be viewed simply as rationales either for the restriction of access to nuclear power or for the legitimising of bulging export order books. Canada, for example, has pursued non- proliferation policies that are costly for its nuclear industries as well as for its capacity to achieve certain foreign policy objectives in non- nuclear areas. Of the exporting nations studied, probably West Germany comes closest to having developed a consistent case for North-South partnership in the transfer and utilisation of nuclear power; but Bonn's approach to international nuclear control issues indicates that the promotion of exports per se, while important, is not the only hinge upon which German policies turn.

What, then, of the nuclear non-proliferation regime? We can note to begin with that nuclear power and nuclear weapons are unlikely to go away. Non-proliferation strategies based on the possibility of their disappearance can be dismissed out of hand. Three broad sets of factors are likely to continue to set limits to the realm of the possible.

The first limiting factor is the spread of capabilities. The creation of purely physical barriers to the spread of nuclear weapons is not a prom- ising route for policy, even though technical barriers on a lower level are an important part of any safeguards regime. Organisational and political factors remain the key. But this in turn raises the problem of consensus, the obstacles in the way of which at the global and at the supplier state levels are prodigious. Some form of consensus can in some situations be manufactured by a dominant power; but even then, there are problems of succession that must be solved if a given order is to survive and adapt, and not be overthrown once that state is no longer in a position to shape broader regime policies. And changes in Northern thinking, including at the least a capacity not to exaggerate the weapons proliferation problem in the South,[1] would seem to be indispensable in the process of consensus-building in the 1980s. Secondly, there is the limit set by the high political context of nuclear power. This provides some basic ground-rules. Thus the US and the Soviet Union will not pursue their rivalries in the Third World to such an extent as to encourage local nuclear forces; they will tend rather to stand together in opposing proliferation.[2] But this then leads to a perspective in which the states of the South are seen as a residual problem, to be dealt with as an afterthought once the great powers have reached their own accommodations with each other. Any regime that fails to go some way towards accommodating Southern interests – diverse though these may in practice be – will either be partial and fragmentary, or else will generate political resistance. A third parameter: states will continue to have a strong interest in civilian nuclear power for reasons of energy independence, and will resist therefore interference by other states or by international agencies with their national power programmes. We may safely assume also that no technological fixes will be forthcoming that will dissolve completely the politically controversial overlaps between civilian and military nuclear technology.

One of the chief benefits of a hypothetical regime resting on a solid basis of consensus would be that a class of "nuclear pariahs" could then more effectively be defined if the need should arise. States clearly violating non-proliferation norms could not point to broadly perceived inequities in the regime to justify their behaviour. In cases where the legitimacy of the regime is itself suspect, on the other hand, deviance is bound to be more common, more acceptable and more difficult to punish. Indeed even the attempt to punish might threaten rather than serve to confirm regime principles. Monitoring nuclear weapons proliferation by identifying high-risk states[3] is, in one form or another, an essential strategy for supplier countries; but incorporating such devices into global regimes is fraught with dangers, not the least of which is lack of agreement on the criteria by which such judgments should be made. More practical steps, however – such as regimes for the management of plutonium stocks or for the supervision of a system of multinational fuel cycle centres – represent useful attempts to reconcile the national desire for a resource with the international requirement of control of that resource.[4]

A successful future non-proliferation regime will thus rest on national nuclear capabilities, where there is a legitimate need; access to internationally-provided goods and services where domestic demand does not justify domestic production; and assurances both of the proper use of national nuclear capabilities, and of access to such goods and services. A nourishing political atmosphere is needed, in other words, as well as technically efficient and political effective safeguards systems. The regime would have to respond to the interests of both suppliers and purchasers, and members of both groups would have to be willing to exercise self-restraint. Ultimately, however, the non-proliferation regime will stand or fall within the limits set for it by states. Some states, though, are more equal than others. The nuclear power resource is not evenly spread among the nations of the world. The six supplier states examined in this volume have found ways during the course of the last decade or so to effect compromises in non-proliferation and nuclear export policies. Keeping this rough-hewn consensus in place while tackling, during the final few and crucial years of this century, the nuclear energy requirements of developing countries will be a task far less easy to accomplish.

NOTES

1. R. W. Jones, "Atomic Diplomacy in Developing Countries", *Journal of International Affairs*, 34, 1 (1980) p. 114.
2. See George H. Quester, "Preventing Proliferation: The Impact on International Politics", *International Organisation*, 35 (1981) pp. 227–32.
3. For a recent discussion, see S. M. Meyer and T. L. Brewer, "Monitoring Nuclear Proliferation", in J. David Singer and Michael D. Wallace, (eds), *To Augur Well: Early Warning Indicators in World Politics* (Beverly Hills: Sage Pubications, Inc., 1979) pp. 195–313.
4. See for example Gene I. Rochlin, *Plutonium, Power and Politics: Inter-national Arrangements for the Disposition of Spent Nuclear Fuel* (Berkeley: University of California Press, 1979) pp. 189–212, 220–35, 260–90.

Index

247